Empowering Teachers and Parents

EMPOWERING TEACHERS AND PARENTS

School Restructuring Through the Eyes of Anthropologists

Edited by
G. Alfred Hess, Jr.

BERGIN & GARVEY
Westport, Connecticut • London

Copyright Acknowledgment

"To Be of Use" from CIRCLES ON THE WATER by Marge Piercy. Copyright © 1973, 1982 by Marge Piercy and Middlemarsh Inc. Reprinted by permission of Alfred A. Knopf, Inc. and the Wallace Literary Agency, Inc.

Library of Congress Cataloging-in-Publication Data

Empowering teachers and parents : school restructuring through the eyes of anthropologists / edited by G. Alfred Hess, Jr.
p. cm.
Includes bibliographical references and index.
ISBN 0–89789–275–5 (alk. paper). — ISBN 0–89789–276–3 (pbk. : alk. paper)
1. Teacher participation in administration—United States.
2. School management and organization—United States—Parent participation. 3. Educational change—United States.
4. Educational anthropology—United States. I. Hess, G. Alfred, 1938– .
LB2806.45.E49 1992
371.2—dc20 91–43394

British Library Cataloguing in Publication Data is available.

Library of Congress Catalog Card Number: 91–43394
ISBN: 0–89789–275–5 (HB)
0–89789–276–3 (PB)

First published in 1992

Bergin & Garvey, 88 Post Road West, Westport, CT 06881
An imprint of Greenwood Publishing Group, Inc.

Printed in the United States of America

The paper used in this book complies with the Permanent Paper Standard issued by the National Information Standards Organization (Z39.48–1984).

10 9 8 7 6 5 4 3 2 1

Contents

Introduction: Examining School Restructuring Efforts

G. Alfred Hess, Jr.

During the 1980s, popular attention in the United States was focused back on public education for the first time since the late 1960s. The report of the National Commission on Excellence in Education (1983), *A Nation at Risk*, claimed that a "rising tide of mediocrity" was engulfing our public schools. The initial focus of reform was on raising standards of performance, for both students and teachers, in an effort to replace mediocrity with excellence. However, it quickly became clear that simply raising standards was not enough. Higher performance would result from higher standards only if the primary issue to be addressed was lack of effort by the nation's students. If the problems were deeper than perennial youth "laziness," the solutions would also have to be more radical.

The second wave of school reform focused on changing the schools our youth attend. It was widely agreed that our schools needed to be "restructured." The questions were how to go about doing this restructuring and who would do it? Richard F. Elmore (1990) has suggested that there are three major themes associated with school restructuring: *empowerment*, *accountability*, and *academic learning*. He suggests that accountability, contrary to popular perception, is quite pervasive in public schools now, but that it is spread among too many diverse interests. Can that accountability be more narrowly focused? If it is, will it be beneficial to schooling, in the long run? The centrality of academic learning as the most important outcome of schooling has gained general acceptance during the past decade. But Elmore warns of overlooking the other major expectations we now have of schools: to provide custodial care for children while their parents are working, to be the locus of social services for children and youth, and to foster skills important for meaningful participation in our democratic society.

The theme of empowerment presents the issue, "Who should be empowered?" Elmore presents two contrasting models of school restructuring with contrasting views of who is empowered. Teacher empowerment focuses upon enhancing the role of educational professionals, particularly at the school level. Under this model, teachers know best what their students need and are best situated to combine subject matter knowledge and judgmental capacity to decide how their students may best be approached. Professional empowerment, then, focuses attention on teacher preparation, entry, promotion and compensation, continuing education, and capacity for decision making. The key assumption is that teachers know better what their students need than do state and local bureaucrats and parents.

The contrasting model is that of parent, or client, empowerment. Under this model, the success of public schools should reflect the degree of satisfaction of the consumers of their services: parents, students, and the community at large. If the clients want different things from their schools and have the capacity to force schools to respond to these changing desires, schools will have to change. Teachers will have to be more responsive to the needs of individual students and the wants of their parents. Schools will be appropriately rewarded if they meet the preferences of their clients.

Elmore and his associates spell out the theories behind these two models and argue for the various values implicit in each. They examine the implications for local and state policy formation. What they are not able to do is examine carefully what happens when schools and school districts attempt to implement either of these models. This book is an effort to fulfill that purpose.

ASSESSING THE IMPLEMENTATION OF SCHOOL RESTRUCTURING

There have been a number of outstanding examples of efforts to restructure schools and the ways that teachers interact with students. The traditional method of improving schools is for academic experts to devise new ways to teach students and then these experts seek to induce teachers and school boards to adopt these new methods or curricula at the local level. Over the last twenty years we have seen many different efforts come and go. There was the introduction of the "new math," which was designed to have students understand the theoretical basis of math, not just memorize multiplication tables. There was mastery learning, with its conception that the various discrete components of learning could be isolated and perfected. More recently a new emphasis has been the heterogeneous grouping of students and the utilization of cooperative learning techniques.

Many of these technical improvement efforts foundered at the point of implementation. Teachers, at the school level, adjusted and accommodated the received improvement until, in implementation, it bore little resemblance to the original model. In other cases, school districts captured a new trend and created abominable distortions disowned by the academics associated with the original development. Sometimes teachers simply rebelled and refused to change their own classroom procedures, regardless of the pressures for change, saying the academics simply did not understand what their children needed. The literature on failed implementation is extensive (McLaughlin, 1978; Elmore, 1978 and 1979; LeCompte & Dworkin, 1988).

EMPOWERING TEACHERS

In response, several efforts have emerged that focus on teacher participation in the development of curricular and teaching improvement. Supported by the Carnegie Forum on Education and the Economy report (1986), these efforts to include teachers in the development of improvement efforts can be seen as a part of the larger effort to empower teachers. Two such efforts are included in this volume. First, Mary Jo McGee Brown examines several efforts to involve teachers in improving math and science instruction in the rural South (Chapter 2). McGee Brown, an anthropologist at the University of Georgia, has studied three education projects in the rural parts of her state. The first project, Kids and Parents at School (KAPS), involves the use of school bus rides to extend the opportunities for math and science instruction for at-risk preschoolers. The second project focuses on high school vocational students. The third involves local participation in a national project to increase scientific literacy among rural students.

The second, more traditional technical improvement model is the much more widely known effort by Ted Sizer and his colleagues at Brown University, the Coalition of Essential Schools. Built on the results of a five-year study of American high schools, the philosophy of the Coalition is embodied in its statement of nine Common Principles, which focus school improvement on the personalization of the schooling process and on envisioning students as learners, not as passive recipients of knowledge (facts). As Sizer lectured on the findings of the study, he found school people eager to try to implement school change based on the philosophy he was articulating. In December of 1985, Sizer launched the Coalition with twelve charter schools. Donna Muncey and Patrick McQuillan were recruited to research the development of the Coalition and to provide an ethnographic documentation of school-level efforts to implement the Coalition's principles. In Chapter 3 they provide three case studies that demonstrate the difficulty of implementing school-level change without adequate attention to altering the dynamics of school-level decision-making and pedagogical practices.

Other teacher empowerment efforts have focused more directly on changing the nature of school-level decision making. In 1983, the president of the American Federation of Teachers (AFT) local union affiliate in Hammond, Indiana, Pat O'Rourke, negotiated a contract that included the initiation of site-based decision making by school improvement teams composed of the principal, several teachers, and a few parents (McPike, 1987). Among other powers, these teams were given the right to request waivers of other provisions of the contract, if to do so would facilitate school improvement planning and implementation. By 1987, every school in Hammond was involved in site-based decision making through school improvement teams.

In 1985, a task force was formed to study the professionalization of teaching in the Dade County Public Schools. Out of that task force, Dade's similar School Based Management/Shared Decision-Making (SBM/SDM) project was launched. Three qualitative researchers, Marjorie Hanson, Don Morris, and Robert Collins, have been tracking the development of Dade's pilot project since its inception. In Chapter 4, they present their assessment of the benefits and limitations of this effort to empower Miami's teachers. They discuss the inception and initial implementation of the pilot project and examine the changing institutional environment within which the project expanded to include nearly a third of the county's schools. They discuss the mixed results the project has thus far attained.

Challenged by the success of the AFT experiments in Hammond and Dade County and spin-off replications in San Diego, Los Angeles, and Rochester, the National Education Association launched its own site-based decision making effort, known as "Schools For the Twenty-first Century." In Memphis, the union and the school board collaborated to launch seven schools on a pilot project in shared decision making. Carol Etheridge and Thomas Collins, two anthropologists at Memphis State University, have been studying the implementation of this project. In Chapter 5, they examine the strained relationships that developed between the principal and teachers in one of those pilot schools. Both the principal and the individual teachers had to make special application to be involved in staffing the school under this pilot project. But good intentions may not be enough to negotiate the shoals of changed patterns of authority and decision making.

The most extensive teacher empowerment effort, to date, is also the most recent. In 1989 the Kentucky Supreme Court declared that the whole system of education in that state was unconstitutional. Ruling on a fairly traditional school finance suit, the court required the General Assembly to thoroughly revamp the state's schools. The Kentucky Education Reform Act of 1990 (KERA) altered the technical methods of educational delivery, mandated the creation of school-based management councils, and significantly increased the funding of most schools across the state. Two anthropologists, Pamelia Coe and Patricia Kannapel, are working with the Appalachia Educational Laboratory in studying four rural school districts across the state as they seek to implement this new legislation. Chapter 6 describes the initial forays of these four districts as they seek to come to grips with the pedagogical, governance, and fiscal elements of KERA. As might be expected, the responses of these districts range from defiance to delight.

William Ayers, an assistant professor of education at the University of Illinois at Chicago, himself a sensitive, long-time preschool teacher, provides a thoughtful overview as to why teachers should be empowered. In the first chapter, "Work That Is Real," Ayers paints a portrait of five disparate teachers and examines the power teachers now exercise, the debilitating context in which many labor, and the alternative learning communities that would better serve our nation's children. He describes what empowered teachers in such learning communities would be like and the real work they would be doing. Ayers makes an eloquent plea for teacher empowerment that is not caught up in politics, but is focused on enabling students to achieve their own proper empowerment.

EMPOWERING CLIENTS

In sharp contrast to the efforts to empower teachers, which might be seen as an extension of worker participation efforts in contemporary business management theory (Deming, 1982; Drucker, 1986; Peters & Waterman, 1982), client empowerment focuses on new ways of forcing educators to be directly accountable to the desires of parents and the larger community. Mary Anne Raywid suggests that school restructuring is an effort at radical and fundamental change in schools and that advocates of restructuring "share the belief that piecemeal supplements, or peripheral modifications that leave most school practices unaffected, are likely to prove futile. . . . [S]chools are no longer in accord with their political environments—that is, with the desires of the parents and communities they presumably serve" (1990: 152). The models of client empowerment are designed to force schools to better meet the desires of parents and communities.

There are two major types of client empowerment in the current school reform movement. The first is an extension of the school-based management model, which is dominated by parents and community representatives at the local level. The second option is to establish schools of choice, in which clients exercise power by enrolling in or leaving schools with different types and qualities of programs. In the first option, parents and citizens exercise direct control over the school's personnel, curriculum, and budget. In the second, the control is indirect and focused on consumer satisfaction.

In Chapter 7, Donald Moore, one of the key architects of the Chicago school reform effort, describes why it is important for parents and community residents to be empowered. He reviews the range of ways in which parents and community residents may participate in the education of their own children and examines the degree to which such involvement leads toward school improvement. Moore suggests that the traditional input-output model of educational productivity (inputs, such as number of teachers, their abilities, or student socioeconomic class, affect the classroom experience of students, which explains student achievement differences) is too simplistic and proposes instead a Quality of Experience Model, which incorporates other aspects that affect student learning, including policies made at the state, federal, and local level, nonschool institutional experiences of young people, and parental support of schooling in the home. Moore suggests that it is when this larger universe of students' life experiences is included in the improvement model that the importance of parental and community involvement in the decision-making and accountability aspects of public schooling comes to the fore.

The Chicago School Reform Act, which incorporates such parent and community involvement, is also unique in the current reform movement in that it represents a state's effort at reforming the major urban school system within its bounds. In Illinois, as in several other "capital place" states that are dominated by one major urban center, there have been essentially two separate school codes: one for cities with more than 500,000 population (i.e., Chicago) and one for the rest of the state. An uneasy and unspoken accommodation focused the state's attention on all other districts but Chicago. But after years of widely proclaimed dismal academic performance and a disastrous nineteen-day school strike, the legislature accepted the recommendations of a movement of Chicago school reformers and mandated change, primarily through the establishment of parent-dominated Local School Councils. In Chapter 8, my colleague, John Easton, and I report on the first year of implementation under the reform act. We describe the trials of newly elected councils of six parents, two community residents, two teachers, and the principal to learn to govern schools while struggling to assert their authority in the continuing tension with a central bureaucracy resistant to giving up power.

At the forefront of much of the recent discussion about improving the nation's schools is the consumer-oriented choice option. Choice has been high on the presidential agenda since 1980 and is a prominent feature in President Bush's America 2000 educational initiative. This conservative Republican political sponsorship has engendered a suspicious backlash in inner-city communities across the nation. The backlash focuses on the threat of vouchers as a means to choice, a process under which the state (or federal) government would provide funds directly to families to allow them to "purchase" education for their children (cf. Coons & Sugarman, 1978; Friedman & Friedman, 1981; Chubb & Moe, 1990). Voucher opponents see this effort as a direct attack on the public schools and as an effort to subsidize middle-class and more affluent families who are currently using their own funds to send their children to nonpublic schools. Voucher advocates say such market pressures would force public schools to get better in order to keep and attract an adequate enrollment of students. Only in Milwaukee, in an extremely constrained pilot project, have these ideas been tested in an urban setting.

But while the voucher argument is carried on in the press and in political circles, public schools of choice have become much more widely available. Perhaps the best known of these choice programs is the system of magnet schools, frequently established to foster desegregation. More dramatic forms of choice have been adopted statewide in several more rural states, including Minnesota, Iowa, Nebraska, and Vermont. Two urban school systems, Cambridge (Peterkin & Jones, 1989) and East Harlem's District 4 (Fliegel, 1989), have adopted districtwide choice plans. In Chapter 9, Diane Harrington, a former administrator in District 4, and Peter Cookson, a qualitative researcher at Adelphi University, examine the claim that student enrollment "choice" was the critical element in the improvement in the schools of New York's upper east-side Spanish ghetto. They describe the early years of creating alternative schools in the district. Although acknowledging the significance of enrollment choice, they emphasize the centrality of the encouragement to teachers to establish differentiated programs that would create the kind of learning communities Ayers describes in Chapter 1.

ROLES FOR ANTHROPOLOGISTS AND OTHER QUALITATIVE RESEARCHERS

Educational research, for the past half century, has been dominated by psychometricians and other quantitative researchers. Too frequently qualitative researchers have retreated into interesting descriptive studies or theoretical projects more designed to advance academic careers than to change educational practice. Some qualitative researchers have banded together to provide minority critiques of what they proclaim to be depersonalizing trends in mainline educational research.

It seems clear that quantifiable results will still be of primary importance in assessing the success or failure of the current efforts to restructure schools. But the quantitative research may not be adequate to isolate which of a number of change variables were most important in schools that do improve, under the current reform effort, a reality many quantitative researchers are beginning to acknowledge (cf. Fowler & Walberg, 1991). And quantitative studies are peculiarly ineffective in understanding the dynamics of restructuring implementation, whether the effort is to empower teachers or to empower clients. Thus a new opportunity has presented itself to anthropologists and other qualitative researchers who choose to engage in policy-relevant research. This book includes the work of a number of such examples. In the final section, we examine some of the ways the task may be approached.

Much of the policy-relevant research being conducted in our nation is funded by the federal government. Thomas Carroll is in a unique position to observe this research effort and to assess its strengths and weaknesses. An educational anthropologist employed in the federal government's program to improve higher education, Carroll has seen the struggle within the discipline to make our work more relevant to our current society at the same time that he has observed the government's need for more descriptive research on the dynamics of improvement implementation. In Chapter 10, he suggests ways anthropologists are particularly equipped to study school restructuring and the values they bring to the restructuring effort. He also examines closely the changing purposes of schooling in the United States and shows why the current restructuring effort is inevitable.

Policy-relevant research in anthropology has been undertaken under a number of different rubrics: applied anthropology, action anthropology, practicing anthropology, and so on. In Chapter 11, John Watkins describes the approach he took to study another dimension of the expansion of Ted Sizer's Coalition of Essential Schools, an approach Watkins calls "critical inquiry." Watkins utilized an approach that is much more interactive between researcher and those researched, an approach that emphasizes collaboration between researcher and innovator, even to the extent of determining the research agenda itself. Watkins acknowledges that "collaborative critical inquiry is messy at best." But he finds great value in an approach that makes both the researcher and other innovation participants the "critical friends" of those whose efforts are being examined.

In the final chapter, I attempt to step back from the specific studies included in this book to examine the trends in educational restructuring that they describe and to assess the importance of qualitative research in evaluating those trends. Anthropologists have not often sought to be active players in the determination of major policy directions in education or in other spheres. But qualitative researchers have the unique opportunity to interact directly and intimately with the persons who are implementing major policy decisions that have been taken by legislatures, boards of education, administrators, and union presidents. It does not compromise their integrity for these researchers to speak out about their findings and to seek to shape the policies they see local practitioners implementing. This book is an effort to give voice to the articulate perspectives of such qualitative researchers.

I Empowering Teachers

1 Work That Is Real: Why Teachers Should Be Empowered

William Ayers

Here are snapshots of five different teachers in action:

Mr. Wilson, an elementary school teacher for over twenty years, tells his fifth-graders on the first day of school that he has only three simple rules: "First, this is a learning community, and everyone needs to be safe here to work and to learn; no one is allowed to hurt anyone else, to hurt anyone's feelings, or to prevent anyone from doing the important work of our class." He explains that this rule applies to everyone—visitors, guests, and even to Mr. Wilson himself. He continues, "We'll discuss this a lot as the year goes on, and we'll discover how complicated it can be to figure out what's fair or what's right sometimes. For now, just keep it in mind, talk it over with each other if you'd like, and be sure to let me know if I do anything that might hurt someone's feelings."

The teacher has set an elevated tone by asking the children to consider something substantive and complex, noting that there are no simple, instantaneous answers and there is nothing patronizing or punitive in it. "Second," he continues, "you *can* wear hats in this room, and third, you *can* chew gum—please don't make a mess with it." These two "rules" contradict school practice, and the announcement sends a wave of disbelief and energy through the students. There is a buzz of excitement, and a few laugh out loud—they are now together resisting an unpopular, somewhat mindless school tradition, and Mr. Wilson is leading the conspiracy. Being part of the resistant community implicitly requires a higher level of strength and responsibility, and the fifth grade is already looking sharp.

Ms. Vaughn, a veteran middle school teacher, has discovered several dollars missing from the top drawer of her desk. She stands her eighth-graders in a line and questions each child sharply about the missing money.

"You're not moving until the thief confesses!" she shouts. The children stand for a long time—sullen and silent. She waits. When the bell rings ending the period, she accuses them angrily, "Some of you are robbers, and all of you are liars. You are the worst creatures I have ever taught." The children, eyes down, file out to their next class.

Mr. Smith has taught elementary school for five years, and he currently teaches third grade. The science fair is fast approaching, and Mr. Smith has been instructed by the principal to develop a science project for his class. He has settled on dinosaurs, a classic standby, and while the children construct model dinosaurs with toothpicks and paste, Mr. Smith makes a poster that begins: "Hypothesis: What are the different names of the ancient dinosaurs?"

When the models are completed, Mr. Smith displays them on a table and announces to the children that "this is a democracy, and so we'll vote for which ones to take down to the fair." One student suggests that they display them all. "No," Mr. Smith replies. "We don't want to embarrass ourselves." Another student notices that his model is missing from the table, and the teacher explains that "I've already weeded out the worst ones."

Ms. Cohen, a new kindergarten teacher, noting a school expectation that children develop an appreciation for different cultures and backgrounds, has taken a unique approach. For "homework" she has sent a note asking that families discuss and write up how each child came to have his or her name: Were you named after someone? Where does your name come from? What does it mean? The children bring back a breathtaking range of responses: Solomon's name is from the Bible, Aisha's from the Koran, Dylan's from popular culture, Malcolm's from the black liberation movement, Lucia's from a grandmother in Cuba, and Veronica's from a comic strip. The names project opens a wide world of affirmation, vitality, and ongoing inquiry.

Ms. Ellis, an experienced elementary school teacher, has labeled every desk in her classroom with the words "left" and "right." "I can't teach them to read," she explains, "if they don't know their left from their right." Ms. Ellis proudly tells a visitor that "we're on page 307 of the math text—exactly where we're supposed to be according to board guidelines." Most of the children are paying no attention, and the fact that virtually every child is failing math is not her major concern. She is doing her job, delivering the curriculum, and it is the children who are failing to do theirs. "I am a good teacher," she declares, "but many of today's children simply cannot learn."

Anyone who spends time in schools could add hundreds, or even thousands, of other snapshots of teachers teaching: glimpses of brilliance, cruelty, heroism, resistance, banality, capacity extended and power abused. No single picture is ever entirely exemplary; no snapshot ever reveals the whole of it. And yet each snapshot embodies pieces of something larger, and looking at just these five, I wonder: Should these teachers be empowered? Are they already powerful in some hidden and some obvious ways? Would I want them running the schools?

THE DEBILITATION OF TEACHERS

I recently attended an orientation for new teachers conducted by a veteran elementary school principal. The administrator spoke about his admiration for the idealism, the energy, and the fresh ideas of his young staff. The tone was light and friendly, if unmistakably patronizing—smiles and good feelings spread across the room. After a lengthy prelude of quips and compliments, the principal, without changing tone or facial expression, got down to business:

> I know you think you're going to change the world—and I admire you for it and I agree with it—but I don't want you to be too hard on yourselves. You think you can teach these kids to read, for example, and some will learn to read. But many come to us from homes where they never learn to listen. There's too much loud music, too much noise. For some of these kids, just getting them to listen would be a good job. The main thing is not to be too hard on yourselves.

All the early praise of youth turns out to be an attack of some substance. These teachers are being told that their aspirations and their expectations are too high, that they are naive and foolish, that soon they can expect to grow out of it. And they are being told that the failure to learn to read, for example, is the fault of the child and the family, not the responsibility of the school or the teacher.

Most teachers enter teaching with a sense of purpose and altruism. They attend colleges of education that muddy that purpose and have disdain for that altruism. They then enter workplaces that, too frequently, neither acknowledge nor nurture nor challenge them. And along the way, they meet a lot of people, like this principal, who patronize and mislead them. The structure of schooling combines with a defeatist and cynical school culture to render teachers silent, passive, and powerless in their own worlds.

All of this creates a teacher who is little more than a cog in a machine. Teachers become glorified clerks, mindlessly shuffling paper and carelessly moving through the workday. Bureaucratic thinking, then, is not simply a problem at the central office; it impacts teachers and youngsters directly. Teachers come to think of themselves as interchangeable parts; they turn their attention to their supervisors (whom they must please) and away from their students (who should, in turn, mindlessly please them). In order to succeed, everyone must follow orders, march in step, become passive, and do the job.

But if, perchance, our larger purposes for children include that they develop a curious and probing disposition of mind, a compassionate and caring attitude, a critical and creative intelligence, and a willingness to participate in public life for the common good, how can mindless, uncaring, detached, alienated, and angry teachers achieve any of this?

What we find in schools, for children and for adults, runs counter to our avowed values and our larger purposes. Too often, we find disrespect in the lunchroom, dullness and conformity in the curriculum, bitterness and anger in the hallways. All the machinery of schooling—the bells, the intercom, the rows of desks, the endless testing of discrete skills—is a context that resists intelligence. Many kids, searching for what will allow them to succeed in school, reasonably conclude that obedience and dullness will bring rewards. And most teachers, having learned the "realities" (the limitations, the politics, the complexities) of life in schools, have learned to seek fulfillment elsewhere.

TEACHER POWER

But would putting teachers in charge change any of this? Of course, teachers do run the schools now, in certain ways. Ask any principal, ask the public, or ask children and youth. Students know teachers directly, immediately. Teachers are the potent embodiment of the entire school experience, from the child's perspective. A wider public knows teachers through the political clout of their unions and professional associations. Periodic strikes are a forceful reminder to the citizenry of teacher strength. And while principals describe their own power as contingent on a wide range of others—school boards, custodians, communities—they calculate their productivity and effectiveness in direct relation to teacher power. Teachers are at the center of the teaching-learning interaction; they are at the heart of the avowed purpose of the whole educational enterprise. Whatever they do or fail to do is, therefore, momentous.

The complexity of schools makes generalizability difficult. Combined with the imprecise and trendy application of language in our culture (and in education particularly), it can be difficult to know if a specific term is referring even to a similar universe of possibilities. A school is "restructured"; a classroom is "technologically advanced"; the curriculum is "revolutionized." But one has to *be there* to know the meaning of any of these terms.

When we talk of "empowerment," an educational buzzword that no one can seemingly live without today, we are on a slippery slope indeed. Are we referring to governance issues, economic issues, contractual issues, or pedagogical issues? Is "teacher empowerment" about the right to control the curriculum, revamp the school day, hire the principal, resist parental interference in textbook selection, discipline students, or protect contractual gains? It might be any of these or none of them.

Teachers appear, to the nonteacher world, to be people of authority, legal sanction, license, and influence. But teachers often experience themselves as powerless, abused, underpaid, and generally unappreciated. This paradox can perhaps best be unraveled by exploring the power teachers actually have.

One focus of teacher power is the whole area of licensure and legal sanction. Every state compels teachers to fulfill specified educational requirements, to be citizens of solid character, to swear certain oaths or make particular affirmations, and, increasingly, to pass some form of standardized teacher test. When every requirement is fulfilled and every gate passed, the state consigns a license to teach; it gives official authority and legal power to the teacher. This license is exclusive, and it endows the bearer with special privileges, responsibilities, and power.

Licensure is, of course, a contradictory kind of power. On the one hand, it provides teachers with privilege and authority: the privilege to be hired and the authority to work in the profession. On the other hand, in practice it can distort core aspects of teaching. For example, while the purpose of sanctioning a specific course of study may be to ensure a certain standard for teachers, this can, and often does, make the college or postgraduate experience exclusively a process of credentialing. Students of teaching become preoccupied with the utility of taking all the required courses for the certificate they want. In the process, they get their first serious taste of what is to come: they feel themselves made into objects within a bureaucracy. It becomes difficult, as a student, to experience oneself as an active subject in a world in need of help, perhaps even of repair. It is difficult, too, to stay alive to teaching as an intellectual and ethical activity. As students pass through their courses of study, the original motivation that drove them to teach—love of children, perhaps, or a desire to share an important part of the world with others—begins to fade and is replaced with a sense of the functional and the technical. Students of teaching begin to submit to the given world of schools, to internalize the taken-for-granted, and not to think too much about it. Thus the power of licensure can also, in effect, undermine the power to teach.

A second center of teacher power is the union or professional association. Teachers' unions are organized and collective expressions of teacher power and a fact of life in U.S. schools. Over 80 percent of public school teachers are members of either the American Federation of Teachers (AFT—700,000 members) or the National Education Association (NEA—1,700,000 members), and more than 60 percent of teachers are covered by collective bargaining agreements. The AFT has spearheaded the negotiated-conflict, trade union approach to teaching; this has led to frequent strikes to improve wages and benefits. The NEA has been more consistently progressive on social issues such as racial justice and union democracy. Each organization has struggled to redefine itself in relation to current school crises and realities. Both have moved in the direction of professionalizing teaching. The AFT has championed career ladders and more learner-centered classrooms. The NEA has fought against arbitrary testing of teachers and the privatization of public schools. Each organization is somewhat defensive toward reform proposals, and each is evolving, however haltingly, from a collective bargaining, conflictual labor-management prototype toward a more professional policy-oriented stance. Together, they have changed the face of U.S. education in the past twenty-five years, and they remain a potent force from the state house to the school house. Two studies in this section (Chapters 4 and 5) examine school reform experiments fostered by each of these unions.

But union power is also contradictory. It has been enormously successful in gaining higher wages and benefits for teachers, and it has provided them with a vehicle for broader political participation. And yet union power has also generated several unintended consequences: it has set teachers off as an interest group engaged in special pleading (e.g., for school funding) that may be perceived to be against the public good (requiring ever-higher taxes). Union power has constrained teachers within a blue-collar framework with its exclusive focus on wages and benefits rather than, say, on issues of curriculum, instruction, and evaluation. And union power has reinforced the problem of size. It has meant building big organizations necessary for the struggle with management, but these organizations have themselves become inflexible, impersonal, and bureaucratic in their own ways. Once again, teacher power proves to be problematic.

Finally, the most obvious and widely recognized venue for teacher power is in the classroom itself. Central to the lore of teaching is the sense that once the classroom door is closed, teachers are autonomous and powerful. So, while reform efforts generally focus on governance, administration, curricular change, and the like, teachers know that all of it depends on them. All reform must be filtered finally through their hearts and their minds; everything in classrooms lives or dies in their hands. Several of the ensuing chapters demonstrate this reality quite graphically. While most often characterized as the base of the educational pyramid, teachers, in this sense, are at the peak of possibility and power.

But this power, too, is contradictory; it can divide and disconnect, isolating teachers from allies and colleagues. Since teacher rewards are mainly rooted in classrooms and teacher goals are primarily classroom-linked, teachers are less likely to seek, or to offer, help in relation to the content and conduct of their work. And since the structure of teaching develops a kind of radical individualism, teachers are typically conservative agents of continuity, rather than dynamic agents of change. Unfortunately, a range of advocated reforms—new math, cooperative learning, critical thinking—are premised on the notion that teachers should be interested in change and should be able to deliver what they currently neither understand nor practice. This is, of course, nonsense. So while the power to be autonomous can be invigorating, it can simultaneously cripple teachers in specific ways.

SCHOOLS AS LEARNING COMMUNITIES

What, then, should schools look like? A school structured around what we know about teaching and learning would look very different indeed from today's schools. Typically schools are little factories, everything neat, ordered, and on schedule, or at least hoping to be so. Children are the products, moving passively along the assembly line, being filled up with bits of subject matter and curriculum until they are inspected and certified to graduate to the next level. Teachers don't think much, don't question, don't wonder, don't care—they are the assembly-line workers. Never mind that between a quarter and a half of the kids fall off the line altogether or that for those who keep moving along the end of the line rarely represents an opening of possibilities. Never mind that teachers are using a fraction of their knowledge and abilities in these classrooms. The line itself has become the important thing, the line and the stuff being poured into the youngsters.

By contrast, schools that are powerful places for teachers to work, vital centers of student action, must be based upon what is known about learning: people learn best when they are actively exploring, thinking, asking their own questions, and constructing knowledge through discovery; people learn constantly and in a variety of styles and at a range of paces; people learn when their emotional, psychological, physical, cultural, and cognitive needs are met; people learn when they are nurtured but also challenged, that is, when they are stimulated through encountering surprising, new ideas and information that don't exactly "fit" their existing scheme of things.

In learning communities, children must be actively engaged with a variety of concrete materials and primary sources. Youngsters must be involved in purposeful work appropriate for their age. Teachers would no longer be clerks delivering a set of predetermined curriculum packages to passive consumers but would act as coaches, guides, and colearners. The first responsibility of teachers, then, would be to see each student in as full and dynamic a way as possible; they would seek to discover the experiences, knowledge, preferences, aspirations, and know-how the children themselves bring to school.

Seeing the student in this way is a complicated proposition, for there are always more ways to see, more things to know. Observation and recording are a way to begin, opening a process of investigation and affirmation. But it is understood that observations are always tentative, always in the service of the next teaching challenge, and always interactive—the observed, after all, are also people with their own intentions, needs, hopes, dreams, aspirations, and agendas. The student grows, the teacher learns, the situation changes, and seeing becomes an evolving challenge. As layers of mystification and obfuscation are peeled away, as the student becomes more fully present to the teacher, experiences and intelligences that were initially obscure become the ground upon which powerful teaching can be constructed.

Teachers would also create environments for learning, constructing laboratories for discovery and surprise. In an early childhood classroom this might mean having a large block area, a comfortable reading corner, and an easel with red, yellow, and blue paints available. Working at the easel, a child might encounter orange and construct knowledge about primary and secondary colors upon this dazzling discovery. Along with the color orange come confidence, self-esteem, curiosity, and a sense that knowledge is open-ended and that knowing is active. In contrast, a lecture and work-sheet would be a rather tame and anemic alternative and would convey collateral lessons about knowledge as though it were finite and knowing as passive.

In learning communities, teachers would struggle to build bridges from the knowledge and experiences of youngsters to deeper and wider ways of knowing. Bridge building begins on one shore with the know-how and interests of the student and moves toward broader horizons, deeper ways of thinking and knowing. In this regard, it is worth transforming the old notion that "you can learn something from anything" into a deeper sense of relatedness and interactivity: "you can learn *everything* from anything."

John Dewey (1914: 157) argues that a big part of the art of teaching "lies in making the difficulty of new problems large enough to challenge thought, and small enough so that in addition to the confusion naturally attending the novel elements, there shall be luminous familiar spots from which helpful suggestions may spring." Children might connect issues in their own lives concerning society and the crowd, group identity, jealousy, and revenge to a deep encounter with *Romeo and Juliet*. It is all there, after all, in their lives *and* in Shakespeare. Teachers might find themselves covering less stuff but teaching everything more deeply.

Assessment would reflect the whole child and would be designed to illuminate strengths and interests as much as areas of need. Assessment would always be in the service of the next teaching question and would be broad and adaptive, rather than narrow and fixed. Teachers would reject the obsession with a single, narrow assessment tool as inadequate to capture the complexity of human growth. It is well known that if the only tool you have is a hammer, you tend to treat everything like a nail. Reinvented schools would develop a range of tools in order to achieve a rich, vital, and contextual portrait of learning.

TEACHER EMPOWERMENT AND THE CREATION OF LEARNING COMMUNITIES

Teachers have all kinds of power—some traditionally held, some won more recently—and yet none of it solves the problem of teacher empowerment or of creating learning communities in our schools. Their existing power is irrelevant to or outside of what teachers need. It does not speak to the imperative for schools to change and the centrality of teachers in defining and building that process. Neither does it address the possibility of a new kind of professionalism and the ways in which teachers could spearhead and benefit from breaking new ground. Finally, it ignores the nature of teaching and learning and the importance of teachers recognizing and wielding their real power in classrooms in new ways. Too much of teacher empowerment simply misses the point.

There are many more examples of failure than of success in the organized attempts to change or improve schools over the past several decades. The inconsistent role of teachers in powering reform is at the heart of much of the problem. Several of the following case studies document this problem. As Seymour Sarason (1971) notes with some irony, the more things change, the more they stay the same. Not only are the unintended consequences of innovations sometimes worse than the problems they were designed to fix, but "existing regularities," the common sense of schooling, frequently prevent us from seeing the wider universe of possibilities. We are often mired in our own limited experiences, curtailed by crises in imagination.

We do, however, know very well by now what kinds of reform projects consistently flop. Failure is practically guaranteed:

- When curriculum packages are brought in from outside and fitted into existing structures and assumptions.
- When "in-services" are given to passive teachers in spite of their own priorities and felt needs.
- When reform is conceived as generic or one-size-fits-all.
- When classroom change is conceived and developed as "teacherproof."

These kinds of things promise easy change and painless improvement and remain dominant in school improvement efforts, despite their consistent failure to deliver.

We have growing evidence of what actually works in attempts to reform schools.

School Change

Successful school improvement efforts tend to be site-based and grounded in the concrete realities of the local situation. Milbrey McLaughlin (1990: 12) argues that "change continues to be a problem of the smallest unit." Successful change is local, not global, and depends heavily on the will and capacity of teachers and other people in the actual situation, a point underlined by the studies that follow.

The participants in successful school improvement efforts—teachers, parents, administrators, students—tend to be visible and accountable to one another. Change is not a treatment done *to* someone or some group, but is an accomplishment achieved with participants acting as partners and allies. The improvement effort draws its power and energy from the needs and intentions of the people in the school community.

Successful school improvement projects are holistic; that is, they are not aimed at tinkering with bits and pieces of the school, but address intellectual and organizational issues, structural and cultural realities. Good ideas, curriculum guides, wonderful materials, all are of limited usefulness without, for example, rethinking the use of time, restructuring the roles of teachers and students, and reworking resources. Expanding roles and capacities, challenging assumptions and the existing ethos, are an essential part of successful change. But, as we shall see, it is easier to describe this process than to implement it.

In successful school change, people actively define and then solve their own problems. Instead of reinforcing passivity and powerlessness, the change process itself is designed to develop agency and efficacy (the sense of oneself as an active agent able to create change). A guiding theme is that the people with the problems are also the people most needed to craft solutions. The process is important, and it leads to an action plan for school people.

What we know about successful school improvement argues decisively for an expanded role for teachers that moves them into the center of the change process—teacher empowerment. This is not something to be granted to teachers, but something teachers must themselves determine is necessary and right. Others may create the context for teacher empowerment, but it is a power that teachers must initiate and exercise themselves.

Professionalization

Professionalism is a second area in which teacher empowerment might effectively be reconsidered. Gary Sykes (1987) calls teacher professionalism "a theme in search of specific policy initiatives and a social meaning appropriate to teaching circumstances." In other words, while everyone talks of teacher professionalism, some mean a stronger union, others mean better wages and higher status, and yet others think of the trappings associated with law and medicine.

While a concern with professionalism is intended to raise the status and rewards of teaching, attract more able and intelligent people to the field, and allow teachers greater control over the content and the conduct of their work, this focus is also problematic. Teacher professionalism can imply a kind of elitism, a distancing from the communities that spawn and sustain teaching. Teacher professionalism could lead to the further degradation of language and the development of more arcane and inaccessible knowledge, things that defy the uniquely shared, inclusive, and democratic nature of teaching. Similarly, professionalism could lead to an overemphasis on developing a "knowledge base" for teaching and a corresponding weakening of attributes like "care" and "compassion" as the heart of the teaching enterprise.

Teacher professionalism could, of course, be developed in partnership with, instead of opposition to, communities, parents, and children. This would take vision as well as courage, for there are no models of a profession of this type. But parents who are actively seeking power and accountability are the natural allies of teachers who see the need for radically restructured schools. Both want to build schools that work dramatically better for all kids; both want to dismantle stifling and unresponsive bureaucracies; both want to build vital, viable learning communities.

The Aristotelian concept of friendship, with its concern for the individual and the community, its attitude of compassion and critique, its focus on mutual pursuit of the right and the good, can perhaps provide a beginning framework for a new professionalism. Teaching, after all, is unlike any other profession in the complex balance it must strike between nurturing and challenging, between private and public, between sympathetic regard and timely demand. A teaching profession built on a model of friendship could become the prototype to revitalize and reshape the other professions, as well.

A new approach to professionalism would also challenge teachers to consider unique and powerful new roles. But once again, this is something teachers themselves must pursue, if it is to have any significance.

Classroom Life

Finally, teacher empowerment is already built into the teaching-learning interaction, the center of classroom life. Power characterizes certain relationships whether acknowledged or not, whether consciously exercised or not, whether overt or not. The power of teachers in classrooms is easily illustrated. For example, in the vignettes at the beginning of this chapter, each teacher wields incredible power and yet each embodies a different sense of teaching, and power is therefore understood, exercised, and experienced differently. Ms. Ellis, whose failing math class was on the "right" page, is a clerk, delivering the curriculum to passive or resistant students. Mr. Smith is workmanlike in creating a science fair exhibition, attempting to shape the raw material that is before him. Ms. Vaughn is a guard, a disciplinarian, and an ineffective detective. Ms. Cohen and Mr. Wilson demonstrate the power to tap into the strengths of children themselves, the power to empower.

SHOULD TEACHERS BE EMPOWERED?

This question is both simpler and more complex than it at first appears. Teachers are already powerful in many ways. Teacher power is contradictory and problematic. Teacher empowerment could be something new and untried. But there may be other, more important questions: Will teacher empowerment, in the ways it is being attempted, lead to better education for youngsters? Will it improve the schools? Will teachers in positions of authority promote the broad public interest or their own self-interest against the interest of others? To whom will teachers be accountable? Are there enough intelligent, competent, and highly motivated teachers to make teacher empowerment a reasonable goal?

None of these questions can be answered definitively, at this point. There has been very little practice in the kinds of teacher power being contemplated here, and the answers are necessarily dynamic and changing. In the chapters that follow, the authors provide some initial glimpses into the struggles of those seeking to empower teachers. Their experiences indicate how difficult this enterprise may be.

Teacher motivation, for example, may be low in a system characterized by coercive control and then spring to life in a restructured school environment. In any case, teacher empowerment will remain only a possibility, a hypothetical proposition, as long as it is conceived as a grant given from outside of teaching. Teacher power can never be simply mandated, legislated, or enforced; it must be taken by people who perceive the possibilities and are willing to overcome real obstacles, create unique alliances, and assume new responsibilities. Greater efficacy, vigor, and energy cannot be imposed on unwilling teachers. Teacher power must be claimed by those who are willing to build and explore and extend it.

People outside of teaching cannot empower teachers, and yet teacher empowerment is essential to the meaningful restructuring of schools and to the reforming of education. Teacher empowerment is a condition of reform, and it is teachers themselves who must choose to rethink and revive teaching.

Still, people outside of teaching can play a part. *Teacher educators*, for example, can structure programs that deemphasize the dominant focus on discrete skills and methods, choosing instead to create opportunities for students to work collectively, to actively construct knowledge about teaching, to resist the passifying, conforming traditions of teacher socialization. If they must teach methods, they can teach methods of creative insubordination. *Educational researchers* can move, as Nel Noddings (1987) suggests, from doing research on teaching, to conducting research for teaching, that is, choosing problems to research that are of collective interest to researchers, teachers, and students alike. They can promote action research, participatory research. And *administrators, advocates*, and *funders* can find ways to reward imagination and courage, to structure opportunities for teacher-initiated, collaborative efforts to take seed in schools and grow. They can remove the structural obstacles that currently debilitate teachers.

EMPOWERING OTHERS

A fundamental goal of all teaching is the empowerment of others. All teachers at all times—regardless of philosophy, method, technique, or approach—want their students to become in some way stronger, to have greater knowledge or capacity, to be more skilled or able or vigorous, to be able to survive or succeed in some way. Empowerment is the heart and soul of teaching, and it cannot be done well by the weak or the faint. There is no way for passive teachers to produce active students, for dull teachers to inspire bright students, for careless teachers to nurture caring students. Should teachers be empowered? Only if we want powerful students to emerge from our schools. Marge Piercy (1973) captured some of this sense in the following poem:

To Be of Use

The people I love the best
jump into work head first
without dallying in the shallows
and swim off with sure strokes
almost out of sight.

They seem to become natives of
that element,
the black sleek heads of seals
bounding like half-submerged
balls.

I love people who harness
themselves,
an ox to a heavy cart,
who pull like water buffalo,
with massive patience,
who strain in the mud
and the muck to move things
forward, who do what has to
be done, again and again.

I want to be with people who
submerge in the task, who go
into the fields to harvest
and work in a row and
pass the bags along,
who are not parlor generals
and field deserters
but move in a common rhythm
when the food must come in
or the fire be put out.

The work of the world is
common as mud.
Botched, it smears the hands,
crumbles to dust.
But the thing worth doing well
done has a shape that satisfies,
clean and evident.
Greek amphoras for wine or oil
Hopi vases that held corn,
are put in museums
but you know they were made
to be used.
The pitcher cries
for water to carry and
a person for work that is real.

Teaching, at its best, is work that is real.

2 Rural Science and Mathematics Education: Empowerment through Self-Reflection and Expanding Curricular Alternatives

Mary Jo McGee Brown

> Believing, with Max Weber, that man is an animal suspended in webs of significance he himself has spun, I take culture to be those webs, and the analysis of it to be therefore not an experimental science in search of law but an interpretive one in search of meaning.
>
> Clifford Geertz
> *The Interpretation of Cultures*

The purpose of this chapter is to discuss the nature of science and mathematics education in rural areas of the United States. Attitudes of teachers and students toward science and mathematics will be presented. Examples of current projects to enhance scientific and mathematical literacy in rural areas will be discussed and compared. Data from three ethnographic case studies involving science and mathematics education will be used to achieve the primary goal of this chapter, which is to allow the "voices" of rural participants in education to be heard. If people are suspended in cultures of their own making, we need to hear the meanings those cultures have to the participants who generate and live out that meaning.

The secondary goal is to generate discussion and investigation among policymakers in rural education about (1) the distinctiveness of schooling in rural areas; (2) needs of students in rural areas as viewed by rural educators, residents, and students who live there; and (3) ways to enhance environments in rural schooling situations that would allow both educators and students to become empowered with educational and vocational choices. It is only through rural educators identifying their own needs, curricular inadequacies, and problems relative to their strengths and available resources for educating children that problems in science and mathematics education in those areas can begin to be resolved. Naturalistic inquiry is proposed as a needed beginning point of investigating rural educators' and students' meanings of rural, science and mathematics literacy, and authentic science and mathematics instruction.

BACKGROUND

Education of students in rural, small school districts continues to be a major part of public formal schooling in the United States, although there is a significant population shift away from some small towns and farming areas in the country. Rural school districts are located in all states, and the diversity across them is great. Toni Haas (1991) suggests that rural schools are different from other schools because of their smaller size, the smaller scale on which education takes place, their isolation from each other, and lack of infrastructures of support present in more populated areas. Rural schools have been characterized (Nachtigal, 1991) as being an integral part of the community where the facilities must serve multiple purposes and where operation is flexible and personnel is versatile. Haas (1991) asserts that state and national policies that treat all schools alike often negatively impact rural schools because they ignore the effects of isolation, size, and diversity.

While there has been interest recently in problems such as inequity of educational opportunity for special-needs students in rural areas (Massey & Crosby, 1983), educational research historically has focused on problems in urban areas (DeYoung, 1987). In a recent article reviewing efforts to improve school science in advanced and developing countries, Herbert Walberg (1991: 31) never directly addresses issues in rural science education, but a quote he uses to describe secondary school science in developing countries ("taught badly by under-qualified teachers struggling with curricula that are urban-biased, scattered with examples unfamiliar and inaccessible to the bulk of the students") could be used equally well to describe science education in some rural areas of the United States.

Attitudes toward Science and Mathematics

Students and teachers nationally and also in rural areas place low importance on science and mathematics. Walberg (1991: 37) cites an analysis of national survey data that shows "that only about one-fifth of high school students said that they needed biology, chemistry, and physics for the future; less than a quarter said they similarly needed geometry and trigonometry." Studies (Hueftle, Rakow & Welch, 1983; Walberg, 1991; Yager & Penick, 1986) indicate that while primary school students enjoy science and feel it will be valuable to them in the future, interest and perceived value plummet by the time students are in secondary schooling. John Goodlad (1984) reported that science and mathematics were ranked near the bottom by students in elementary through high schools in their choices of favorite subjects. One statewide survey in Kansas (Horn, Davis & Hilt, 1985) revealed that teachers, in rating the importance of general studies to the success in teaching, ranked mathematics, physical science, and biological science sixth, seventh, and eighth, respectively, out of eight areas of preparation. Teachers in small rural schools and large schools alike felt that these three subjects were relatively unimportant.

Recently projects to enhance rural teachers' attitudes toward science and mathematics have been attempted. Based on Paul Nachtigal's notion: "If rural education is to be improved, it will be because rural communities define their problems in ways that make sense to them," Gail Shroyer and Larry Enochs (1987) conducted a two-week summer workshop (science education, biology, and astronomy) for rural science teachers to enable them to identify strengths and needs for development of an action plan for improved science instruction in their schools. The focus of the training was to prepare participants to become leaders of rural science education improvement in their own school districts. Shroyer and Enochs do not present effectiveness data on this project but indicate that action plans developed in the workshop were implemented the following year by participating teachers in their schools.

Betty Bitner (1990) reports on a year-long in-service science workshop to enhance attitudes of K–7 teachers toward science and science teaching. The thirty-three elementary teachers were from rural and small city schools in Arkansas. Topics in the workshop included scientific reasoning, the structure of science, and a variety of topics from state instructional objectives. Teachers engaged in learning through lectures, field trips, experiments and activities, and individual projects. They found that the year-long workshop had a significant positive effect on the attitudes of the participants and also had a significant positive effect in reducing apprehension toward science and improving attitudes toward using science equipment, doing scientific laboratory work, and discussing science topics.

Some projects in science and mathematics are based on workshop models to target specific teachers who can impact students in their schools (National Science Foundation [NSF], 1989). The focus of the Nebraska

Mathematics Scholars Program for Secondary School Teachers is to enhance mathematics background and provide professional development for sixty exemplary secondary school mathematics teachers. Science Networks: A Model for Science Teacher Leadership is a three-year project to enhance the scientific competence of rural elementary teachers and equip them to motivate their students toward careers in science.

Other projects are more global, as they attempt to affect whole school districts or large numbers of students and teachers in rural school systems. Fundamentals of Pre-Engineering: Networking for School Math and Science Teachers is a project to organize a network of science and mathematics teachers in rural districts in south and central Georgia to increase their understanding of the engineering field. The project targets 300 teachers and 6,000 students over a three-year period in summer workshops and school-year activities. Project LITMUS (Leadership Infusion of Technology in Mathematics and its Uses in Society) is a project to implement comprehensive instructional computing in the K–12 mathematics classrooms of two rural Georgia school systems. Project LITMUS will include approximately 300 classrooms serving 8,000 students.

Isolation is a key problem of teachers in rural areas. Goals of the Nebraska Mathematics Scholars Program were to strengthen mathematics knowledge of sixty-six outstanding secondary school mathematics teachers and assist them in developing dissemination activities through which their knowledge and expertise could be shared. A common theme emerging from teacher evaluations of the project statewide (Thornton, 1991) was "the *tremendous* value in forming a *statewide* community of math teachers." Advances in technology are providing alternative solutions to the isolation problem of rural educators and curricula deficiencies. Training elementary science teachers in the use of a microcomputer telecommunications system in the Better Elementary Science Teaching Project in Montana (Jinks & Lord, 1990) has resulted in 92 percent of participants accessing the network to share information. Ward Worthy (1988) describes a system where advanced placement chemistry courses are offered to rural secondary schools via satellite and microcomputer links with Oklahoma State University.

Student Views of Science and Mathematics

More studies are needed in rural areas to understand how students and educators construct understanding of science and mathematics and to identify the constructions they have produced. Elisabeth Charron (1987) conducted a naturalistic inquiry in a small rural county served by a single school system to determine students' understandings of science. She interviewed students, educators, and community participants about what science means and how children learn science. She found differing attitudes about science, from "You can learn more about the future with science. Science is the future," to "Other things you use more, like math. When you grow up you can use adding and multiplying, not science." She asserted that the latter quote is more representative of people's views in this rural community. Young students defined science as doing things, making things, naming things in science, and understanding ordinary things. Older students defined science as thinking, learning ideas, learning how things are put together, learning already discovered facts, and providing single answers to particular questions. Students at all levels equated science with natural history. Older students preferred involvement in science and criticized less interactive approaches. To adequately meet the needs of rural students in science and mathematics, more studies like this are needed across different types of rural situations so that local instruction can be modified to address students' constructions and misconceptions about mathematics and science.

Meeting Student Curricular Needs

Bruce Barker (1985) conducted a random sample mail survey of large (enrollments in excess of 1,000 students) and small (enrollments of less than 500) schools in the United States to determine how broad the disparity is in curricular offerings between them. Results indicated that larger high schools can and do offer greater variety in their curricula than do their small school counterparts. In the areas of mathematics and science, the percent of schools offering certain advanced courses was significantly higher for large schools than small schools (see Table 2.1). Barker suggests that school administrators should investigate alternative delivery systems and innovative practices that will expand program breadth in small high schools, yet he acknowledges problems in small schools such as inadequate finances, shortages of teachers, changing social values, and pressure from special interest groups.

Realizing the curricular inadequacies in mathematics and science in rural school systems, educators across the country are using summer workshop models to enhance student learning and experiences (NSF, 1989). The Rural Model for Connecting Young Scholars is a nine-day workshop of lab and field experiences for fifteen high-ability and high-potential eighth- and ninth-grade students in Montana. The Science Enrichment for Nebraska

Table 2.1
Advanced Course Availability in High Schools

Courses	Small Schools	Large Schools
Advanced Geometry	37.2%	79.0%
Calculus	55.6%	90.2%
Computer Math	42.3%	76.8%
Probability/Statistics	21.6%	44.3%
Advanced Placement Math	23.5%	62.5%
Geology	16.6%	32.3%
Advanced Placement Biology	24.5%	52.2%
Advanced Placement Chemistry	13.7%	48.6%

Talented Youth Program is a two-week laboratory-based experience in biology, chemistry, physics, and computer science for forty participants from small rural high schools. The Summer Science Institute for Rural Minority High School Students is a six-week program of hands-on laboratory experiences, computer workshops, and field trips in the areas of mathematics, science, and engineering for thirty minority high school students in North Carolina who possess academic potential for pursuing careers in the sciences and engineering. Teaching Chemistry for Rural Students with Chemical Research is a program of technical writing, research methodology, and Special Topics in Chemistry for twelve high school students in Texas. A Summer Science Experience for Young Rural Scholars is a four-week peer/mentor program of analytical and communicative science skills for twenty-four eighth-grade students in rural schools with minimal science opportunities in Texas. All of the above workshops include a career counseling component for the participants. While each of these programs for scholars demonstrates a concern for reaching targeted students, they do not address the science and mathematics needs of all individuals in formal schooling K–12 in rural areas of our country. Components that are common to most of the projects are hands-on experiences and field trips. If these are targeted to future potential scholars in the areas of science and mathematics, it is reasonable that educators in rural areas might consider incorporation of these instructional strategies to enhance student learning and improve student attitudes in science and mathematics courses.

Parents Affecting Student Learning

Historically rural schools have been the center of the community and parents have been directly involved in school activities and children's learning. As more rural areas consolidate schools, parent involvement is decreasing. A number of projects are exploring the role that parents play in student learning and the effectiveness of hands-on and field experiences for young children. The Families in FAMILY MATH: A Research Study (NSF, 1989) is a study to determine how children's interests and proficiency in mathematics are affected through a program designed to help parents of low-income minority students become more effective partners in their children's mathematics learning. Mary Williams-Norton, Marycarol Reisdorf, and Sallie Spees (1990) report success in the SPACE (Science Parents and Children Explore) project, in which more than 95 percent of families in Poynette, Wisconsin, joined in science learning with children through carefully designed experiences using materials commonly found around homes and in outdoor settings available to all students and their families. William Kyle, et al. (1990), report that students in K–6 who participated in the ScienceQuest Program preferred inquiry-oriented, process-approach science and that participation in the program increased student attitudes toward science as a favorite subject.

RURAL PERSPECTIVES: THREE CASE STUDIES

I will present data from three case studies of education projects in rural Georgia to provide an emic perspective (participant's view) of the nature of rural education and some approaches that are achieving success in addressing some rural issues in science and mathematics education. The first project focuses on active involvement of at-risk rural preschool children and their parents in the learning process; the second is a ninth-through-twelfth-grade project to enhance science, mathematics, and communication skills for vocational students in a rural area; the third is the rural team of a K–12 national scientific literacy project.

Kids and Parents at School—the School Bus as a Science/Mathematics Lab

Kids and Parents at School (KAPS)[1] is a project in the rural south Georgia town of Waycross to involve parents in preschool education. The targeted population for KAPS is at-risk (low-income, single-parent home situations) preschool children. The racial composition of the group of four-year-olds the first year of the project was half African-American and half Caucasian. The goal of the project is to reduce the children's risk of failing in school and later dropping out. To accomplish this, both children and their parents are provided instruction in an informal educational setting in half-day sessions throughout the school year. Children attend class Monday through Friday, and parents attend class on Thursdays.

Many things are happening in this preschool interdisciplinary learning environment to enable students to learn science and mathematics concepts and skills: mathematics manipulatives, science manipulatives, science field trips to different natural environments (e.g., a swamp), stories and songs that relate science and mathematics concepts, and a variety of media with which students can "write," "read," draw, and produce artifacts and projects that enhance science and mathematics learning. One little girl told me that the science center is her favorite center to choose to work in because "that's where I learn everything and see how heavy things are here [large plastic scale] and the ants live here in the jar—and we let roly-poly bugs live in a jar too." One of the most interesting lessons I observed was one in which students listened to a children's story about butterflies and sang a song about a butterfly emerging from a cocoon; then all the children got together on the floor and formed a caterpillar, crawled in formation around the room, hibernated into a cocoon, and then emerged, "flying" around the room with their arms waving slowly as butterfly wings.

I could tell many other stories of science and mathematics awareness for these children and their parents in the classroom, but the most striking instructional time I observed utilized the school bus as a learning environment. In that county, like most rural counties, the long bus rides some of the children have to take to attend consolidated schools create problems. On the buses children get bored and cause discipline problems. In general, bus time is a waste of time and causes the school day to be extended.

In the KAPS preschool, the situation is quite different. The teacher rides the school bus with the children, and the community becomes the natural learning laboratory. One method of bus instruction is music. Most of the songs reflected mathematical principles of counting where numbers of certain things were added or subtracted one at a time. In some of them, individual children were pointed out to get the right number; in others, it was a group effort. Children counted numbers of trucks, cars, people, and any other things that they were observing in the environment. Science instruction included things like the teacher pointing out clouds and leading a brief discussion of rain and clouds. The group talked about the temperature outside that day compared to previous days, and they talked about the weather forecast for the next day. This occurred on one twenty-five-minute ride as the sunny afternoon evolved into a light, then heavy rain. During a unit on the swamp (prior to the field trip to a swamp) the bus driver stopped at different points along the route for the teacher to get different things to place in the "swamp" that she and the students were making in the plastic swimming pool at the center. Other times, different types of animals were pointed out and children were asked how one type differed from another (chickens from bantam hens was one example). Functions of things in the environment that they passed, such as the landfill, were discussed. Comparisons such as open/closed, tall/short, two-story/one-story, light and dark colors, big and little, and others were continually made.

I was surprised that students were as involved in the observation, discussions, and questioning as the teacher. As the teacher walked children to their doors as they were taken home in the afternoon, the bus driver continued instruction, pointing out things in the environment and answering students' questions about things they observed.

Mathematics and science were not the only things students were learning in the bus. They learned geography, proper manners, rhymes, general songs, and a variety of things to enhance language and communication skills. At the project on-site evaluation that summer the teacher said, "Teaching on the bus may be the most important aspect of this project, since we consolidated this year and students way out in the counties will have much longer bus rides next year." Since extended time on the school bus is characteristic of rural school systems in which sparse populations are spread over large geographical areas, the concept of bus as learning environment for preschool and primary students could be an important instructional strategy. The one potential problem that emerged with this structure is that the teacher's day is extended by a couple of hours. Financial compensation for the extended day, hiring teacher aides to provide instruction, or some other arrangement would be necessary to effectively implement this model.

Reinforcing Basic Skills of Vocational Students

Historically vocational education has played a central role in schooling in rural areas of the United States. Courses in agriculture, home economics, auto mechanics, and metal and wood shop, for example, met the needs of populations of students who would remain in rural areas and assume occupations of their parents. More recently, however, vocational programs have expanded to include computer technology, principles of technology (physics-based), word processing, computer programming, computerized technology of automobile mechanics, and other courses whose goal is to prepare students for a technologically focused workplace. Some (Rosenfeld, 1983) argue that this transition in vocational education must occur because mechanization has replaced many agricultural opportunities and that employment in industry is becoming scarcer in rural areas of the United States as industries locate in other countries. Walberg (1991: 36) goes beyond calling for changes in vocational education to assert: "Thus, education in basic scientific theory and its applications seems a better investment than vocational training that may soon be obsolete and, in any case, is better learned on the job as needed with the facility-specific equipment required." Vocational training, however, remains a prominent theme in rural education literature, and educators are trying to identify curricula that will match rural students' science, mathematics, and technology skills and content knowledge with that which is needed in occupations in which they will be employed in the next decades.

The Southern Regional Education Board—State Vocational Education Consortium: A Regional Focus

The Southern Regional Education Board (SREB)—State Vocational Education Consortium has been working with schools in fifteen states to help improve mathematics, science, and technology skills of vocational students. The following goal statement includes the rationale for this endeavor.

> More than half of the high school students in America are in general and vocational programs. Students who complete vocational programs, however, score significantly lower on science achievement tests than do students in the academic curriculum nationwide. As work in business and industry becomes more technologically based, the differences between vocational and academic learning must be drastically reduced. How well vocational students perform in high school and later will determine, in good measure, how well America performs in an increasingly global economy. . . . In science the goal is to close, by one-third, the gap between the achievement scores of vocational students and the scores of 1986 students nationwide who indicated they were in academic curriculum. (SREB, 1989)

Based on data from the National Assessment of Educational Progress tests, the SREB report (1989) asserts that in 1988 vocational students were better prepared in mathematics than in science. Further, students completing programs in vocational education performed better in the earth and life sciences than in physics and chemistry. Survey data from participating SREB schools indicated that vocational students are not encouraged to take higher-level mathematics and science courses, that content in the lower-level courses is highly repetitive, and that approximately 50 percent do not take mathematics and 75 percent do not take science courses in their senior year of high school. Yet one year after graduation, approximately 40 percent of the students who had completed a vocational program indicated that they needed to understand more scientific principles underlying their vocational field of study.

A Case Study of One Comprehensive High School

Cedartown Comprehensive High School, located in a rural area of northwest Georgia, is beginning the fourth year of a project to enhance mathematics, science, and communication skills of vocational students through cross-disciplinary instruction as a part of the SREB effort and also with the support from a state innovation grant. The focus is not to integrate science, mathematics, English, and vocational education instruction, but rather to reinforce specific skills in the academic areas as they are needed in vocational courses and to use vocational examples in academic courses. Over 90 percent of the students in this high school take vocational courses during their high school experience, and many of the students in college preparatory courses also get a vocational degree.

The most important outcome of the project to date is the interaction that academic teachers have had with vocational teachers in project meetings to learn about the curriculum in each other's areas in order to identify skills that need to be reinforced for students. Formerly, academic and vocational education within the school were viewed as separate entities by both teachers and students. This was intensified by the vocational education building being physically separate from the academic building. Vocational education courses were formerly seen as a "haven" from academic concerns by most students, who felt these academic studies were unnecessary for the jobs they would assume in their rural hometowns. All teachers in the project are more aware of the mathematics, science, and communication skills that are necessary for students in the types of jobs that they will acquire after graduation, and the vocational students are becoming more cognizant of the importance of mastering academic skills even if they do not plan to attend college. Teachers say that working collaboratively has provided them with a holistic view of education for their students and they are working with counselors to enhance science and mathematics program requirements for vocational students.

When asked in a questionnaire whether rural students should be taught mathematics and science differently than students in urban and suburban areas, all teachers in the Cedartown project said no. In a focus group interview with a small group of academic teachers and individual interviews with vocational teachers in the project, they asserted that while rural students may not all go to college or may get jobs locally, they needed the same science and mathematics understanding as students from urban areas and that they could not think of any reasons that rural students should be taught differently. One teacher said that she felt that in any context it is important to use examples from students' experiences and that especially in science, instruction might reflect examples from agriculture and the different types of local industries in rural areas. Teachers felt that skills, content, and instructional strategies should be the same in mathematics and science and that only examples and experiences would differ from rural to urban/suburban areas.

Vocational, mathematics, English, and science teachers at Cedartown High School *are* teaching differently, however, as a result of the project. Vocational students are benefiting. Rather than assuming that vocational completers do not need science, mathematics, and communication skills to strengthen preparation for their selected vocation, teachers are providing students with knowledge, principles, and skills understandings that support the relationship between the academic and vocational areas. Teachers are using examples from vocational education and from "real world" examples reflecting issues in the local rural businesses and industries where the students work. Further, teachers and administrators are encouraging vocational students to take more science and mathematics courses. Educators feel that these approaches will expand students' opportunities, make them more competitive in their selected occupations, and enable some to pursue college careers who might otherwise have dismissed that option.

Project 2061

The last example is the most comprehensive change proposed by any projects previously discussed. The American Association for the Advancement of Science (AAAS), with funding from NSF, is sponsoring a longitudinal and holistic effort at scientific literacy reform in public school education. It is a visionary interdisciplinary K–12 curriculum development project to enhance scientific literacy for all American schoolchildren. Scientific literacy (embracing science, mathematics, and technology) includes using scientific knowledge and concepts, knowledge of the natural world, and scientific ways of thinking for personal and social purposes. The goal of *Project 2061: Science for All Americans* (AAAS, 1989) is to develop curriculum models based on identified key scientific concepts, principles, and interconnections determined essential for all Americans.

Project 2061 consists of three phases. The first phase was to have panels of experts develop an interdisciplinary conceptual base. Through collaborative efforts of educators, scientists, mathematicians, social scientists, and technologists in Phase II, the conceptual base for reform has been translated into alternative curriculum models. Phase III will be a collaborative effort of educators and scientific literacy consultants to combine resources and materials from Phases I and II to pilot in school systems to "move the nation toward scientific literacy" (AAAS, 1989: 4).

One of the goals of the AAAS staff was to have curriculum models that would be appropriate for educational needs of different populations throughout the United States. They identified six areas representing diverse geographic areas and life-styles: rural, urban, suburban, and inner-city models from six geographic locations around the country. The rural model was developed by the Georgia team during Phase II.

The Georgia "rural model" team was composed of public school educators (administrators and teachers) from areas of mathematics, science, social science, and technology and represented different grade levels from primary to secondary school. The Georgia team, along with members of the other five teams, was introduced to the conceptual base and goals of Project 2061 by AAAS staff members and carefully selected consultants during the summer of 1989 at Boulder, Colorado. Members of all six teams met again during the summer of 1990 at Madison, Wisconsin, to share progress on model development and use additional consultants in scientific literacy and education to augment their efforts.

The goal of the Georgia team was to develop a model of authentic scientific literacy acquisition for rural students. Brian Martin, Heidi Kass, and Wytze Brouwer (1990: 552) discuss a number of meanings of "authentic science" and summarize their presentation by asserting: "A science education that is tending toward authenticity would be one that draws in as many relevant aspects of science as are appropriate at a given point in the student's life. . . . All along the way, the teacher would face the peculiarly pedagogic question: What is appropriate for this child, now?" This is the same philosophy that guided the Georgia team development of components of the model.

The team became most focused on their curriculum model task as members began to grapple with the question "What is rural?" because this provided guidelines for the development of educational experiences that would reflect a rural life-style. While all members teach in rural counties, some have lived and taught in urban and suburban areas previously. The diversity of internal and external perspectives about rural, however, did not facilitate the task of answering the question "What is rural?" in the context of what it meant for formal schooling in general and scientific literacy instruction specifically. The following excerpts from their "Rural Science Education" statement at the beginning of their model reveal some of the characteristics they feel are unique to rural students and schools and how those differences should be addressed educationally.

- A clear-cut definition of rural is difficult to phrase, because no one definition of rural encompasses every condition falling under the term.
- Within rural diversity, there are some characteristics of schools in sparsely populated, relatively isolated settings which require that they be viewed as different learning environments. . . . [S]ome rural schools represent a consolidation of several rural communities, giving these schools some advantages of large schools, but also bringing the disadvantages of distance from the students' homes and the communities they represent. Other smaller schools have limited numbers of faculty and thus may have only one science teacher, who must be expert in all sciences at every level.
- Because of widespread mass communication, we believe that rural students today differ less from their urban counterparts than they have in the past. Those differences that remain are important, however. Rural students bring disparate kinds of knowledge and experiences to school, many of which are uncommon to students in an urban or suburban environment. For example, many children raised on farms come to school already having experienced a "living lab" at home. . . . Some rural students live substantial distances from their schools and from other students which can leave them isolated when at home and can make access to after-school activities difficult. This directly impacts school social life. Both kinds of factors, academic and social, contribute strongly to the final outcomes of schooling.
- Regardless of differences between rural and urban schools and students, the Georgia team does not believe that "rural-ness" should affect radically a school's curriculum or instructional practices for science. . . . We do not feel that rural students should be dealt with differently educationally. . . . This should not affect what is to be taught or how it is to be taught. It might only affect the examples to be used.

At the end of Phase II, team members responded to an open-ended questionnaire asking them to justify keeping a rural model in Phase III of Project 2061. Rather than arguing for retaining the rural model as developed, the following responses represent views of respondents:

> The Georgia model is NOT a "rural" model—rural is a state of mind!
>
> We don't consider ourselves rural! However, our experiences for students will use the natural and human resources available to our students in the areas they live. All curriculum models should do this.
>
> The Georgia model is not "rural" nor should it be given that title alone. We do call for experiences which might be difficult to achieve in urban areas, however. Our experiences we propose do naturally flow from our experience base and would be things students could relate to.

The Georgia rural curriculum model does not differ from the other models in terms of content. It includes all of the science, mathematics, and technology concepts and principles as they relate to human existence as proposed in *Project 2061: Science for All Americans*. The Georgia team members did not identify any content, skills, or attitudes proposed that "all students should acquire as a consequence of their total school experience from kindergarten through high school" (AAAS, 1989) which they felt should be eliminated from the rural model. The only content that was discussed as periodically problematic in some conservative rural areas was evolution. One teacher pointed out, however, that this is not a phenomenon that is distinctively rural, since there are conservative persons in urban and suburban areas who oppose teaching of the general process of evolution in science.

Although reflection and discussion in Phase II led team members to reject the notion that they are rural and that their students should be taught differently, the process of sharing models with the other five teams at the beginning of Phase III in August 1991 led the members to rethink their position. They now hold that they are in fact rural. However, rural cannot be equated with agricultural. The characteristics that emerged for them as descriptive of their rural educational situations were small scale, less variety in curriculum, less specialized teachers, and technological inadequacies. Through this process they now feel empowered through their own recognition of rural problems and identification of alternative ways to resolve them to enhance national science, mathematics, and technology education in rural areas. The team vision is that "students participating in this educational experience (student centered local experience-based curriculum) will be empowered as continuing learners to access knowledge about how the world works and make informed higher education and career choices that transcend local rural boundaries."

The national staff of Project 2061 has purposely integrated into its curriculum development the challenge for a group of educators from rural school districts to define rural as it affects scientific literacy; identify characteristics specific to rural students, schools, and communities; and develop longitudinal experiences within the framework of a curriculum model for preschool to high school students that would mesh their rural experiences and environment with the scientific content and skills identified as those that all U.S. students should acquire as educated citizens. What teachers have done in the units of this rural model is integrate examples and experiences that are familiar and accessible to the majority of rural students and that reflect issues and real problems in modern society. The goal is to have a model and exemplary interdisciplinary curriculum units that can be adopted and adapted by rural school districts across the country. Some teachers are already piloting the ideas, as team members from one of the rural counties formed an interdisciplinary instructional team last year focusing on science, mathematics, technology, and social studies.

The final rural model that evolves during Phase III will be useful to rural school districts. It will address the curriculum inadequacy problems by demonstrating instructional strategies to teach scientific skills to rural students through targeted key concepts in an interdisciplinary manner. Further, it will include ideas for experiences to enhance scientific literacy that reflect rural, rather than urban, human and natural resources. Teachers in adopting districts, following the process used by the Georgia team, can collaboratively construct the meaning of rural for themselves and identify how it affects meanings of science, mathematics, technology, and the pursuit of scientific literacy for students in their rural areas.

EMPOWERMENT OF EDUCATIONAL PARTICIPANTS

There are some common elements across the three case studies:

1. At all three sites, educators assert that the science and mathematics concepts and skills needed by rural students are the same as those for children in other areas.

2. Educators feel that instructional strategies, examples, and experiences must be different for rural students.
3. Teachers reflecting on rural problems in schooling feel empowered because they are the ones making curricular decisions to address the problems.
4. Parents and students feel empowered both because of the knowledge they have gained, which expands opportunities, and because of the change in their worldviews to include themselves as active players in the educational process.

In each of the cases the process rather than the product seems to be of most value. The basic process is collaborative problem solving in rural educational settings. Thus it is self-empowerment, not being empowered by outsiders. Each group has defined what rural does and does not mean in its particular context. After initially rejecting the notion of being rural, teachers at two of the sites realized that they were rejecting the notion of being agricultural, not rural. Additionally, barriers to effective education offering maximum curricular and technological options in those areas have been identified (for the 2061 team local barriers were only seen after cross-site comparisons in dissimilar settings). Methods have been employed to give teachers a voice in curriculum changes to enhance concept and skills development for students. Educators are employing strategies for science and mathematics education that address issues specific to their students and parents in their rural contexts. This process of self-examination, problem identification, and expansion of worldview is what will begin to free rural educators from the constraints of urban-based curricula and allow them to creatively generate alternative instructional strategies in their cultural contexts.

DISCUSSION

Problems and educational issues faced by people in rural areas are being addressed by many projects. Rural educators and residents are the key to solving the scientific and mathematics literacy problems of their young people as they begin to define what it means to be rural and the roles scientific and mathematical knowledge play in a rural life-style as we move into the twenty-first century. Through reflection and input into the structure of rural schooling, educators and parents will empower their own students by providing educational and career experiences and choices that have meaning in a rural environment and global society. Rural science and mathematics curricula must neither restrict students to life in rural areas nor function as a springboard to propel them out of small-town life, but rather provide the knowledge, skills, and career opportunity awareness necessary for informed choices from among all alternatives.

NOTE

1. KAPS and Reinforcing Basic Skills of Vocational Students are both projects sponsored by Georgia State Department of Education innovation grants.

3 The Dangers of Assuming a Consensus for Change: Some Examples from the Coalition of Essential Schools

Donna E. Muncey and Patrick J. McQuillan

From the White House to the National Governors' Association, in education journals and in the popular press, there has been a widespread call for school reform. The words of Mary Futrell, recent president of the NEA, summarize this perspective:

> We are finally arriving at a consensus on the need for meaningful reform of U.S. schools and on the direction which that reform shouid take. . . . We have forged a new consensus on the necessity of providing a high-quality education to all children. We have also come to realize that achievement of that goal will require a radical re-formation of our schools. If we can hold on to this consensus and build around it a new coalition—characterized by mobility—we will finally be ready to undertake the hard work of meaningful education reform. (Futrell, 1989: 10)

Despite claims that schools are failing our children and our society and concomitant calls for change that have filled the public media and education journals for years (e.g., Holt [1964], Kohl [1967], Kozol [1967], the

An earlier version of this chapter was presented at the 89th Annual Meetings of the American Anthropological Association in New Orleans, Louisiana, November 1990. This research was supported by grants from the Exxon Educational Foundation and Pew Charitable Trusts. The authors would like to thank these funders and the following individuals, who provided assistance and critical feedback on earlier drafts: Sarah Uhl, Liliana Costa, Thomas James, Robert Hampel, G. Alfred Hess, Jr., Gail Bader, James M. Nyce, William Graves, and Jeannie McQuiggan. The authors also wish to thank the faculty and administrators from the three study schools for their cooperation and feedback, even though confidentiality agreements preclude our mentioning them by name. We alone are responsible for the contents of this chapter.

National Commission on Excellence in Education [1983], the Twentieth Century Fund Task Force on Federal Elementary and Secondary Education Policy [1983], and the Task Force on Education for Economic Growth [1983]), we found that many teachers and administrators in the schools we studied did not think that their schools or their personal situations needed to be changed. Further, whether they wanted school reform or not, teachers in our study schools would not agree with Futrell's optimistic assessment of the existence of a forged consensus.

We found that assuming there is a consensus regarding the need for school reform has powerful ramifications for efforts at reform and for their eventual outcomes. That is, assuming there is a consensus, and therefore support for change, obscures powerful factors that strongly influence the change process and leaves proponents unprepared to deal with opposition when it arises. School restructuring is a political process, and insufficient attention to this point from the start can prove detrimental to the educational dimensions of restructuring and to schools as a whole.

Drawing on four years of ethnographic research at eight "Coalition" schools and with the Central Staff of the Coalition of Essential Schools (CES), we discuss a common pattern that emerged at seven of the schools, which derived from the assumption of consensus. With the support of the school's administration and the superintendent's office or Board of Trustees, a faculty "vanguard" initiated what they perceived to be the first stage of what would eventually become a more encompassing restructuring effort. This vanguard assumed that those who at first were disinterested would eventually become supporters. These early efforts, rather than building support, quickly became enmeshed in the political life of the school, raised issues of teacher equity and school and personal philosophy, and did little to promote comprehensive, schoolwide change.

THE COALITION OF ESSENTIAL SCHOOLS

The Coalition of Essential Schools was founded in 1984 by Ted Sizer, former dean of the Harvard Graduate School of Education and former headmaster at Phillips Academy, Andover, Massachusetts. Coalition philosophy is the product of thinking, research, and writing that emerged from a five-year multisite study of American secondary schools, A Study of High Schools.[1] Drawing on his experiences in schools and the general shortcomings he perceived in American education, Sizer wrote a compelling narrative about his findings, *Horace's Compromise*, and devised a philosophy, codified in the Common Principles, that has formed the basis for the Coalition. These principles urge schools to maintain an intellectual focus, to concentrate on academic essentials ("less is more"), to acknowledge and meet the diverse needs of all students, to personalize learning, to promote trust and decency, to make students active learners, to see teachers as generalists, to judge mastery by demonstrated exhibition, and to maintain an 80–1 student-teacher ratio while keeping per pupil expenditures within 10 percent of existing costs. (See Appendix A.)

Prior to and at the time of his book's publication, Sizer and his associates made numerous speeches promoting his philosophy (Hampel, 1990, personal communication). Based on what he perceived as an enthusiastic reception for his ideas among the teachers and school administrators he met, Sizer recruited schools willing to experiment with his philosophy and put together a small, university-based staff to assist this effort. From an initial membership of twelve charter schools in December of 1985 and a Central Staff of three persons, the Coalition has grown to include over 140 schools nationwide (Sizer, 1991) and a Central Staff that now numbers nearly forty persons.

In proclaiming the diversity of its membership, the Coalition stresses that it is a grassroots reform movement focused on improving classroom teaching and learning and helping students to "use their minds well." Unlike many reform efforts, the Coalition emphatically rejects centralized and standardized solutions to school problems. Moreover, the nine Common Principles that form the foundation of this reform are ambiguous by design: each member school is to interpret and act upon the principles within its own cultural and institutional context.

To understand the political tensions that arose in our case studies, it will help to keep three aspects of Coalition reform in mind: First, as with the national rhetoric, the Coalition, too, assumes that change is needed. Second, by promoting an intellectual focus as the basis of their reform ideology and stressing the idea of the triangle of learning (i.e., the relationship between the student, teacher, and subject matter) as a school's most important priority, the Coalition Central Staff and member schools, at first, overlooked the political issues associated with school reform. Third, the Coalition asserts that a strength of its reform program is that there is no single model for change; instead, it emphasizes local interpretation of the Common Principles.

THE SCHOOL ETHNOGRAPHY PROJECT

The School Ethnography Project (SEP) began a multiyear ethnographic documentation and research effort focused on the schools and staff that

Appendix A
The Coalition of Essential Schools—The Common Principles

1. The school should focus on helping adolescents learn to use their minds well. Schools should not attempt to be "comprehensive" if such a claim is made at the expense of the school's central intellectual purpose.

2. The school's goals should be simple: that each student master a limited number of essential skills and areas of knowledge. While these skills and areas will, to varying degrees, reflect the traditional academic disciplines, the program's design should be shaped by the intellectual and imaginative powers and competencies that students need, rather than necessarily by "subjects" as conventionally defined. The aphorism "Less Is More" should dominate: curricular decisions should be guided by the aim of thorough student mastery and achievement rather than by an effort merely to cover content.

3. The school's goals should apply to all students, while the means to these goals will vary as those students themselves vary. School practice should be tailor-made to meet the needs of every group or class of adolescents.

4. Teaching and learning should be personalized to the maximum feasible extent. Efforts should be directed toward a goal that no teacher have direct responsibility for more than 80 students. To capitalize on this personalization, decisions about the details of the course of study, the use of students' and teachers' time and the choice of teaching materials and specific pedagogies must be unreservedly placed in the hands of the principal and staff.

5. The governing practical metaphor of the school should be student-as-worker rather than the more familiar metaphor of teacher-as-deliverer-of-instructional-services. Accordingly, a prominent pedagogy will be coaching, to provoke students to learn how to learn and thus to teach themselves.

6. Students entering secondary school studies are those who can show competence in language and elementary mathematics. Students of traditional high school age but not yet at appropriate levels of competence to enter secondary school studies will be provided intensive remedial work to assist them quickly to meet these standards. The diploma should be awarded upon a successful final demonstration of mastery for graduation—an "Exhibition." This Exhibition by the student of his or her grasp of the central skills and knowledge of the school's program may be jointly administered by the faculty and by higher authorities. As the diploma is awarded when earned, the school's program proceeds with no strict age grading and with no system of "credits earned" by "time spent" in class. The emphasis is on the students' demonstration that they can do important things.

7. The tone of the school should explicitly and self-consciously stress values of unanxious expectation ("I won't threaten you but I expect much of you"), of trust (until abused) and of decency (the values of fairness, generosity and tolerance). Incentives appropriate to the school's particular students and teachers should be emphasized, and parents should be treated as essential collaborators.

8. The principal and teachers should perceive themselves as generalists first (teachers and scholars in general education) and specialists second (experts in but one particular discipline). Staff should expect multiple obligations (teacher-counselor-manager) and a sense of commitment to the entire school.

9. Ultimate administrative and budget targets should include, in addition to total student loads per teacher of eighty or fewer pupils, substantial time for collective planning by teachers, competitive salaries for staff and an ultimate per pupil cost not to exceed that at traditional schools by more than 10 percent. To accomplish this, administrative plans may have to show the phased reduction or elimination of some services now provided students in many traditional comprehensive secondary schools.

(The Coalition of Essential Schools, 1985)

were partners in the Coalition of Essential Schools in August of 1986—when schools were still in the initial stages of their restructuring efforts. Data collection concluded in June of 1990. Our research did not involve a formal educational evaluation of the Coalition of Essential Schools; rather, we sought to document broadly what occurred as a consequence of the Coalition's reform efforts. To accomplish this documentation, we collected data on four interrelated components of the reform movement:

1. Individual schools involved in the project.
2. The Central Staff's activities and the role(s) they played in developing the movement's philosophy.
3. The interaction between the Central Staff and the individual Coalition schools at workshops, symposia, and conferences.
4. The developmental history of the Coalition itself.

The majority of our research was conducted in individual schools and focused on two broad questions: How are the Common Principles interpreted by individual schools? And how do those involved in Coalition schools (teachers, administrators, and students) implement the principles as they are developed in each setting? We consciously included an array of perspectives in our research—for example, Central Staff members, students, teachers, and administrators in CES schools, including both supporters and opponents of Coalition philosophy and practices.

We will now look at three schools that adopted different approaches to Coalition reform—a school-within-a-school (SWAS) effort, a whole-school effort, and a school that never went beyond planning for its Coalition program—to illustrate the emergence of common difficulties in these diverse school settings.

CASE STUDIES

Silas Ridge High School[2]

Silas Ridge is an eastern city of 65,000 inhabitants. Located in the heart of the city, Silas Ridge High School is a comprehensive high school that serves a student population of slightly more than 1,000 students. Academically, most students are grouped according to a five-tier tracking system—advanced placement through basic. Although historically most students have been white and middle-class, in recent years Silas Ridge has enrolled increasing numbers of minority and immigrant students, primarily Southeast Asians and Eastern Europeans. Between 1983 and 1987, Silas Ridge won numerous awards for excellence.

Silas Ridge High School's relationship with CES was initiated by a school committee member who became familiar with Ted Sizer's ideas through her graduate work. As part of the professional development activities of the city Teachers' Association, Sizer was invited to speak to faculty members from both city high schools. Following his talk, and with encouragement from a supportive superintendent, the "Sizer Committee," a volunteer group of teachers from Silas Ridge High that included a woman who would soon become the school's principal, explored the possibilities of Coalition membership, then authored an application to CES. In January of 1985, Silas Ridge High School became a "charter" member of the Coalition of Essential Schools.

Silas Ridge spent the next year and a half (from January of 1985 through the summer of 1986) planning its Coalition program. This process had five primary components: (1) sponsoring and attending professional development activities intended to promote school change; (2) investigating other schools' attempts at restructuring; (3) creating new structures and positions to facilitate the change process (such as a Steering Committee to direct Coalition-related work and a Coordinator to oversee this work); (4) consulting and collaborating with the Coalition Central Staff; and (5) generating support for their Coalition effort (through holding faculty dinner "seminars" and meeting with the School Committee, for instance). Two final points about the planning phase are significant: first, in order to participate, faculty and administrators had to assume additional responsibilities to their existing workloads; and second, to avoid forcing disinterested faculty into becoming involved or accepting responsibilities they had never sought, no one was required to participate in any Coalition-related activity; all involvement was voluntary.

In translating Coalition philosophy into practice, Silas Ridge adopted a school-within-a-school (SWAS) structure, with the intent of gradually expanding the program's size. In its first year the Coalition program consisted of a team of four teachers (from the English, history, math, and science departments) who taught the same eighty ninth-grade students—two general-level classes, one college preparatory class, and one honors class. These teachers taught four periods each day, had two periods to plan with their Essential School colleagues, and one free period. (Most of their larger school colleagues had five teaching periods, one supervisory period, and one free period.) To help administer the program, an assistant principal served as Coalition Coordinator. During the program's first year, there was also a "shadow" Coalition team of four teachers who represented the same disciplines and participated in SWAS-related work and who would form a second SWAS team when the program expanded, as planned, the following year.

In its first year, the SWAS proved relatively uncontroversial for the school as a whole. Most Coalition teachers preferred the SWAS structure to their previous teaching situations and felt that they and their students benefited both from this structure and from their efforts at interdisciplinary teaching, heterogeneous grouping, and cooperative learning. Yet internally the team encountered problems. Some team members, for example, were more enthusiastic than others about grouping students heterogeneously, changing the schedule, or experimenting in general. Cooperation became increasingly difficult. Furthermore, one teacher's personal problems had a powerful impact on the team and strained the team's energy and enthusiasm. There were two common reactions to the Coalition SWAS among the rest of the school's faculty. When polled, nearly half the faculty expressed a willingness to assist the program in various capacities (e.g., as a participant in professional development activities, offering professional assistance to the program, etc.), but few volunteered to be actively involved. Second, faculty viewed the SWAS as an interesting experiment.

In its second year (1987–88), the SWAS expanded to include four more teachers and an additional eighty students. During the first quarter, the Coalition program experienced some unexpected faculty turnover and since the assistant principal found it difficult to add SWAS-related business to her other responsibilities, a teacher from the shadow team, a relative newcomer to Silas Ridge High, became the Coordinator.

During this second year, both the SWAS program and the Coalition Steering Committee expanded—the latter in part because of a controversy about the SWAS program. The previous spring, the Steering Committee had voted to expand the SWAS. Since the program would also continue to enroll general, college, and honors students, SWAS faculty were guaranteed to have a second group of the school's honors students, a contentious issue for some Silas Ridge faculty who viewed teaching honors sections as a professional privilege. When some non-SWAS teachers realized that this expansion could limit the number of honors sections available to them, they voiced their concerns to the administration. The administration, however, was adamant that this decision would stand. These teachers then decided to mobilize other faculty members to monitor the workings of the Steering Committee, to ensure that similar developments would not recur. Resistant faculty members, who were influential, experienced, and respected, then joined the Steering Committee.

Whereas during the first year of implementation the Steering Committee had focused on aspects of the triangle of learning, its work thereafter became much more politically charged. One opponent of the SWAS and Silas Ridge's Coalition affiliation described her role as a new member of the Steering Committee:

> The second full year that [the school-within-a-school] was in place, I joined the Steering Committee. . . . I went to every meeting. I am not a negative person. I work *for* things. I work *with* people. . . . But I spent one year as a member of a two-person team of hinder, stall, and delay. And we hindered, stalled, and we delayed that Coalition school-within-a-school right into the ground. We questioned every vote. . . . We made them accountable for who was involved and what was involved, the reasons behind the changes.

As the year progressed, faculty divisiveness and disaffection with the SWAS program and structure worsened. The dispute over assigning the SWAS a second honors section was only one of myriad concerns faculty expressed. Many faculty contended that the SWAS teachers received preferential treatment. As one teacher commented: "We had some teachers who had eighty students, no duties, and fewer classes. How could anybody think that that wouldn't create tension?" These accusations were exacerbated by perceptions among the faculty that the principal hired only those persons who were philosophically compatible with her ideals. Additionally, some questioned whether this effort represented a democratic change coming from the faculty or an administrative mandate driven by the principal and a core of teachers. As one teacher said: "The perception within the school was that it's not coming from the faculty; it's coming from the principal." Although all agreed that faculty members had been involved in each stage of the planning process, some faculty maintained that the process excluded those teachers who could not attend the voluntary before- and after-school meetings so critical to this reform effort. Still others contended that the faculty never voted about whether to be affiliated with the Coalition, nor on the "form" of their Coalition involvement. In the words of one teacher: "What started out as tacit agreement—because why would you be against change; why would you be against improvement?—all of a sudden turned into a school-within-a-school. And that was not voted on by the full faculty."

A third source of resistance and resentment by those not directly involved concerned what they viewed as an implicit criticism of their conventional teaching practices embedded in Coalition rhetoric (e.g., teachers are lecturing too much). One experienced teacher, who was not involved in the SWAS, remarked in a newspaper article that reflected on these tense times:

> Whether it was real or perceived, I don't know, but there was a feeling that what [older] teachers were doing and had been doing was not good and should be changed, and the new people were doing things right. You just can't suddenly say to people who thought that they were doing a good job all along that what you're doing is all wrong.

Finally, during the course of the restructuring, there was a growing sense that SWAS members and the Coalition Steering Committee (the first Silas Ridge governance body with formal power) were now exerting power within the whole school and becoming prominent and identified with success in the local community. And many of those perceived to be the most supportive of Silas Ridge's Coalition work were women with Ivy League educations new to the community. Thus, it was commonly perceived that a clique of relative newcomers was now changing Silas Ridge High.

Recognizing the problems, in February 1988 the Steering Committee voted to abandon the SWAS structure and "to encourage innovation and creativity among the entire staff." The school-within-a-school then became the "teacher teaming project," just one of several Steering Committee efforts. That spring, the faculty created the Faculty Forum, a faculty governance committee intended to ensure faculty input into any restructuring efforts. Recommended after a needs assessment, done as part of an application for a restructuring grant from the State Department of Education, the Faculty Forum was a seven-person committee elected by the faculty and given authority subject to the principal's veto. Subsequent to the formation of the Faculty Forum, the Coalition Steering Committee was dissolved. Some people argued that the creation of the Forum was merely an effort by those opposed to the principal or the SWAS to limit the power of both the Coalition Steering Committee and the principal. So although officially tied to the grant application, the creation of the Forum also signaled the faculty's disaffection with both their principal and the somewhat unanticipated effects of the SWAS expansion.

Silas Ridge's Coalition program spent the next three years in a state of limbo. The Forum named a Coalition Subcommittee to maintain contact with the Coalition Central Staff, to attend Coalition-sponsored events, and to inform the faculty of Coalition-related developments. During the 1988–89 school year, in the name of the Coalition, there was an effort made to allow interested teachers throughout the building to team, but in practice, it proved difficult to promote teaming on such an ad hoc basis and few teaming proposals were ever implemented. In 1989–90, Silas Ridge had one interdisciplinary team of three teachers (two of whom were members of the Coalition Subcommittee) who taught a humanities course, but perhaps more important, the school held a faculty referendum on whether to remain in the Coalition. When the vote was taken, there was faculty endorsement for Coalition affiliation, yet only one-fourth of the faculty expressed a desire to actively participate in Coalition work at the school. Membership continued in 1990–91, following the departure of the principal, but it remained uncertain what the future direction of Coalition involvement would be.

Barrett Preparatory School

Barrett Preparatory School is a small K–12 private school in a large, multicultural metropolitan area. A strong commitment to minority recruitment on the part of the administration has meant that the sizable Greek, Italian, and Soviet Jewish populations at the school have been complemented by an increasing number of African-American students. The student body is heterogeneous in ability as well. Members of the administration often cited the students' needs for personal attention as their primary reason for attending Barrett. Some attend the private school as an alternative to a heavily criticized public system, while others attend on merit scholarships. Some have had problems at other schools. Most students plan to attend college, and increasingly the school has placed students in more desirable colleges and universities.

Barrett's first contact with the Coalition resulted from the arrival of a new headmaster at the school in the fall of 1984. During the first year of the new headmaster's tenure, the faculty read *The Paideia Proposal* (Adler, 1982), *Horace's Compromise* (Sizer, 1984), and other books about educational philosophy and school change and formed a committee to consider reform. Toward the end of the school year the headmaster prepared the Barrett Educational Plan, a statement of the school's guiding philosophy. It was discussed among the faculty and formally accepted by the school's Board of Trustees. One teacher said:

> [The headmaster] came in with a structure [for] the school because the school was really amorphous. It had no structure. It had no goals. It was floundering academically, student population–wise; there

> weren't fewer students, but the quality of the students was very poor. The kids came here just because their parents didn't want them to go to public school. [The headmaster] came in and had a vision and set up this core curriculum. It happened about the same time Sizer's [1984] and Adler's [1982] books came out and it seemed to fit and *so basically, it was all the headmaster's idea because, as a faculty, we were just no place*. It had been turmoil the year before.

Because the Barrett Educational Plan was similar in intent to the Coalition's Common Principles, the headmaster approached Sizer at a national meeting of independent schools about joining the soon-to-be-formed Coalition. Barrett was accepted as one of the earliest member schools in 1985.

Most of the faculty (still at the school in 1986 when this research began) described themselves as enthusiastic about the initial change-related discussions. For various reasons, however, many became resistant to the changes as they were implemented during the next school year (1985–86). One reason was that the schedule created to institutionalize the new educational plan called for each of the four core subjects (math, science, English, and history) to be taught by teams of teachers in a lecture, seminar, and tutorial arrangement. Concerns abounded about how the teaming would be accomplished, whether the seminar and tutorial periods would be productive, and who would be responsible for grading students. According to one administrator:

> The teachers were unsure about what was going to happen in seminars and they were really concerned about coverage of material. The math and history people were the biggest on coverage. They were really upset that they would not have enough time to cover the material as they previously had because of the seminars.

Other teachers felt their disciplines to be threatened by the Coalition philosophy as incorporated into the Barrett plan. One teacher said:

> The way it was presented . . . almost made it seem like the Coalition did not feel that modern languages, art, or music were as important as the four core courses.

Another said:

> The first year, I think it was exciting because a lot of ideas were being thought about, about how we could be at the forefront of educational

> reform. I only found out later on that languages, my area, really is on the periphery . . . that the headmaster never really saw languages as being part of the plan. We were more or less tacked onto the schedule.

The emphasis placed on student-centered pedagogical techniques such as Socratic questioning raised other concerns. Some teachers felt that this was just one successful technique they used in their daily teaching and that other techniques were being unjustly criticized as ineffective. One English teacher summed up this position:

> As a seminar teacher I felt I had been told that there was just one kind of teaching that I was to be doing and that was what Mortimer Adler recommended and the kinds of things . . . that Sizer recommended. So that meant that as a teacher who had been successful using a full arsenal of things . . . [I was now told to use only] the Socratic method. I felt limited.

While administrators were aware of these criticisms, they felt it was appropriate to stress the Socratic method to the exclusion of other approaches in the seminar classes.

Between 1986 and 1990 the turnover of teachers in the secondary school was substantial. But a small group of teachers committed to or interested in the ideas of the Coalition continued attending conferences and workshops and offering professional development activities for their fellow faculty members. They were surprised and discouraged by the resistance they encountered as they attempted to "help" the faculty operationalize student-as-worker and personalization in their classroom practice. In 1987–88 some of the criticisms faculty raised about the schedule were addressed by removing the tutorial period, reducing the number of lectures for each core course, and adding an additional seminar period. Additionally, this reduced the number of people on each of the teams and reduced the number of preparations for each teacher. Many faculty were pleased that their input had been considered and acted upon. However, criticisms about emphasizing student-centered pedagogies, less-is-more rhetoric (and its apparent contradiction with the exceedingly demanding curriculum the school listed for each grade level), and problems that teachers had coordinating their efforts to team remained.

In 1988–89, at the request of the faculty, the schedule of the school changed again. All English and history classes were blocked back-to-back five periods per week. The same was true for math and science courses. Additionally, each interdisciplinary pair had two single periods for lesson presentations. Teachers agreed that this schedule furthered student-centered pedagogies and promoted "teacher-as-generalist." It also meant that while they taught two subjects to the same group of students, they now teamed with even fewer teachers and had fewer preparations.[3] Some teachers prepared interdisciplinary curricula for their classes; others divided the ninety-minute period into the respective English and history or math and science periods and taught the two subjects as distinct. In other words, while the headmaster saw these changes as improving and institutionalizing a schedule that emphasized student-as-worker and personalization, resistant teachers saw it as a slow return to previous practices, particularly because of the decline in expected teaming—even though there were expectations that teachers working with the same grade level would "coordinate" their efforts. People with both views could comfortably interpret the changes made as supporting their position.

Complaints about the lowly status of all subjects other than the four core courses were continuous throughout the implementation of various schedules. No changes were made to accommodate the objections of these teachers or others who supported them. The continually high turnover in faculty at the school meant that new faculty, who voiced support for the Coalition ideas as codified in the school's educational plan, could be hired.

In 1989–90 some adjustments again were made in the schedule. A limited number of electives in the upper grades were offered. This made interdisciplinary pairing difficult, so the math and science courses at the junior and senior levels reverted back to being independently scheduled. An advisory period was added for grades 6–11. The scheduling of the English/history classes and the noncore subjects was unchanged. In June 1990, the headmaster and two of the most vocal proponents for change at the school left to take new jobs.

Resistance to Coalition philosophy and the schedule have been intertwined at this school from the start. Barrett, a small school, was one of the few schools that attempted to change the entire secondary school simultaneously. However, the effort was hampered by a lack of clarity about the overall goals of the reform. One teacher said that early in their efforts the "faculty . . . gave some degree of lip service to the reform, but . . . they didn't understand the nature of the reforms partly because of the way the reform was implemented." Faculty did not feel prepared to teach differently simply because the schedule changed. And as another teacher said, scheduling decisions "became" the embodiment of the Coalition at Barrett:

> I don't think we can really separate the two from one another. We were all introduced to the Coalition principles at the same time all the

> new changes in scheduling were made along with cutting back on electives, etc. . . . so they really go hand-in-hand. . . . [P]eople who were upset with the removal of electives or change in the schedule, as a result . . . became anti-Coalition.

No movement was ever made to reconsider membership in the Coalition at Barrett, partly because the school was struggling to survive when it joined and received some much-needed favorable publicity as a result of its Coalition membership. Those most opposed to the Coalition left or were asked to leave the school throughout the change process (unlike public school teachers, teachers at Barrett have a one-year contract). Those still at the school learned the language of the Coalition and, regardless of their personal beliefs about the philosophy, were comfortable using it. In private, the terms frequently were used in unflattering comparisons or jokes. With the departure of the headmaster and the arrival of a successor whose views about the Coalition and its philosophy were unknown, it was uncertain whether the schedule modifications that have characterized this school's operationalization of Coalition philosophy will continue. The new headmaster arrived, again, at a time of fiscal crisis for the school—an expensive addition to the physical plant and the local effects of the current recession on enrollment have pushed the school into a precarious financial situation. Whether the course charted by the previous headmaster continues and how the faculty who have had mixed reactions to the changes to date react to the departure of the school's most vocal proponents of the Coalition remain to be seen. At the end of five years of Coalition membership, then, it is unclear how much genuine support for Coalition philosophy exists in the school, but it is certainly apparent that passive resistance as well as outright opposition has characterized the attempts at change undertaken thus far.

Elliston High School

Elliston High School is part of the Elliston Central School District, located just outside a medium-sized northern city. There are approximately 25,000 residents in the school district, and the suburban communities from which the school's 1,000 students are drawn are primarily white-collar, middle-to-upper-middle-class. The high school boasts high completion rates, for example, 98.5 percent in 1982–83. Most students (85–90 percent) pursue higher education. Elliston's curriculum is broadly comprehensive, and there are numerous opportunities for extracurricular activities, independent study, and technical work. The high school offers several advanced placement courses as part of its tracked system and has won numerous awards for excellence.

Elliston's first contact with the Coalition of Essential Schools occurred during an informational meeting in December 1984. Between 1984 and 1986, the Elliston principal and interested faculty engaged in activities to increase their awareness and understanding of Coalition philosophy and practice. These included faculty seminars that explored Coalition ideas, a visit by Ted Sizer, participation in Coalition summer workshops, and the creation of a "Sizer Study Committee" to consider the implications of Coalition affiliation.

In February 1986 the Sizer Committee distributed a proposal for Coalition membership to the Elliston faculty that emphasized six of the nine Common Principles: intellectual focus, simple goals, personalization, student-as-worker, graduation by exhibition, and an atmosphere of respect and decency. The Committee also summarized what the principles implied for them and stressed that the "same level of commitment will not be required of the entire faculty." In a survey/vote in April of 1986, faculty affirmed their support for the six principles *as outlined by the Sizer Committee* (75–14), as well as for allowing interested faculty to implement these principles through Coalition membership (53–29). Yet on their response forms twenty-two faculty members said they were not presently interested in the project, twenty-two said they were interested but lacked the time to participate, fifteen wanted more information, and thirty-one volunteered to help plan the program. In November 1986 the Elliston School Board voted to join the Coalition. To direct this effort two co-coordinators were appointed.

The 1986–87 school year was primarily used to plan, because Elliston was on double sessions at the junior high school while the high school was being renovated. In 1987–88, the co-coordinators organized a school and community project based on Coalition practice, created a Steering Committee, provided teachers with opportunities for professional development, published an occasional newsletter, and developed a pilot program for implementation in 1988–89. In addition, one coordinator wrote: "We have decided to narrow our scope to three of the nine Common Principles . . . 1) Less is More, 2) Student as Worker and 3) Decency." Beyond this work, each co-coordinator continued to experiment with his or her own interpretations of Coalition pedagogy and presented their work at various Coalition symposia. A few other Elliston teachers also experimented with their teaching, and several teachers and administrators from Elliston attended Coalition workshops.

Although the co-coordinators felt progress was being made in these areas, opposition to Coalition affiliation also emerged. In the fall of 1987, one teacher, who described himself as philosophically opposed to Sizer's ideas and skeptical of their practical feasibility, circulated to all faculty members copies of an article that derided the process approach to learning as ignoring context and questioned whether the Coalition might have similar problems. Other faculty questioned the procedure used for joining the Coalition—had there been a vote or not? Also, issues of faculty divisiveness and concerns about how to provide nonthreatening support for colleagues arose repeatedly.

Late in the spring of 1988 the Coalition Steering Committee suggested that a school-within-a-school format might be an appropriate structure for piloting Coalition ideas. But at a Steering Committee meeting in December, more than two years after the school joined the Coalition and with little in place except the Steering Committee and some attempts at change in a few classrooms, the larger issue of what being a Coalition school meant for Elliston was raised again and the Committee decided that a SWAS program would *not* be acceptable. The Committee's report ended by raising the larger concerns discussed at the meeting:

> What we don't know . . . is what being a coalition school could mean for us. What do we want it to mean? The Coalition Steering Committee feels that we as a staff and school community have to define what the coalition principles mean for our school and for us as teachers. It is the hope of the committee that this process can be an open one which does not preclude the possibility of rejecting some of the principles or even all of them.

Other events affected the discussion of the school's relationship to the Coalition as well. During the 1988–89 school year Elliston High School received an A+ Award for Excellence from the National Education Association—based on an application that highlighted the work the school had undertaken through its Coalition membership. The award was announced while debate over Coalition membership was "heating up" again, and some of those opposed to Coalition membership viewed this award as an effort at résumé building by the co-coordinators, not as an achievement in which the entire school should take pride. Also, as part of the debate about membership, several strongly worded memos that outlined key issues were circulated among the faculty throughout the 1988–89 school year, including a letter from Ted Sizer to all member schools that encouraged schools to commit themselves to schoolwide implementation of Coalition philosophy:

> [I]t is virtually impossible to pursue one of the nine Common Principles without ultimately engaging with them all. . . . [I]mproving the work in conventional classrooms is a wonderful thing but insufficient for this particular Coalition's work. Our goal is more ambitious—to effect a new, demonstrably higher level of educational quality by breaking out, where necessary, of existing constraining structures. (Sizer, 1989)

The February (1989) faculty meeting at Elliston included a lengthy debate about Sizer's letter, particularly whether the school was required to implement all nine Common Principles to remain a Coalition member.

At the end of March, in preparation for a faculty vote on continued Coalition membership, the Steering Committee raised four questions:

1. Does Elliston have to implement all nine principles in order to remain a member of the Coalition?
2. What does each principle actually mean? What do we currently do with each principle?
3. How do the principles apply to our [proposed] new mission statement?
4. Should Elliston continue its affiliation with the national Coalition?

Numerous communications with the Coalition Central Staff requested clarification on the first point and inquired about the "boundaries" of local interpretation; for example, could individual principles be completely rewritten? Additionally, Coalition proponents indicated to the Coalition Staff that many faculty questioned whether there was a need for change at their school. One coordinator wrote: "Some teachers question the need for change. After all, we are doing very well as measured by standardized instruments and college placement. We often hear the question of 'Why fix what doesn't need fixing?' " In late April Sizer responded to the coordinator's letter with a ten-page letter that elaborated upon his January letter but still emphasized that all nine Common Principles were interrelated.

In May, a faculty survey listing the nine Common Principles and each of the proposed Elliston interpretations was distributed. The survey portion asked faculty to indicate the extent of their agreement with the Steering Committee's interpretations, which were identical with the Coalition Principles only for universal goals, exhibitions of mastery, and values of unanxious expectation. There was an explicit redefinition of the principles concerning the comprehensive high school, student-as-worker, and teacher-as-generalist. The remaining principles (simple goals, personalization, and budget) were reworded but not completely challenged. Generally, there was strong agreement with the Common Principles as rewritten. In the comment section of the survey, however, strong disagreements and criticisms were recorded, indicating that previous interpretive differences had not been erased by what seemed to be greater consensus about the Committee's interpretation of the Common Principles. Some of the opposition's comments were:

> Less is not necessarily better;
> We are losing our comprehensiveness when we drop courses and programs in the elective areas; and
> I am opposed to Sizer's concept of teachers being generalists.

Two other faculty comments addressed wider issues:

> If we want to rewrite so many of these, why are we in the Coalition? and,
> What are the school's goals?

Finally, in June 1989, the Elliston faculty voted 55 opposed and 30 in favor of the statement: "Elliston High School should continue its formal affiliation with the National Coalition of Essential Schools." The school requested permission from the Coalition for interested faculty to attend and participate in Coalition-sponsored activities. That summer a few teachers participated in Coalition workshops at Brown University. No further participation in Coalition activities has occurred.

COMPARATIVE PERSPECTIVE

Based on these case studies (and research at our other study schools) perhaps the most important point to be made is that there was no consensus at the schools that fundamental changes in school structure and/or teaching practices needed to occur. Instead, at each school a "vanguard" of interested faculty voluntarily embraced Coalition philosophy and saw themselves, and were viewed by the administration, as "harbingers of the future." Their noninvolved colleagues viewed them quite differently, as the recipients of preferential treatment. They called the Coalition core the "principal's favorites" and argued that they had received all sorts of benefits, from fewer and better students, to more free periods, to more opportunities for travel and greater access to professional development funds. Conversely, the teachers and administrators involved with reform saw a need for the support Coalition faculty received and expected that their efforts would eventually benefit the entire school. Further, since faculty involvement often entailed volunteering free time, involved teachers dismissed the label of preferential treatment.

Several changes occurred as a result of these developments within the schools. For one, new "we/they" distinctions emerged within the faculties. Moreover, teacher equity issues continually arose that further reinforced these "we/they" distinctions—such as when class size requirements of SWAS pilots were believed to increase other teachers' class loads. In all cases the perception of favored treatment and reactions to CES membership were linked to some teachers' opinions about the principal. For the principal's opponents, then, attacking the "favorites" or the program was viewed as an attack on the principal as well.

Since there was no consensus about the need for change, Coalition schools and programs could not simply try "anything" they might have wished. Instead, the usual starting points for reform were aspects of the Common Principles that individual teachers (or small teams of teachers) could implement with little disruption to the school as a whole. For example, Coalition reform began in each case school with an emphasis on student-as-worker and personalization[4] and these changes were implemented without faculty consensus concerning their appropriateness as a schoolwide philosophy. (This was less true of the schedule changes at Barrett that affected the entire school, although there, too, the initial emphasis was on student-as-worker classroom activities.) Further, our study schools did not implement the Coalition principles that proved most contentious, such as: applying the aphorism "less is more" to their curriculum; integrating exhibitions (as defined as schoolwide assessment measures required for promotion or graduation) into their programs; having faculty function as "generalists" who teach in more than one discipline; or reducing their student-faculty ratios to 80 to 1, unless it was for certain faculty members only (e.g., SWAS faculty).

Nevertheless, by defining the individual classroom as the arena within which to make changes and evaluate their success, reports of success by Coalition teachers have been impressive. Focusing on student-as-worker and personalization often revitalized teachers and demonstrated to them a potential for personal efficacy in the classroom that many felt had been lost. Over time, however, concentrating on these two principles focused the change process on the teacher–student–subject matter relationship and tended to ignore larger issues of schoolwide change, such as changing the schedule or the student-to-teacher ratio or restructuring schoolwide into houses. (Again, this was less true of Barrett, where there was more schedule change but less consensus about the value of student-as-worker pedagogy.) While the classroom was the locus of change most emphasized in early Coalition rhetoric, because of the fundamental interconnectedness of so many aspects of school life, a lack of attention to schoolwide issues has impeded the scope of change possible in individual classrooms.

The divisions created within schools as a result of Coalition membership also restricted communication among the faculty—a consequence of the perceived criticisms of existing practices, the sense that the vanguard received preferential treatment, and the tensions, power struggles, and personal misgivings these feelings generated. In turn, noninvolved faculty rarely developed a clear sense of the reform effort, what changes were being enacted, or what their effects had been on students, teachers, or the institution as a whole—beyond how certain changes might directly affect their own situations.

Finally, Coalition supporters have been politically naive in their use of power, in their negotiations with their less interested colleagues, and in their expectations about what school change would require. For the Coalition as a whole, there was, at first, naiveté about the degree to which school reform could be effected solely by focusing on academic concerns, specifically, the triangle of learning. Paralleling this trend, Coalition supporters in our study schools focused on the triangle as well—for instance, concentrating on program structure, curriculum, and their pedagogy—while giving limited attention to political concerns and the consequences of exerting influence within the school. Since the tensions that emerged within faculties were largely unanticipated, most pro-Coalition faculty members were unprepared to deal with resistance when it arose. On top of the other difficulties these teachers faced—developing curriculum, organizing their schedules, and generally dealing with the uncertainties associated with something new and ambitious—political opposition at the school site was an unpleasant surprise that few faculty had the time or energy or appropriate forum to resolve.

The naiveté of Coalition supporters was especially apparent in the tendency of Coalition proponents to define those not currently involved with or uninterested in their reform efforts as potential supporters, instead of viewing them as equally liable to oppose their efforts. Yet, as some of those initially unconcerned about these reform efforts, or even supportive of the ideas *in theory*, realized the ramifications of these changes *in practice*, what seemed like a good idea or, at worst, a harmless experiment became the basis for controversy and contention. In addition, in order to exert counterinfluence to change efforts, those opposed did not need a consistent theoretical or political basis. All the opposition required was to be upset with some aspect of the changes they were experiencing. Given that the Coalition advocates changing multiple aspects of school life, these reforms held the potential for considerable opposition to arise. And opposition did emerge, over and over again in the same schools, sometimes for the same reasons, sometimes in modified arguments or assertions.

FINAL REMARKS

In closing we would like to make four general remarks about school change. First, it might be productive to ask two distinct questions about change before beginning:

- Is change necessary?
- If it is, are the proposed changes appropriate?

Second, from the discussions about change and the need for change at the schools we studied, it became apparent to us that a desire to promote change is not value-neutral. Whether or not the rhetoric of an organization (like the Coalition or a school) suggests that everyone can benefit from school reform, efforts to create change implicitly criticize the status quo and create a sense that there are winners and losers. Being an advocate for school change precludes approaching the topic neutrally: regardless of intention, advocates are vested in viewing change as "improvement" and they are perceived as judgmental by both those who support change and those opposed.

Third, the divisiveness and conflicts that arose in our study schools may have been inherent to the change process. People responded differently—resistantly, embracingly, obliviously—to a call for change, thereby creating a more contentious atmosphere at the school than previously existed. If the expectation is that change or specific changes will become part of the life of the whole school, eventually contentious issues will have to be addressed. In the cases we discussed, political opposition threatened the vanguard, in part because it was unexpected and they were not prepared to deal with it. Because restructuring efforts cannot simply focus on philosophical, pedagogical, or even structural concerns, political consciousness raising may need to be part of the preparation for change. Those interested in restructuring schools will need to juggle the structural concerns reforms raise with philosophical and pedagogical issues in ways that are respectful of the group dynamics of the workplace and savvy about the political and personal tensions that change can both uncover and create. As part of this political socialization, it would seem reasonable to warn potential change agents that what is considered "opposition" at a school may vary; opposition can potentially include anyone not actively involved in the change effort, not just the outright hostile.

Fourth, teachers may want to consider how to make their school's philosophy, the proposed changes, and the change process the objects of regular reflection by the entire faculty. As change occurs, a school's philosophy may become contested. It might be useful, therefore, to recognize that *change* and *philosophy* are terms continually negotiated (more or less actively) among the factions and individuals within a school. This view might encourage more frequent, structured conversations about contentious issues that could help reveal and resolve some of the tensions, productive or otherwise, before they threaten an entire reform effort.

Our work may appear to denigrate efforts at change that are occurring in Coalition schools. This is not our intent. Our motivation in preparing this chapter is simple and straightforward: schoolwide reform as advocated by the Coalition, and more generally, is going to be extremely difficult to accomplish. It will be time- and labor-intensive and will require rethinking and relearning by all participants. It will, as David Tyack said, mean that if teachers "are really to be free to experiment, they may also fail, as do doctors or politicians" (1990: 187). For, as Phillip Schlechty (1989) observed, these reform efforts are on "the cutting edge of ignorance," implying that change of the scope and nature presently being undertaken has no historical precedent. To deny this is to believe that there are quick fixes or miracle cures. Structural constraints and power issues are realities in all institutions (Sarason, 1990). For current reform efforts to avoid ending up "on the margins of the schools" (Cohen, 1988: 242) like so many other educational innovations, those wishing to make change more central to their school may benefit from considering these points about whether there is a consensus about the desirability of change, about the political nature of change, and about the fundamental interconnectedness of all aspects of school life *before* beginning change and *throughout* the change process.

NOTES

1. A Study of High Schools generated three books: *Horace's Compromise: The Dilemma of the American High School*, by Sizer (1984), *The Shopping Mall High School*,

by Arthur Powell, Eleanor Farrar, and David K. Cohen (1985), and *The Last Little Citadel*, by Robert Hampel (1986).

2. All school and individual names (except that of Ted Sizer, the chairperson of the Coalition) have been changed or omitted.

3. It is hard to separate the effects of declining enrollment from the effects of schedule changes on teacher teaming.

4. We are not alone in noting the rapid acceptance and incorporation of these two principles into school life at Coalition schools. See also Hampel (1990, personal communication), CES Committee on Evaluation (1988), and Sizer (1989).

4 Empowerment of Teachers in Dade County's School-Based Management Pilot

Marjorie K. Hanson, Don R. Morris, and Robert A. Collins

In this chapter, we shall examine the extent to which teachers were empowered during the first three years of Dade County's pilot of school-based management. We shall look at one aspect of teacher empowerment, participation in key decisions. We define empowerment as the extent to which teachers influenced the outcomes of decision processes traditionally under the control of the principal. This, we maintain, is an indication of the extent to which influence relations between teachers and principals have been altered. Our examination makes use of information gathered in the evaluation of the school-based management pilot (Collins & Hanson, 1991) and data published annually in the *District and School Profiles* (1987 through 1990).

First, we shall provide some background information and outline the concept of school-based management as it is practiced in Dade County. Then we shall examine the extent to which school-based management empowered teachers or altered influence relations between principals and teachers. We shall close the chapter with a discussion of the conclusions and implications of this study.

THE CONTEXT OF SCHOOL-BASED MANAGEMENT IN DADE COUNTY

Development

School-Based Management in the Dade County Public Schools (DCPS) was one outcome of a task force formed in 1985 that joined the efforts of

The authors are employees of the Office of Educational Accountability, Dade County Public Schools. The views expressed in this chapter are those of the authors and are not necessarily shared by Dade County Public Schools.

district management and the United Teachers of Dade (UTD) to study the professionalization of teaching (Fernandez, 1991). The program, which is officially designated School-Based Management/Shared Decision-Making (SBM/SDM), was under the jurisdiction of two committees designated by that task force, one consisting of principals and chaired by a deputy superintendent, the other consisting of union stewards and chaired by the UTD executive vice president. A January 13, 1987, memorandum described the committees' deliberations. The principals' committee focused on increased budgetary discretion, alternative staffing and scheduling patterns, and alternative models for delivering support services. The primary focus of the union stewards' committee was "shared decision-making and the development of a model(s) to be used in implementing shared decision-making at pilot schools" (Collins, 1988, Appendix A: 3).

In January 1987 the committee chairs sent requests for proposals (RFPs) to building principals and union stewards inviting schools to become pilot SBM/SDM schools and participate in a three-year "test" of the idea. Staff at schools were to develop proposals that included three elements: (1) a description of the means by which school personnel decided that they would like to participate; (2) a description of the proposed procedures for shared decision making; and (3) justification for and description of as many innovations as the staff desired to pursue. Thirty-three of the almost 300 Dade County schools were accepted into the program, based on the proposals they had submitted. These pilot schools—eighteen elementary schools, ten middle schools, four senior high schools, and one technical education center—implemented their proposals during the 1987–88 school year and participated in an evaluation that began that year and continued through 1989–90.

Since participation in this SBM/SDM pilot was voluntary, it might be expected that the schools would not be representative of the entire spectrum of the DCPS student population. In fact, with the exception of the four senior high schools, which all had lower proportions of students who qualified for free or reduced-price lunches than the Dade County average for senior high schools, pilot schools represented the broad socioeconomic range of the county. The professional staff (both principals and teachers) of the pilot schools were more predominantly white than the staff of district schools in general, but in terms of proportions of staff with graduate degrees and average years of teaching experience, the pilot schools were no different than their counterparts districtwide (Morris, 1991).

In July 1987, the deputy superintendent, an enthusiastic supporter of the SBM experiment, became the superintendent. Other Dade County schools entered the SBM/SDM program toward the end of the second year of the pilot

(1988–89). The superintendent tendered his resignation in the fall of 1989, leaving DCPS the following January, midway into the third year of the pilot program. Despite this and other inevitable "contaminations" of the experiment, the length of the pilot program evaluation offered a rare opportunity to examine school-based management implementation and impact over a three-year period for a subset of schools in a large and diverse urban district.

School-Based Management and Empowerment

School-based management, whereby school staff are freed to chart their own courses, is one way of restructuring the educational system. It is based on the assumption that units closest to clients understand their needs better than remote central office or state policymakers. Often this restructuring involves greater teacher roles in school-level decisions, in addition to greater school-site freedom from central office dictates (AASA/NAESP/NASSP School-Based Management Task Force, 1988; David, 1989).

Although public media, professional literature, and school practice have focused extensive attention on school-based management in recent years, there is neither clarity nor agreement on its definition or impact (David, 1989; Malen, Ogawa & Kranz, 1991). Observing that there are few systematic investigations of implementations of the concept, Betty Malen, Rodney Ogawa, and Jennifer Kranz (1991) question whether school-based management actually alters influence relations among district office and schools or principals and teachers. It is the alteration of influence relations between principals and teachers that we address in this chapter, in an effort to identify the extent of teacher empowerment that occurred in Dade County.

Formal provisions that laid the foundation for the alteration of influence relationships between principals and teachers are to be found in the requirements for preparing proposals to become SBM/SDM schools. In particular, the RFP called for involvement of the union steward in preparation of the proposal and development of a model for shared decision making. It also allowed for innovations that involved different roles for teachers. Two points are particularly relevant.

First, RFPs were sent to both the principal and the union steward at each school in the county. This enabled persons filling either position to initiate participation in SBM/SDM. Furthermore, the completed proposal was to be signed by both the principal and the union steward, with a provision for "actions taken to insure consensus of decision to request participation" (Collins, 1988, Appendix A).

Second, the model for shared decision making was a required part of the proposal. Although the intent to involve teachers (as well as students, community members, and parents) was clear from the stated philosophy and goals of the SBM/SDM program, no particular structure for such involvement was mandated. School staff were free to develop structures of their own and provide for alteration of relationships as they desired. Thus the opportunity for teachers to influence key decisions with respect to defining the roles they might play in school affairs was a part of the initial decision to participate.

DATA, METHOD, AND RATIONALE

The question is whether teachers have been able to take advantage of the opportunity for increasing their influence in school affairs. A reliable answer to that question is not easily reached. We examine here two major indicators to explore the question of altered influence relations. First, we look at the extent and nature of teacher involvement in innovations as described in administrative reviews prepared by the individual schools. Next, we examine briefly and more generally indications of reservations of principals at the pilot schools toward shared decision making, as reflected in responses to staff surveys.

Innovations

Innovations are a particularly relevant framework from which to examine the question of teacher empowerment, since they represent actual outcomes of deliberations at schools. The level and nature of participation by teachers in design and implementation of the innovations is an indicator of shift in influence relations between teachers and principals.

School staff were free to propose any kind of innovation for which they could provide a rationale and outline an anticipated benefit. Even if the innovation involved overturning district or state policy or teacher contract provisions, it could be proposed for possible approval by the appropriate office. This provision allowed for all kinds of creative new types of teacher involvement in schools. One, peer evaluation of instructional staff, was even featured as an example in the RFP.

Administrative reviews were prepared by individual SBM/SDM pilot schools at the end of each school year of the pilot evaluation (1988, 1989, and 1990). The reviews were self-evaluations planned and carried out by school staff with the technical assistance of staff from the DCPS Office of Educational Accountability. While administrative reviews varied among schools, they generally included descriptions of the SBM/SDM innovations and thus often provide rich descriptions of teacher involvement in innovations.

The Principal's Perspective

To further investigate the extent to which empowerment is genuine, we examine briefly the occasional points of contention between principals and faculty. The reasoning is that if SBM/SDM is "working," if authority to make meaningful decisions is being shifted from principals to faculty, there is likely to be some resistance.

Whenever some or all of one of the valued social commodities wealth, prestige, and in this case, influence (authority, power) is transferred from one group to another, we observe what political scientists call a redistributive policy. Such policies are rarely effected smoothly. Principals will resist if they believe that control may be lost to the point that it appears their ability to meet their responsibilities will be jeopardized. That resistance should be detectable. And that resistance, whether justified or not, may be regarded as evidence that the principals themselves recognize a potential on the part of teachers (or a subset of them) to meaningfully influence decisions.

There is some evidence of this resistance, reported in the first year of the pilot, and in the changing responses principals made to certain survey questions as recorded in the evaluation report. Since opinions questioning shared decision making ran counter to district policy and in opposition to the superintendent's personal views, they may not have been openly discussed or officially acknowledged. Consequently we rely on reports and survey responses intended for other purposes to make inferences about situations for which, although often unofficially acknowledged, no overt documentation is available.

SIGNS OF TEACHER EMPOWERMENT

Teacher Involvement in Innovations

SBM/SDM pilot schools proposed and implemented a variety of innovations ranging from programs for at-risk students to a "wellness room" for staff sponsored jointly with a local university. Four types of innovations—different roles for teachers, block scheduling, school-within-a-school, and teachers-as-advisors—were most prominent, each being implemented by five to eleven of the thirty-three schools. Many innovations underwent change over the three-year period, with innovations being added and deleted by decision of school staffs and because of funding variations. Although the original innovations were modified in subsequent years, over 90 percent of these innovations initiated during 1987–88 remained in place at the end of 1989–90.

Since distribution of decision-making power was formally left to individual schools, the involvement of teachers in the innovations and nature of roles played by teachers in their implementation illustrate how influence relations among building administrators and teachers were altered.

Level of Involvement

Views of teacher involvement in school innovations may assume involvement in every relevant aspect of the implementation. Larry Cuban (1988) asserts that the success of school improvement depends upon "professional accountability," which he defines as teachers, principals, and central office administrators holding each other accountable for implementation. This definition of "professional accountability" implies joint involvement of administrators and teachers throughout implementation of innovations.

In actual practice, however, unassigned responsibilities tend to fall to the individual who is available when decisions need to be made. Since principals serve twelve-month contracts and are more available even during the school year than teachers, there is a tendency for day-to-day decisions to fall to them. The extent to which "professional accountability," or accountability shared among teachers and principals, prevailed over the traditional arrangement of principal accountability is an indicator of the extent to which the influence relations between principals and teachers were altered.

Teacher involvement in innovations depended on the magnitude of the innovation and the stage of implementation. The entire faculty was usually involved in initial approval and annual reconsideration of innovations. However, teachers participated to varying degrees in defining, initiating, planning, and overseeing implementation.

Almost all teachers tended to participate in carrying out single-task innovations like block scheduling in elementary schools. This activity took place once a year, and since all teachers were affected by it, they tended to be involved in annual schedule adjustments. Only special area and primary teachers were sometimes left out of the scheduling process.

On the other hand, decisions regarding different roles for teachers tended to involve only a subset of the school staff in part of the implementation process. Typically, shared decision-making cadres, including both administrators and teachers, defined and subsequently evaluated the roles to be played by teachers in these innovations. Additionally, cadres, personnel committees, or ad hoc groups selected and evaluated persons filling some roles. Other roles, notably peer evaluation and collegial hiring, were filled by principal appointment. Furthermore, principals alone supervised incumbents in all these different roles.

There were some exceptions to the general trend of total involvement in single-task and partial involvement in multitask innovations. These exceptions included both more and less involvement by teachers.

Teachers were more involved in at least one type of innovation. In high schools, they not only planned and evaluated school-within-a-school innovations, but also supervised day-to-day operations. Affecting only a subset of the school population and involving only a few teachers, both the content and the administration of these programs were under the strong control of teachers.

In contrast, in middle schools, school-within-a-school and teachers-as-advisors innovations were guided primarily by administrative decisions, from both central administrators and building principals. The district assigned schools to specific timelines for transition to middle school status and provided guidelines and training to ensure similarity. Principals were responsible for overseeing implementation. Staff contributed to structure and content and provided support in the form of training and materials development. Staff, however, had little say in whether or not such innovations would be pursued.

Evidence of this administrative control may be found in a comment district staff gave regarding the success of one middle school's advisement program. Success was attributed to the commitment of the principal to the middle school model. At that school, advisement was well integrated into the other aspects of the model and commitment to the model was a strong consideration in hiring new staff.

In short, professional accountability that includes teachers existed in the implementation of innovations. It was more prominent in some types of innovations than in others. Innovations in which schools had some discretion, that is, different roles for teachers, block scheduling in elementary schools, and school-within-a-school in senior highs, were subject to faculty approval and were initiated, modified, and reapproved by formal faculty consent. On the other hand, district-initiated innovations associated with conversion to middle school status, that is, school-within-a-school and teachers-as-advisors, although also subject to faculty input, ultimately moved forward according to the central administration's prescribed format. Additionally, building administrators had the most involvement in day-to-day implementation of all innovations and in any supervision required. Only for school-within-a-school in senior highs was professional accountability shared with teachers in all phases of the implementation process.

There were interesting concomitants of more or less teacher involvement. When teachers shared more of the accountability for innovations, the innovations were less stable and more likely to diminish in scope. In senior high schools, teachers redesigned school-within-a-school programs after one year so that they resembled supplementary programs more than distinct "schools." Innovations related to conversion to middle school, on the other hand, were quite stable.

Nature of Roles

Each innovation involved teachers taking on formal roles that were not traditional. Almost all of these new roles were administrative in nature; only teachers-as-advisors innovations involved teachers taking on new nonadministrative roles. Different roles for teachers included discipline deans, lead teachers, assistants to the principal for student activities, and peer evaluators.

Although teachers had input into decisions regarding new roles, the most successful roles were devoted to aspects of administration that were removed from teaching. Thus, at the end of three years, roles like collegial hiring and student discipline seemed securely in place. Roles that countered this tendency by bringing teachers closer to each other's classrooms experienced difficulties in implementation. One example was a peer evaluation model that involved voluntary participation of teachers. With its goal of schoolwide training in classroom observation and informal observation and feedback from other teachers, it exemplified mutual instructional support. However, existing training opportunities and the personal satisfaction derived from observing colleagues voluntarily were not sufficient to encourage widespread participation.

In addition, roles that underwent substantial change or rethinking often reflected a distancing of these teacher-administrators from the classroom. One middle school staff had created lead teachers whose job description included mentoring new teachers and supporting the professional development of all staff. At the end of the three-year pilot, staff redefined the role to entail student discipline. In each annual school administrative review, teachers at this school had called for clearer definition of goals and more direct involvement with teachers from the incumbents. Similarly, teachers conducting peer evaluation at a senior high school found their program temporarily suspended at the end of the third year. The reason given was lack of clarity in the role. Perhaps these roles were too close to the classroom to survive social constraints on proper teacher roles (Smylie & Denny, 1990).

Some innovations involved only brief periods of assuming a nontraditional role for teachers. Block scheduling, for example, involved teachers in arranging the schedule. Others, like team leaders or lead teachers in school-within-a-school innovations, took on varied responsibilities involving a small team of teachers throughout the school year. Some entailed release from one or two class assignments in order to fulfill the duties. Others involved assuming such roles full-time. Instituting most different roles for teachers involved the sacrifice of some other resource, sometimes an assistant principal.

The new teacher roles not only encroached upon administrative tasks and some actual positions, but also caused the administrative structure in schools to proliferate. Teachers took on administrative duties in addition to or in lieu of their own. Although three new teacher roles replaced assistant principals, the net impact was a greater proportion of personnel devoted to administrative tasks than had been previously. Additional part-time administrative roles were developed for other teachers. Some teachers gained a larger view of the school as a result of participation in administrative tasks. However, other teachers gained little involvement through the creation of these special roles at their schools.

In conclusion, most nontraditional roles that teachers took on in carrying out innovations were administrative in nature. They participated in administration in areas that ranged from advice to actually carrying out policy in hiring, teacher evaluation, and student discipline. This practice altered the influence relations between teachers and principals in that teachers influenced the design of the administrative functions, participated in administrative tasks, and, in some cases, even replaced administrators.

Principals and Shared Decision Making

The occurrence of participation in decisions and the creation of new roles, even nontraditional ones, do not of themselves ensure changes in influence relations. The skeptic may argue that there is no convincing evidence of altered influence relations to be found in the innovations and that only the appearance of empowerment is evident, with teacher opinion prevailing only where the principal had no real objection.

Unfortunately, we have no information on where the principals of these schools stood concerning decisions involving the innovations just considered. However, we do have evidence of the concern of principals generally about the loss of control over decisions. While not directly related to the innovation decisions, it does offer some independent indication of the presence of increased influence on the part of the teaching faculty.

Writing of the first year of the pilot, Joseph Gomez (1989) reported: "Some of the principals in the pilot schools felt uncomfortable with their role in shared decision making." His comments are worth quoting at length. He goes on to state:

> If a decision by the cadre resulted in a major blunder, they said, it would be the principal who would be held accountable, not the cadre. For this reason, some principals retained veto power over cadre decisions—in effect, reducing the cadre to an advisory committee. Other principals restricted the jurisdiction of the cadre to areas they considered safe, such as curriculum issues. This solution eased some anxieties, but in the process, these principals might have undermined shared decision making. The pilot schools have yet to find a workable solution to this problem. (1989: 22)

There was, through all the three years of the pilot, an exceptionally high turnover of principals in the district, as compared to the previous three-year period, and the SBM schools at the elementary and middle levels showed higher turnover rates than the other schools (Morris, 1991). (There were a variety of reasons for this high turnover, including the creation of new regional-level administrative positions and the opening of new schools.)

As a result of this turnover rate, by the spring of 1990 fewer than half of the principals who had been in SBM schools in the first year remained. One might have expected this to resolve the problem of reservations about shared decision making, since presumably only principals supportive of the shared decision-making concept were appointed to those schools after they were so organized. However, from 1989 to 1990, the percent of principals agreeing with the statement "My relations with staff have become more open/friendly since SBM" dropped from 78.6 to 59.1 percent (Collins & Hanson, 1991: 20).

More to the point, there is a question on the Principal's Survey administered annually in the evaluation of the SBM/SDM program that directly addresses the problem Gomez reported arising at the beginning of the pilot. Respondents were asked to agree/disagree along a five-alternative Likert scale: "I believe that SDM places principals in an untenable position with respect to being held accountable for all aspects of a school's operation while, at the same time, being expected to share decision-making prerogatives with staff" (Collins & Hanson, 1991, Appendix C).

In 1987–88 only 20.6 percent of the principals answered the above question "agree" or "strongly agree." The next year it was 17.2 percent. But in 1989–90, this jumped to 56.5 percent, triple the previous levels. The percent agreeing remained low in the first two years while the strongly supportive superintendent was present and then increased abruptly. This, along with Gomez's observations quoted above, suggests that many principals remained uncomfortable with shared decision making throughout the period, withholding comment until the climate was more amenable.

This discomfort or concern reflects the principals' belief that control over the decision process could potentially be more determined by the cadre than by the principal, supporting the position that effective or meaningful decision sharing was occurring. However, it also suggests that countermeasures were being taken to limit the effects and/or scope of such sharing. It further points to the impact that the position taken by central authorities (stated or tacit) was likely to have had on the degree of decision sharing.

WHERE DOES TEACHER EMPOWERMENT STAND NOW?

The leadership supplied by the central administration during the first two years was an important part of sustaining the SBM/SDM momentum. Shared decision making for teachers benefited greatly from the superintendent's strong and unwavering support for the concept. Although SBM/SDM has remained a high priority since this superintendent's departure at the end of 1989, it has had to compete with other concerns and priorities. In this climate, can teachers retain whatever influence gains they have made in the schools? A consensus among teachers on the goals of professionalism and shared decision making is an important part of the answer. Indications are that such solidarity is lacking. However, structural inroads made during the SBM/SDM movement by organized teachers may assure their continued representation at various district levels.

Nontraditional Roles and Traditional Perspectives

As the discussion of innovations has shown, the Dade County model has involved teachers taking on nontraditional roles both as decision makers and, in certain innovations, as quasi-administrators. Certain structural and social constraints associated with the teaching profession may prevent the acceptance of new types of roles (Smylie & Denny, 1990). For one thing, the structure of teachers' schedules may not permit the time or the opportunity for interaction between teachers and teacher-leaders. This may be particularly true in SBM schools, where time must be found for participation in school affairs. Evidence of burnout in the SBM schools has been noted by both Gomez (1989: 22) and Donald Morris (1991: 11–12).

Perhaps more important, social norms of the teaching profession have been found to include "strong commitment to norms of equality, autonomy, and privacy" (Smylie & Denny, 1990: 253), which conflict with ideas of teachers as instructional leaders or supervisors. These ideological conflicts may have contributed to the undermining of teacher solidarity at the school level.

Antagonisms among teachers were generated by the decision-making structure itself and by the division of faculty into activists and nonparticipants. Gomez found intrafaculty stresses arising between activist teachers and their constituents who remained "more provincial"; because of the broader scope of their new roles, the activists were perceived as "sounding like the principal" (1989: 22).

Underlying such cleavages were what might be termed ideological divisions, and the indications are that these increased over the three years. Collins and Hanson (1991) show responses to the question: "Which of the following best describes your current and ideal teaching situation?" The three alternatives—to which each respondent indicated both an ideal and a current selection—are: (1) free to teach without interference (independent); (2) part of group of competent teachers who work together (collegial); and (3) part of a school organization, goals spelled out by principal (hierarchical). The table showing the response percentages is reproduced here as Table 4.1.

The responses in percents are given for four years, 1987 through 1990. The "current" situation (i.e., the actual situation at the time of response) percentages show what is expected, that the individual and particularly the collegial situations have gained ground decisively at the expense of the hierarchical. However, distribution of the perceptions of ideal situations (the way things ought to be) changed much less over that period than the

Table 4.1
Present as Compared to Ideal Teaching Situations

	% responding							
Which of the following best describes your current and ideal teaching situation?	Fall 1987		Spring 1988		Spring 1989		Spring 1990	
	Ideal	Current	Ideal	Current	Ideal	Current	Ideal	Current
free to teach without interference.	35.7%	28.4%	33.7%	40.7%	31.9%	33.8%	31.1%	39.4%
part of a group of competent teachers who work together.	33.7%	42.0%	38.5%	45.6%	38.1%	48.6%	36.4%	47.1%
part of a school organization; goals spelled out by principal.	30.5%	29.5%	27.8%	13.6%	30.0%	18.0%	32.5%	13.4%

Source: Reproduced from R. A. Collins and M. K. Hanson, Summative Evaluation Report: School Based Management/Shared Decision-Making Project 1987-88 Through 1989-90. Dade County Public Schools, January, 1991.

perceptions of current situations. If one adds up the absolute differences between perceptions of ideal and current across all three categories for each year, it turns out that the total in percentage points for 1987 was 18.0 and that it increased to 38.2 percentage points in 1990. Insofar as the discrepancy between ideal and actual can be regarded as a dissatisfaction index, there was less harmony among SBM school faculties in 1990 than there was in 1987.

Evidence of dissatisfaction surfaces elsewhere in the evaluation reports also, especially between the teacher surveys of 1989 and 1990. When the teachers were asked about their level of satisfaction with job and school, the percent of satisfied responses remained about the same for job, but dropped by 10 percentage points for school. Again, when asked whether the "Project [SBM/SDM] produced [a] more satisfying work environment," the number of teachers answering "agree" or "strongly agree" fell from 52.4 percent in 1989 to 41.8 percent in 1990 (Collins & Hanson, 1991: 10f).

Contributing to the dissatisfaction among SBM school staff was the apparent persistence of traditional views. The percentage of responses naming the hierarchical as the ideal situation remained essentially the same throughout the pilot period; about 30 percent of the responding teachers continued to prefer administrative leadership. In 1987, the difference between the percent naming hierarchical the ideal and the percent naming it the current differed by only 1 percentage point. In 1990 that difference had increased to 19.1 percentage points.

Other evidence of the persistence of traditional views can be found in the fact that 14.7 percent of surveyed teachers gave as a reason for lack of participation in SDM "school should be run by administrators" (Collins & Hanson, 1991: 12). Clearly some teachers had not been won away from the administrative model.

In general, the teacher surveys show that support among teachers for the SBM/SDM experiment dropped following the departure of the superintendent who had championed it. Local empowerment of teachers as individuals through shared decision making, insofar as it had existed in the three years of the pilot, appears to have been highly dependent on the active support of the district administration.

Empowerment at the District Level

While teachers as individuals may not have sustained empowerment, teachers as an organization appear to have been more successful. As a consequence of the superintendent's restructuring in the context of continued joint district/union planning, teachers in Dade are now formally better integrated into the district decision-making structure.

This came about because the SBM/SDM concept was extended to encompass the feeder patterns of the (then twenty-four) senior high schools. The reorganization by feeder pattern designated twenty-four selected principals as "lead principals," who in addition to continuing with their own school responsibilities now coordinated distribution of services, articulation, and other functions among all of the schools in the feeder pattern.

Feeder pattern councils, consisting of the lead principal, a lead union steward, and other professional, parent, community, and student representatives, were established. A major purpose was "to move educational decision-making closer to schools and their communities." It is the position of lead steward that is significant to teacher empowerment. In the words of the former superintendent, the lead steward position was established "[i]n order to be consistent with . . . the commitment of the district and the United Teachers of Dade to share decision making." The superintendent was also specific as to what this decision sharing was to mean: "The lead steward will represent the union on the feeder pattern council" (Fernandez, 1991: 246).

Thus the shared decision making concept was formally extended beyond individual schools to the feeder patterns, implicating all the district's schools, whether or not they had volunteered to accept SBM/SDM status internally.

CONCLUSION

Summary

Within schools, teacher involvement in defining, planning, and deciding whether to continue innovations actually altered influence relations between teachers and principals, in that the outcomes of their participation in these decisions resulted in changes in the functions and roles of some or all teachers at a school. Teachers have been participating in school governance in unprecedented ways, many of them administrative.

Nevertheless, principals retained authority in certain innovations and in certain aspects of innovations, notably supervision of implementation. More important, principals appeared concerned over the loss or potential loss of too much decision-making authority. There appear to be grounds for their fears. The middle school innovations show quite clearly that when districtwide policies are to be carried out, it is the central office and building administration that take over. The district formally began the process of adopting the middle school model in 1986, and the school board targeted the 1991–92 year for full implementation. In such a context, there was little leeway for deliberation or slack for bargaining.

The pattern seems clear. Where there is a centrally defined goal or assignment, it is the principal who is given the responsibility to get it done. The account of the middle school innovations gives weight and substance to the principals' concern about retaining the authority to meet responsibilities, and these innovations also show how the question was resolved. It is reasonable to assume that—in the final analysis—this will be the result whenever concrete district goals are set and responsibilities assigned.

Implications

We are restricted in what we can say about the alteration of influence relations, given the limitations of the data. The main difficulty lies in the fact that we are unable to link opinions or actions of principals directly to the decisions for which we have information on teacher participation. For this reason we cannot know whether principals regarded any of them as being of any real significance, in the sense of constituting a meaningful sharing of decision-making authority. With this important caveat in mind, we draw the following tentative conclusions concerning teacher empowerment in the Dade County SBM/SDM pilot schools.

Alteration of Influence

The innovations seem to show that under certain specific conditions some teachers can affect decisions that appear to be important, in the sense of bringing about outcomes that generate unprecedented kinds of teacher participation. Teacher empowerment as meaningful participation in shared decision making seems to be a case of "yes, but . . . " Yes, it is significantly greater than before, but it is subject to a couple of caveats.

First, teacher empowerment was well below the level of determining or changing the direction of a school. Second, their newfound influence was apparently precarious, subject to changes over which teachers have little control. Teacher-dominated innovations were found to be less stable, and support for their involvement in decisions as reflected in attitude statements on both principal and faculty surveys appeared to change with the "downtown political climate."

Local Limits

The apparent desires of some principals to place limits on the extent of decision sharing, and disagreement among teachers as to their role, delineate the limits to alterations in influence. The principal's role as policymaker is presumably strengthened by the estimated 15 to 30 percent of teachers who endorse the legitimacy of the authority of that office as the source of school policy. Whether and how effectively this support may have been employed by principals to sway decisions we do not know.

External Limits on Both Principal and Teachers

The plans, goals, and desires of central authorities limit the decision making of both principal and faculty. The practical limit on influence alteration is probably that it is restricted to affairs so local that any decisions with effects beyond the scope of the school are always reserved to the principal, as the appointed representative of the central administration. This is another way of saying that it may matter little to the downtown administrators whether principal or cadre prevails where district concerns are not in question. Therefore, a superintendent, say, can favor one or the other or neither in purely local affairs without effect on district policy, but with profound effects on the outcomes of school-level decision making.

Lasting Effects

Whatever local empowerment there was in the school-based management pilot schools seems to have rested more on informal than on institutional foundations. In contrast, the lead steward position on the feeder pattern council—giving formal representation to the union—is at the mercy of neither a school vote nor the central administration's goodwill. For this reason, the council may turn out to be the most successful vehicle for shared decision making, and thus for this aspect of teacher empowerment.

5 Conflict in Restructuring the Principal-Teacher Relationship in Memphis

Carol Plata Etheridge and Thomas W. Collins

> This is my school where I graduated. I've always wanted to be here. I don't want to be a principal at another school.

So saying, Walter Corley[1] applied, was interviewed, and retained his position as principal at Southwest High School. Southwest was to be one of seven Memphis urban schools that would adopt a school-based decision-making (SBDM) strategy of school management.

In 1989, as a last resort effort to catalyze change in its inner-city schools, Memphis City Schools designated seven schools as deregulated by releasing them from many contractual agreements and district policies. This enabled establishment of school-based decision making. Not to be confused with school-based management (SBM), SBDM is a participatory decision-making process that shifts decision making to the local school level, giving all parties affected by a decision a voice in making the decision. School-based management, however, does not have a precise meaning. It sometimes is equated with SBDM, but can also refer to a simple shift of management to the local school level without widening decision-making authority. SBM can also mean assignment of decision-making authority to only one group at the local school level while precluding other local school groups from that authority. In Memphis, school-based decision making is based on Carl Marburger's (1989) model. It is intended to be a horizontal process whereby principals, teachers, parents, students, and community residents, the people closest to the school and students, consult and come to decisions through consensus (Herenton, 1989).

This chapter examines processes and issues related to restructuring traditional top-down school administration to a more democratic school-based approach. Southwest High School during the first two years of this management reform is a prototypic case illustrating what happens when all key players have been immersed in a traditional authoritarian bureaucracy but engage to change to the new shared management style. This case is part of a larger study[2] examining how SBDM is simultaneously implemented in the seven urban schools. Descriptions included here synthesize two years of observation, participation, and interviewing at Southwest High.

THE MEMPHIS PLAN

Decentralization and school-based management are not new. Since the 1970 inception of decentralization in the New York City public school system there have been efforts to increase community control of urban schools and bring the schools closer to the people. Memphis planners drew heavily from recommendations of Marburger (1989), James Lewis (1990), and the National Education Association (1989) when establishing school-based decision making. The uniqueness of SBDM in Memphis is the strategy with which personnel volunteered to work under SBDM. The seven targeted inner-city schools were closed and reopened as deregulated, SBDM schools. All professional staff were asked to resign their positions, which were then posted as vacant. The assumption was that inner-city schools can successfully teach students only if the professional staff desires to work in the inner city. Likewise, successful implementation of SBDM hinges on people desiring to work under that management structure. The technical closing of the schools provided the opportunity to completely restaff the schools and created a psychological break with past practice.

A local school council and a professional advisory committee are the primary vehicles through which the various groups participate in decisions. The local school council is the primary vehicle through which the decision-making authority is shared (Etheridge, et al., 1990; Etheridge, Terrell & Watson, 1990; Memphis City Schools SBDM Advisory Council, 1989). Two parents, three classroom teachers, and one community member are elected to the council by their peers in the school's attendance zone. Start-up elections were held in October 1989, after student enrollments were final and new faculty were settled in their schools. Thus initial parent representatives were elected by parents of currently enrolled students and teacher representatives were elected by the new faculty.

The principal automatically serves on the council but cannot be its chairperson. The chair must be a parent or community resident; this is an effort to avoid automatic professional dominance of the council. The council's role is to set school goals and advise and recommend operational and program procedures and local school expenditures. In addition, the council interviews all potential professional personnel, including the principal, and submits recommendations of assignment or reassignment to the superintendent, who makes final personnel decisions. Each council member's task is to represent and present the issues and perspectives of his constituent group. Decisions are to be made through consensus.

The professional advisory committee is composed of grade or department heads in the school. In addition to conducting department meetings, they disseminate professional materials and are the liaison between the teachers and school administrators. In addition, they advise the principal on programmatic needs related to curriculum, instruction, and pupil service.

A recommendation basic to successful establishment of SBDM is that the personnel involved be trained. In Memphis, after new personnel had been hired, the first year was designated for training and establishing the SBDM governing and decision-making mechanisms in those schools.

SOUTHWEST HIGH SCHOOL

Southwest had a long tradition. Under the old racially segregated school system that legally existed in Memphis into the 1960s, attending this school was the symbol of upward mobility for several generations of prominent black middle-class families. Under segregation, the black principal held a position of influence, respect, and high esteem in the community. Invariably, he was a male who had achieved community prominence. He knew all the important people. In some respects, his role was like that of a ward heeler who "could get the job done" with the white establishment. In terms of community power, he was an equal with those local pastors of the largest black churches. With this influence, he could operate his high school like a fiefdom, disciplining teachers, bending the rules to "save" a student, and staffing as he pleased.

Under court-ordered desegregation in the late 1960s the principal's status was altered. Racial balance for all schools in the system was impossible (the entire system is now 79 percent black and 21 percent white). Black principals remained in predominantly black schools. With open housing achieved, a major shift occurred in existing demographics.

The black middle-class families moved out of Southwest's district to integrated and more affluent neighborhoods to the east. Southwest, left with poor and working-class children, became a typical inner-city school. Attention and esteem followed the middle class to the suburban and optional schools. The principal's extensive status and power in the greater community was limited to the local inner-city school and its community. Thus, in 1989–90, the principal at Southwest, like similar inner-city principals, had no bragging rights but retained absolute power within the school and high status and considerable influence within the school's immediate low-income neighborhood.

Southwest's Principal

Walter Corley administered Southwest during the three years prior to the 1989 restructuring. Within the school, he was the absolute authority and commanded respect from the low-income community served by the school. His influence beyond Southwest, however, was minimal. His efforts to improve conditions at Southwest resulted in positive publicity in the local press and support from the superintendent. However, among teachers, he was reputed to be a tyrant, holding teachers in low esteem.

"Conditions of practice have become the most commonly cited explanation for the shortage of good urban teachers" (Haberman, 1987: 20). Conditions of practice include large class size, clerical demands, lack of instructional materials, poor safety conditions, and students who are culturally different from the teacher. Faculty turnover at Southwest just prior to the administrative restructure approached 50 percent annually; central administration and Southwest's principal routinely attributed the teacher attrition rate to the conditions of practice in the inner-city school. Southwest's teachers, however, reported that the pattern occurred because of the principal's dictatorial and demeaning style. Regardless of his reputation among teachers, parents and central office staff considered the principal to be a good leader. During his tenure the school reported a decline in student discipline problems while attendance rates and achievement scores increased. He was able to wrangle funds for a new school building during a time of tight budgets and declining high school student enrollments.

Walter Corley dreamed of bringing the black elite back to the neighborhood school. He believed that alumni would send their children to Southwest after the new building was completed and its academic reputation improved. The school's current low status and the principal's sense of mission intensified his autonomy and authority within the school. He held to an autocratic view whereby he was the only person capable of delivering the vision. To accomplish the task he had to rally community support and, in his words, "hold the whip over the lazy teachers." He would be Southwest's savior. The SBDM reform was the means to accomplishing these goals because SBDM, he believed, would increase his autonomy.

Southwest's Teachers

> I became a part of a competent, enthusiastic, creative, and experienced group of professionals. I have [the] opportunity to share my [expertise] with others through a site-based decision-making approach.
>
> Southwest teacher

With the SBDM reform, teachers from all parts of the school system applied to teach at Southwest. Corley recruited many; all who were hired were interviewed and selected by the local school council. Conversations with teachers during August and September staff development sessions revealed that their enthusiasm equaled the principal's and they too envisioned Southwest becoming the best school in the system, making a difference for disadvantaged youth. They embraced Corley's vision for the school and ignored his reputed leadership style. Unlike Corley, however, teachers also envisioned a school where they could work collaboratively to build an educational school program where teachers would truly be professionals. This expectation was based on the design of the SBDM model and messages delivered during early training sessions. At these sessions, teachers learned about consensus decision making and working as teams and were told they would participate in school decisions.

ESTABLISHING SHARED DECISION MAKING

During the fall of 1989, the first semester of implementation, initial euphoria over the school management restructure soured for both principal and teachers. The principal discovered his new faculty would not simply do what he told them to do—they asked questions; they had their own ideas; they expected to participate in decisions and for those decisions to be by consensus. Teachers discovered that their leader would not allow them to be involved in school decision making of any kind and especially not in the consensus decision making required in the SBDM design.

Planning committees were established but were expected to adopt the principal's ideas rather than to discuss them or generate new ones. For example, Mr. Corley believed that all students at Southwest should be prepared to enter college. Thus without consulting teachers he selected a curriculum to be implemented, ordered the materials, and then announced to the teachers that they would implement it. Teachers, surprised that they were not included in this decision, asked Corley to be included in such decisions, but they were not. As he completed the first SBDM year, a math teacher talked about his administrator. His description of Corley reflects the faculty's view of their principal:

> Mr. Corley doesn't have a [cooperative] bone in his body. He doesn't. He's a go-getter. He works hard and he will come in and do everything, but that's the point; he wants to do it all and that's not what the process calls for. That's not what [SBDM] is about. . . . The principal exhibited a pure "X" leadership style.[3] We were in trouble.

Teams that share decisions and responsibility do not occur spontaneously because someone decides such a team will exist or because people decide to join such a team. It takes time. It takes skill. It takes stamina. It takes support (Bradford & Cohen, 1984). Successful transition to SBDM also requires training (White, 1989; Marburger, 1989). Training in defining SBDM, participant roles, communication, team building, and consensus decision making was ongoing for all seven SBDM sites. Teachers at Southwest, hoping their principal would change, requested and participated in staff development sessions additional to what was being delivered to all seven schools; training especially designed for them included intensive team-building workshops. The teachers believed that over time and with training they were capable of "birthing, incubating, and nurturing" their autocratic administrator into a democratic one.

Initially, Corley adamantly opposed the additional training, but he subsequently seemed to participate wholeheartedly. However, administrative practices at Southwest did not change and the principal repeatedly told faculty that SBDM was simply another experiment and soon all would be back to business as usual.

The differing expectations of teachers and principal and the inability of the principal to change resulted in conflict over how the new school governance should occur. Both teachers and principal understood that they would have increased power, but the principal expected to remain an absolute authority; teachers expected automatic empowerment. Neither expected to have to fight to realize their expectations.

The Principal's Struggle to Control

Some researchers have suggested that participation in SBDM should be voluntary, particularly for pilot programs (White, 1989); those who volunteer will more readily adopt the new behaviors and roles required. This premise was followed at Southwest, but it did not hold true. White reported that SBDM can result in power struggles between the teachers and principals when principals want more control over their own destiny but are resistant to change (cf. also Malen & Ogawa, 1988). At Southwest, the principal did not believe that SBDM was a permanent change, that the council was the governing body of the school, that he was one equal member of the council, or that he shared decision-making authority with teachers. Though by applying for his position he tacitly agreed to implement shared decision making, he did not allow teachers to be involved in curricular, instructional, or budgetary decisions and he allowed the council to serve only as councils have historically served, as a rubber stamp to the principal's decisions.

He used several strategies to maintain control of the council and teachers. First, he countermanded teacher decisions. These ranged from teachers deciding to work on Saturday to how teacher sponsors should work with cheerleaders. In their struggle against what they viewed as arbitrary orders teachers often refused to do what the principal directed. One teacher's description of a series of events exemplifies the nature of the relationship:

> In September [the cheerleaders] complained to the principal about practice sessions. Without speaking to the three teachers who cosponsored the cheerleaders, he told the girls he would get someone else to work with them if they did not like the sponsors. The relationship between the sponsors and the cheerleaders deteriorated. [In January, after heated discussion with sponsors about how cheerleaders who do not come to practice should be disciplined,] without informing the sponsors or the cheerleaders, the principal disbanded the squad. He asked the girls to turn in their uniforms and said there would be no squad. In the same week he told the girls they could cheer again and in the subsequent week he retrieved the uniforms and [again] declared that there would be no squad.
>
> In a faculty meeting he [chastised] the staff for not sponsoring enough student activities. The cheerleading sponsors requested opportunity to work with the cheerleaders again. [The principal's] response was, "No!" He said it was an administrative decision and he

> was not going to be "wishy-washy" about the issue. But then [in February], he asked each of the three original cheerleader sponsors if one sponsor would attend each of the remaining basketball games to chaperon the cheerleaders that "he" had selected. The teachers refused the assignment.

A number of other strategies were used by the principal to maintain control:

1. Misinforming the local school council about policy and budgets.
2. Limiting communication between the council and teachers by forbidding distribution of council meeting minutes or rewriting the minutes before distribution.
3. Submitting proposals for curriculum revisions to the local school council but refusing to allow teachers' views to be expressed.
4. Providing perks to teachers and parents in return for their support.
5. Intercepting mail to teachers from the professional association or central office.
6. Eavesdropping on teacher phone calls.
7. Telling anyone who would listen how lazy the teachers are.
8. Harassing teachers who did not agree with administrative decisions, who insisted on being involved with planning and decisions, or operating on the belief that teachers on the council represented the school's faculty.

A teacher described her harassment:

> Students tell me that I am intimidated. When I am called to the office my students say, "Oh, oh, what did you do? You are in trouble now!" My students beg me to cover the window on my door so nobody can see in. One day a child put his head down on the desk. He had just put it down and [the principal] charged into the room, snatched the child up from the desk, and yelled at him for putting his head down and [at] me for allowing him to do it. My children beg me to cover the window.

Initially, the principal was able to completely dominate teachers and the council with relative ease. Maintaining complete control, however, was not easy. It depended upon the cooperation of the teachers and the council chairman.

Teachers Struggle for Empowerment

In an effort to be included in school decisions, a small cadre of teachers, one of whom was a teacher representative on the council, turned to the project director (an assistant superintendent) and the professional association representative assigned to work with the SBDM schools for assistance. Teachers increasingly met with the project director and the union representative to clarify issues and discuss how to proceed with SBDM. These meetings occurred at the school and were open to any faculty and the principal. From the union and the assistant superintendent teachers became informed of their rights and advocacy procedures. The principal attended few of these meetings. As teachers advocated to the council and principal for increased involvement in school decisions Walter Corley became increasingly punitive toward those who were most active in the effort and whom he termed "troublemakers." In contrast, teachers who supported the principal were treated more benevolently. The faculty became increasingly fractionalized. All the while, teacher issues continued to be barred by the principal from council consideration, but teachers continued to bring them forth.

Finally, a combined meeting of the faculty and local school council was called by the project director at the principal's request. Mr. Corley explained his interpretation of the roles and responsibilities of the council and asked council members to "please not entertain any complaints that the teachers have against either the administration or school or whatever because the council was not the vehicle [for this]." He said that he sent a letter to the superintendent suggesting "maybe my teachers simply could not understand the function of the council." The director, who was asked to comment, explained that the principal's interpretations of council responsibilities were incorrect. In response, the principal yelled at the assistant superintendent and left the meeting. This confrontation marked the beginning of open battle between teachers and principal to determine whether the principal would remain at the school. Principal and teachers alike fought for their survival. In the process one local school council teacher representative resigned under pressure from colleagues after they learned the teacher, in a meeting with the superintendent, had not supported teachers when parents and principal complained about "lazy" teachers at the school. A new teacher representative was elected who was less aligned with the principal.

The project director and union representative continued to advise teachers in meetings open to the principal until a confrontation occurred between Mr. Corley and the union representative. The principal badgered the union representative, accusing her of being a troublemaker; she was reduced to tears. The principal subsequently reported to the superintendent that the union was "meddling." Concerned about being perceived as the cause of strife, both the union representative and the project director stopped attending meetings at the school but continued to advise individual teachers who sought assistance.

The project director met with the chairs of all seven of the local school councils to inform them of system and state policies and procedures. At this meeting Southwest's chairperson, a parent who had supported the principal, learned that Mr. Corley had misinformed the council about expenditures and the availability of monies for school supplies. Her support for the principal began to wane as she began advocating for teachers.

In March, the council remained dominated by the principal and teachers had minimal involvement with school decisions. One teacher representative emerged as leading the struggle for SBDM as originally designed and as interpreted by the school's teachers. She initiated communication with the superintendent and, with a few colleagues, pressured for the principal's removal based on failure to include teachers in decision making as prescribed by SBDM and based on grievances charging mistreatment of teachers. Over half of the school faculty threatened to request transfers if the principal was not removed, and the union and assistant superintendent recommended removal of the principal.

Teachers continued to plan as though they would return the next year, explaining, "We can't afford to do otherwise." In June, after school closed for the summer, the issue was not yet resolved.

Though he recognized the need to remove Southwest's principal, the superintendent, who was under attack from the school board for much-publicized personal involvements, was reticent to take action that might garner more unfavorable publicity. In July, following close of the first academic year and after repeated teacher efforts to quietly have the principal removed based on inappropriate leadership style for SBDM, teachers went public. Through the local newspaper and before the school board, they reported the principal's punitive management style and requested his removal based on his incompatibility with SBDM. But the principal fought back with favorable articles in the newspaper, and he brought parents to the school board meetings, where they advocated for him. No action was taken by the superintendent or the school board.

Finally, teachers reported irregularities in Southwest's attendance reports; these were reported in the newspaper. Within two weeks of this news, the superintendent recommended to the school board that the principal be removed for approving alterations of student attendance records and allowing repeatedly absent students to graduate, which were violations of school board policy and state law. The superintendent made it clear that the sole reason for dismissal was violation of state law, "not the result of pressure groups." Walter Corley was placed on "at-large" status but subsequently obtained a position in the central office. Within two months the superintendent announced his retirement one year hence and the project director announced she would take a year's leave of absence from the school system before her retirement in one year.

In August 1990, school opened at Southwest with the assistant principal serving as interim principal and 83 percent of the prior year's faculty returning. That semester, the local school council went through the process of finding another principal. The atmosphere changed at Southwest. Procedures were established for consensus decision making. Departmental and topical committees were established that generated ideas for curricular and instructional changes. Open and often heated discussions occurred regularly on a variety of schoolwide and departmental issues. Teachers came early and worked late. The rampant talk of applying for transfers disappeared. In May 1991, teachers continued to be enthused and optimistic, and only one teacher expected to request a school transfer. When asked about burnout, they explained that burnout comes from frustration and they were no longer frustrated.

But they worry. Though in January 1991 three candidates for principal had been recommended to the superintendent by the local school council, no appointment had been made. A core of parents and central office administrators continued to advocate for Corley to regain his principalship. The professional staff at Southwest suspect that "everyone is waiting for us to make one mistake at this school." The superintendent, having been selected by a coalition to run for mayor, had not yet appointed a principal in May 1991. Still, the teachers say, "We will never go back to the old way."

Context

Southwest High School is one of seven schools engaging in SBDM in Memphis. At the end of the second year of the reform three other schools were engaged in power issues similar to those occurring the previous year at Southwest. In the other schools, teachers did not assert themselves until the second year. It appears that similar strife will occur in those three schools before everyone settles into shared decision-making processes.

DISCUSSION

> Whenever democracy comes from the top the people at the bottom are probably not ready for it. . . . When school personnel are professionalized they will not have to be urged to shape curricula, make policy, and exercise leadership. Instead, the administration will be hard put to prevent them doing so.
>
> Harry S. Broudy
> *Paradox and Promise*

Events at Southwest illustrate Broudy's point. SBDM was mandated from the central school office. The teachers were ready; the principal was not. The door to SBDM was opened by the top of the Memphis City School bureaucracy—the superintendent and school board. Even with the door open, restructuring school management from authoritarian to a shared process is difficult when the principal is steeped in authoritarian school power traditions. Mandating, volunteering, and retraining did not make shared decision making happen. Volunteers must intend to change and not be threatened by sharing authority. Though the principal voiced willingness to change administrative style, he misinterpreted SBDM as consolidating his power, not sharing it. Thus he either could not or would not change. Instead, the principal fought to retain his traditional position of absolute authority.

New York City's earliest experiences demonstrated the necessity of a strong superintendent who could manage and make decisions according to the needs of the district (Rogers, 1981). Southwest's circumstance was complicated by the fact that the superintendent twice did not make a timely decision regarding the principal. The superintendent had resigned from his own position and was attending to his own political agenda.[4] Thus he not only was a lame duck superintendent but had abdicated his decision-making responsibility. This probably served to prolong the teacher-principal conflict during the first year and has allowed uncertainty to exist during the second year.

Events at Southwest High School also illustrate how teachers, when given the mechanism by which they are empowered to influence the nature of schooling, can and will change their traditional roles, responsibilities, and behaviors. In addition, Southwest's experience illustrates how teachers, when denied their expectation to share decisions, will fight for their new roles and responsibilities. First they attempted to change the principal. Failing this, the teachers worked to have the principal removed.

Usually, teachers do not have much political power, especially in controversial changes such as principal removal. In the absence of superintendent decisiveness, Southwest's teachers had to rely on individualized assistance from knowledgeable and powerful supporters in the district's central office and the teachers' union. This suggests that the central office and union support that reformers recommend for successful implementation of SBDM must be specific to the situation at hand and at times might approach interference. In such circumstances the participants are susceptible to criticism. Thus reform leaders must have a good reservoir of stamina with which to weather the conflict.

Because shared leadership was not the dominant leadership mode in the school system, the conflict that occurred at Southwest should be considered a normal and necessary part of the change process until a new equilibrium is reached that includes a common understanding of shared decision making as the norm. Indeed, the existence of conflict is considered to be normal in the corporate world, where shared decision making is new (Bradford & Cohen, 1984).

This instance of teachers willing to change and able to actively advocate for their own empowerment suggests that restructuring school management and teacher empowerment can occur from within the school bureaucracy, but not easily and not quickly. Further, the events at Southwest suggest that the restructuring of school curriculum that some envision SBDM catalyzing will take considerable time. After two years, the management in this school is restructured, but curriculum and instruction are still far removed from being changed. Logic tells us that there must be comfort with the new management strategy before other changes follow. Events at Southwest and other SBDM schools must be observed for longer than two years before the full impact of SBDM can be determined and the processes understood.

Finally, Southwest's experience suggests that school-based decision-making processes must be thought through in advance. Guidelines must be clear regarding what decisions can be made by whom. They should be made either at the school level or at the central office, not some of each. In this case, political agendas served to prolong strife and stress and impede progress.

NOTES

1. Pseudonyms are used for names of people and schools to protect anonymity.

2. Support for this study has been provided by the Center of Research in Educational Policy, College of Education, Memphis State University. The center is a Center of Excellence for the state of Tennessee.

3. The teacher was referring to Douglas McGregor's (1960) management theory based on assumptions about human behavior. Theory X assumes the worker dislikes work and avoids it when possible and so must be coerced, controlled, directed, and threatened with punishment.

4. The former school superintendent was elected mayor of Memphis in November 1991.

6 Rural Responses to Kentucky's Education Reform Act

Pamelia Coe and Patricia J. Kannapel

In June 1989, the Kentucky Supreme Court handed the state's General Assembly one of the most difficult tasks faced by any state legislature in recent history—to restructure completely the state's system of public schooling. The decision, resulting from a suit filed by sixty-six of the state's poorest school districts, declared the entire Kentucky system of schools unconstitutional (*Rose v. Council for Better Education*, 1989). This decision went beyond the original complaint that state funding of the schools was unfair and set in motion a fast-paced and dramatic redesign of the state's system of education.

The Kentucky Education Reform Act of 1990 (KERA) was adopted by the General Assembly just nine months after the court decision and was signed into law on April 11, 1990. For the most part, KERA follows what some researchers have called the "second wave" of reform, restructuring schooling primarily through decentralization and the professionalization of teaching (Murphy, 1990).

STUDY OF FOUR RURAL KENTUCKY SCHOOL DISTRICTS

Because massive school restructuring is taking place statewide in a predominantly rural state, KERA has provided two qualitative researchers associated with the Appalachia Educational Laboratory (AEL) the opportunity to study restructuring in rural and small, independent school districts. During the fall of 1990 they worked as a team to study six districts, each working primarily in the three districts closest to her home (Coe &

Kannapel, 1991). They undertook to make a baseline study of attitudes toward KERA in the six districts prior to implementation of most of the law's mandates, relying primarily on structured interviews but also on attendance at board of education and PTA meetings, document review, and general observation. In the two months they had available for field observation they were able to spend about five working days in each district and to interview 171 people, including superintendents, central office staff, principals, counselors, teachers, classified employees, school board members, and, if accessible, parents and students.

This baseline study laid the groundwork for a five-year study of KERA implementation in four rural county or small, independent Kentucky districts. (Many county districts in Kentucky have small, independent districts within their limits.) While seeking to negotiate entry into a central Kentucky district, at the time this chapter was written, the authors were working in four school districts, whose pseudonyms are Orange County, Humphrey County, Lamont County, and Newtown Independent. All four were part of the baseline study. In the longitudinal study, the researchers are using typical ethnographic methods: participant observation, interview, document analysis, and—sparingly—videotaping of key events. They anticipate spending approximately one week a month in each district over the next five years.

These four districts are the basis for this case history. A brief description of the major provisions of KERA follows. The major part of this case history, however, is four vignettes, describing each district and the impact restructuring has had on each to date.

THE REFORM LAW

KERA is a massive piece of legislation—a bill of over 900 pages contained in four volumes (Kentucky General Assembly, 1990). It is to be implemented incrementally over five or six years. The law is divided into three primary sections: curriculum, governance, and finance.

Curriculum

The curriculum section of KERA reflects the philosophy that all children can learn and that the primary role of the state is to ensure that this learning occurs by defining what students must learn (outcomes) and to hold schools accountable for producing these outcomes. Toward this end,

KERA removes all curriculum mandates and adopts instead a list of capabilities that all students will be expected to achieve—capabilities that emphasize the practical application of skills, particularly critical-thinking and problem-solving skills. Over a period of five years, all schools in the commonwealth are expected to switch to school-based decision making (SBDM), under which a council of one administrator, three teachers, and two parents will be formed at each school to set school policy designed to help students acquire the mandated capabilities.

KERA abolishes the standardized testing program and mandates the development of a new performance-based assessment that will be administered to a sample of students in each school biennially. Schools will be expected to demonstrate a specified level of improvement in the proportion of students demonstrating the required capabilities from one testing period to the next. Schools that reach this level will receive financial rewards; schools that fail to improve or actually decline in performance will be sanctioned. Sanctions involve, at the least, being required to develop a school improvement plan and receiving state assistance. At the most, the school would be placed on probation and all students allowed to transfer to the nearest school judged successful. All faculty and administrators could be dismissed if improvement were not demonstrated after a probationary period.

In addition to outcome-based components, KERA mandates a number of inputs aimed at eliminating extracurricular sources of student failure. They include preschool programs for at-risk and handicapped four-year-olds, social service centers (Family Resource Centers and Youth Services Centers) at or near all schools in which 20 percent or more of the student body is at risk, a statewide program for utilizing technology in the schools, replacement of grades K–3 with a nongraded primary program to eliminate early school failure, and a program of extended educational services for students who need additional time to meet the mandated outcomes (Hornbeck, 1990; Kentucky General Assembly, 1990).

Governance

The governance section of the law is primarily designed to rid the school system of political influence and to return the focus of schooling to students.

At the state level, the governance section transfers the duties of the elected Superintendent of Public Instruction to the newly created appointive office of Commissioner of Education and abolishes all positions in the state department of education to allow the new commissioner to reorganize the department. At the local level, KERA transfers nearly all hiring and firing authority from local school boards to the superintendent and prohibits board members from attempting to influence the hiring of school employees. While the board is still responsible for hiring the superintendent, it must accept recommendations from a screening committee and cannot dismiss a superintendent without the approval of the Commissioner of Education. Relatives of school board members and superintendents cannot be employed by the school district, and relatives of principals cannot work in the same school as the related principal (except in certain limited circumstances). School district employees are prohibited from donating to or campaigning for school board candidates. To ensure that these mandates are carried out, the Office of Education Accountability has been established under the legislature to monitor reform implementation.

The governance section also contains a number of features designed to improve teacher and administrator certification and training, such as the establishment of a teacher-dominated professional certification board, regional service centers under the state department of education, and training and assessment centers for principals and superintendents.

Finance

The finance section of KERA attempts equalization of funding. It establishes a new funding mechanism that provides each district a guaranteed amount of money per pupil and additional funds allocated to cover the cost of educating at-risk and exceptional children and of transporting students. Local districts are required to contribute their share by levying a minimum equivalent tax rate of 30 cents per $100 of valuation (35 cents to participate in the state school construction fund) and by assessing all property at 100 percent of its fair cash value. Local districts may provide up to 15 percent beyond the revenues guaranteed by the state, and the state will match these funds up to a specified level (known as Tier I funding). Any additional revenue generated at the local level must be approved by a vote of the people, will not be matched by the state, and cannot exceed a set level (Tier II funding).

In addition to this new funding structure, KERA guarantees all districts an 8 percent to 25 percent increase in state funding for the 1990–91 year and a 5 percent to 25 percent increase for the 1991–92 year. Teachers are guaranteed a 10 percent salary increase for 1990–91. To fund the new reforms, the legislature raised the state's sales tax one penny, raised the corporate tax 1 percent, and made some changes in the state income tax code (Kentucky General Assembly, 1990; Miller, Noland & Schaaf, 1990).

CASE STUDIES OF FOUR RURAL KENTUCKY SCHOOL DISTRICTS

The districts varied widely in their characteristics. Some traits are common to all four districts: they are small, they are rural or small-town, and they have very few minority students or staff. The student body minority population ranged from 0.08 percent to 2.5 percent—a figure somewhat less than the statewide average for the 1989–90 school year of 10 percent. Likewise, the percentage of minority school employees was less than the state average of 4 percent, ranging from none to 1.5 percent.

In all four districts teachers and central office staff—with the significant exception of the superintendent—were most enthusiastic about the KERA reforms, while school board members were the only group in a set of structured interviews with a majority who had negative opinions about KERA. In all districts a majority of classified (nonprofessional) school staff, parents, and students were not well enough informed about the law to have a considered opinion, even though all the parents we interviewed were school volunteers and about half were PTA or PTO presidents (cf. Coe, Kannapel & Lutz, 1991).

Orange County School District

> I think our administration at the top will make [implementation of KERA] as easy as possible, probably a lot easier than a lot of districts . . . because we have a very innovative superintendent. He's great as far as trying to implement things, and he doesn't want Orange County to be on the bottom of anything. If we come out on the bottom, we'll all have to work a little harder. And he inspires motivation by being the way he is, by working as he does.
>
> An Orange County central office staff person

The District

Orange County is situated near the West Virginia border of Kentucky. Historically the economy has been largely dependent on coal mining, but most of the coal has been mined out. The district has a mixed economy, and the county seat is a market town that attracts customers from nearby counties as well as from Orange County.

An independent school district in the county has a higher tax base than the rest of the county. Assessed property value per pupil in the Orange County district is about $62,000, putting the district in the bottom 10 percent of districts statewide. The state median property value per pupil is $124,892; the state mean, apparently skewed above the median by a few large, affluent districts, is $171,101. In addition, Orange County ranks in the highest 20 percent of school districts for the proportion of students who are classified as economically deprived (65 percent).

Orange County has over 4,000 students in one high school, seven elementary schools, and an alternative school for potential dropouts. The high school, one elementary school, and the central office building are all located on a large campus, which also boasts playing fields for different sports and an indoor sports center. It is fairly easy for all the schools to interact, as none of the outlying elementary schools is more than ten miles from the central campus. Students are bused frequently from outlying schools to the central campus for intramural games or other events.

Serving a large number of nonprivileged students, Orange County has historically had very low academic achievement. At the outset of the current superintendent's tenure, an administrator was sent from the state department of education to help the district improve. This administrator worked with the district for about a year, recommending improvements in every area of school life from fiscal accountability to academic instruction. He was withdrawn when the county district showed evidence of improvement, and one local administrator declared that state assistance was "the best thing that ever happened to us." There was a dramatic improvement in test scores in 1989–90, attesting to the efficacy of the improvements that have been made. For the 1989–90 school year, Orange County students at the third- and seventh-grade levels ranked in the top 30 percent statewide on the standardized test. Students in the fifth and tenth grades, however, performed less well, with fifth-graders ranking in the bottom 40 percent and tenth-graders in the bottom 10 percent. The attendance rate was 94.4 percent (Kentucky Department of Education, personal communication, 1991).

Orange County schools exhibit some political strife. There are allegations of favoritism in hiring practices and also some conflict between teachers and the superintendent as to how KERA should be implemented. This conflict is most apparent at the high school, where there are three identifiable factions of teachers.

Responses to KERA

Twenty-three persons in Orange County responded to our structured interviews. Most expressed positive attitudes toward KERA: 65 percent were more positive than negative, in the opinion of AEL staff rating each interview as a whole. Twenty-two percent were neutral or ambivalent, 9 percent were more negative than positive, and 4 percent were judged to be too uninformed to have an opinion about KERA. The general level of receptivity to the reform was the highest of the four school districts.

Orange County respondents felt, by and large, that they had received adequate information on KERA. Nearly half said their information was adequate, and about one-third said that it was as good as possible considering the lack of guidelines on most KERA mandates at the time. It was the only district we studied in which no one reported having totally inadequate information.

The Orange County School District is implementing KERA requirements on schedule. The superintendent has assigned one central office administrator full-time to the task of informing staff and community about KERA and overseeing reform implementation. District leadership is encouraging the development of innovative instructional programs compatible with outcome-based education, such as cooperative learning and hands-on mathematics and science instruction.

A key to the recent innovations in the Orange County School District, as well as the district's response to the challenge of KERA, is a strong commitment to staff development. Respondents referred frequently to training staff members have received during the past year, often involving considerable investment by the school district in sending teachers as well as administrators to workshops in various parts of the state. According to the superintendent, professional development was the second largest item in the 1990–91 budget, after normal operating expenses, but training will be in-house next year, now that both administrators and teachers have been trained as trainers. The major concern that administrators expressed about KERA was whether enough training could be provided in the time frame set by the bill to allow local staff to implement the law adequately.

At the time of the baseline study, the high school principal said that he thought it unlikely any school would vote to adopt school-based decision making (SBDM) and that he planned to suggest to the superintendent that the high school be assigned to do so (since the board is required to designate a school to undertake SBDM if none votes to adopt it by the 1991–92 school year). An elementary school principal said that her staff was excited about SBDM and she thought they would vote for it when they were ready. In fact, the elementary school staff has since voted to adopt SBDM and a school council has been elected but postponed meeting regularly until July 1, 1991, by which time they would have received training.

In response to a series of open-ended questions, Orange County respondents revealed a preoccupation with SBDM. Other KERA features mentioned by respondents (none mentioned by as many as one-third) were the new testing program, the antinepotism measures, and a number of finance provisions (funding in general, funding equalization, and tax increases required by KERA).

Orange County respondents listed fewer weaknesses of KERA than strengths. A few complained about the lack of a research base for many of the KERA features. Some felt that the provisions for professional development were inadequate or that the attempt to remove politics from the school system would not be successful.

Asked what steps the district had taken to implement KERA, about half of the Orange County respondents said that staff development had been increased. (None of the other three districts had so high a percentage of respondents who cited increased staff development.) A few mentioned other actions, mostly planning for or implementing curriculum features of the law. Few respondents had much to say when asked what impact KERA had had on them personally. Three said they had not yet been affected at all.

General Prognosis for Successful Implementation of KERA

When asked whether reform would be particularly easy or difficult in their district, Orange County respondents identified many more facilitators to reform than barriers. The chief facilitator of reform they cited was that the superintendent and central office staff are receptive, innovative, and supportive of KERA. One teacher voiced a philosophy supportive of the basic intent of SBDM:

> I don't think it's going to be difficult. We're eastern Kentucky people; we are . . . independent people, and it's good that we're going to be able to assert our independence. . . . With the reform, we will be able to do that. . . . As independent people, we've relied too long on Frankfort [the state capital] to tell us what to teach and how to teach it. They don't really understand our children. . . . Our kids have not got the same problems you'd find in Louisville or Lexington or Frankfort. . . . They may think they know what our kids are like, but they don't, and we do. And it's time that we started teaching the way we know that they're going to learn . . . and get them ready for the life they're going to be living.

The only barriers to reform mentioned for the district as a whole had to do with lack of support for education in the community. At the school level, elementary school respondents primarily named facilitators of reform, while high school respondents mostly named barriers. Two teachers at the elementary school commented that the principal would make implementation easier because she is innovative and keeps teachers well informed about KERA. A central office administrator said she believed reform would be easier at the elementary level because there are better working relationships in elementary schools than in the high school. Two people identified the chief barrier to reform at the high school as a fragmented faculty that does not work well together.

Political divisions may undermine some reform efforts. The local Kentucky Education Association (KEA) affiliate, with leadership from high school teachers, has filed a lawsuit against the board and superintendent because the SBDM policy adopted by the board differs from the bill's formula by adding a nonprofessional staff member to each council. (According to local rumor, the high school teachers fear that the principal would be able to dominate the council by exerting influence over the parent and classified staff members.) The council elected by the elementary school that has already adopted SBDM includes a classified staff person. The KEA affiliate also objected to a provision in board policy that if two members of the same family work at a school, neither can serve on the council.

Orange County has strong leadership from the superintendent and central office staff. Thus, even with the divisions that were apparent in the school district, Orange County district appears to be a well-led system, well organized to provide excellent education in a relatively low-income community with very little historical interest in education. Unless political rivalries escalate beyond their present level, the district appears to be in a position to use KERA to multiply the educational improvements already taking place.

Newtown Independent District

> There's scarcely enough funding [from KERA] for us to cover salaries, a 10 percent salary increase. This is true largely because our independent district has a lot more employees than are funded by the Minimum Foundation Program. We are what is termed by the Department of Education as being "overstaffed".... In order to have the proper program, we must employ an elementary art teacher, elementary music people, elementary physical education.... And also, at the high school, in order to have a quality program, we must employ a teacher to teach classes that might not have what would be considered a full load (for example, a physics class).... It's simply a situa-

> tion of small districts that you must be "overstaffed" . . . (as far as the Department of Education is concerned) in order to have a quality program. Now, if we give a raise . . . , we must cover this "overstaffing." Some districts can give a high percentage because they aren't overstaffed. . . . , but those districts do not have quality.
>
> Newtown district superintendent

The District

Newtown Independent District is a small city district in eastern Kentucky. It is located in a medium-sized town that is considerably more affluent than the surrounding countryside, even though it is not particularly affluent by national standards. Assessed property value per pupil is about $141,000, compared with a state median of $124,892. About 30 percent of the student body is classified as economically deprived. (The state average is about 39 percent.)

The community, which has a history of strong local support of education, has raised local taxes for the schools far above the minimum required by Kentucky law to qualify for state financial aid. The district has been able to provide higher teacher salaries than surrounding county districts, and administrators feel it has been able to attract the best teachers in that area of the state. There are only two school buildings in the district, serving about 950 students: a combined middle and high school and an elementary school. The two buildings are only about a block apart, and high school students can easily walk to the elementary school to eat at the only school cafeteria in the district.

Staff and parents proudly report that, for at least the past ten years, Newtown District's test scores have been among the top twenty and often the top ten school districts in Kentucky. In 1989–90, twelfth- and fifth-graders had scores that put them in the top 10 percent, while seventh-graders tested in the top 20 percent and third-graders in the top 30 percent statewide. The attendance rate in 1989–90 was 95.6. When this high level of achievement was publicized in local newspapers, the Newtown District began to attract tuition students from nearby county districts. While the city's population is remaining steady or declining, the school district's student population is growing from an influx of tuition students, resulting in 1990–91 in overcrowded classes (Kentucky Department of Education, personal communication, 1991).

Administrators and teachers all emphasize that the school district functions as a big "family." Many are related to one another. All staff are involved in decision making. The district has apparently been relatively free from political strife. No one mentioned politics as a problem during the interviews, and several respondents emphasized that even though Newtown District is in eastern Kentucky (notorious for political abuses), the school system is free of partisan infighting.

Not only do teachers have a great deal of informal access to administrators and board members, but the school board has for some years set aside time to listen to teachers' concerns. The elementary school PTA is very strong and has been honored by the state PTA organization as one of the best in Kentucky.

Responses to KERA

Twenty persons in Newtown District responded to our structured interviews. Of these, only 35 percent were more positive than negative toward KERA. Thirty percent expressed generally neutral ("wait and see") attitudes, while 20 percent were more negative than positive, and 15 percent were judged to be too uninformed about the law to have an opinion. Almost 70 percent of Newtown Independent respondents felt either adequately informed about KERA or as well informed as possible, given the lack of guidelines. However, more than 30 percent felt inadequately informed.

While the district is meeting KERA requirements, it is not so proactive as other Kentucky districts. Because of the high level of achievement and participation by teachers and parents in decision making, many respondents in Newtown District (from administrators on down) expressed the opinion that KERA is not needed here. Neither school faculty requested a vote on adopting SBDM. When the administrators—knowing they would be required to assign one school to implement SBDM in 1991–92—required that teachers in both schools vote on SBDM in May, over 80 percent of each faculty rejected SBDM. One of the principals summed up the district's apparent position:

> We haven't made a lot of changes up to this point. In the last five years, our school has ranked very high in statewide testing. . . . I always believed that if you don't have a problem, there's no reason to change. Now, the new reform bill will cause us to make some changes. But we've always had success, and we have a very dedicated faculty, and I think that's number one. If you have good teachers, everything will fall in place.

As in other districts we surveyed, respondents were focusing primarily on SBDM, mentioned by thirteen respondents as a particularly significant feature of the reform. Opinion was divided about the value of SBDM: seven persons said it was a strength of the reform, while four felt it was a weakness. Other KERA provisions mentioned by a few people as significant features of the reform were the nongraded primary, the nepotism provisions, the funding formula, and increased funding and the effort at funding equalization.

Newtown Independent District respondents listed almost as many weaknesses of KERA as strengths. Six respondents listed the funding formula as a weakness of the legislation (reflecting their dissatisfaction with the district's relatively low increase in state funding), while an equal number said that funding (primarily the increase in state funding) was a strength. Those who listed financing as a negative feature felt their district was being "penalized" for having supported the schools financially in the past. One classified employee commented, "I wish they'd have given the independents a little more cut out of the pie. I think they have penalized them . . . for attempting to do a good job over the years. Our tax rate is higher than the county system's, but we're going to fall behind them."

Some Newtown respondents criticized the nepotism provisions, mentioning specifically that they were causing the district to lose a particularly valued school board member. Others complained about specific aspects of SBDM and about the general lack of KERA guidelines. The nongraded primary program was of great concern in Newtown District. Six respondents felt it was a strong point of KERA, while two considered it a weakness. A central office administrator reported that the district had experimented with a nongraded primary program in the past and that it had not been a success. In late May, however, the superintendent reported that the primary teachers were enthusiastic about the nongraded primary and well prepared to implement it. Some respondents also expressed uneasiness about the proposed new performance-based testing program.

General Prognosis for Successful Implementation of KERA

When asked to list school district traits that would either facilitate or hinder implementation of KERA, Newtown Independent District respondents identified more facilitators than barriers. They emphasized that teachers and parents had been involved in decision making for years. Some respondents also felt that the small size of the district and the good communication and strong sense of trust that already exist in the district should make implementation of KERA easy. One of the few barriers to reform they identified was that KERA does not really benefit the district, since it did not receive a large increase in state funding and was already doing many of the things mandated by the law.

The reform law is viewed with more trepidation here than in the other three districts because Newtown Independent District respondents are afraid of losing what they have or of having to change when no change is needed. The fact that the district received a smaller increase in state funds under KERA than neighboring county districts has resulted in the perception that the school district has been "penalized" by the new funding formula. One classified staff person voiced a fear that may underlie many other fears: "Somehow I feel it's sort of the beginning of the end of independent schools. I don't see how they'll keep up, particularly in this system, because the city's not that big and the tax base is not that big." The superintendent has also voiced the fear that KERA may be designed to put an end to small, independent districts.

However, most respondents expressed optimism that the district would continue to be one of the best in Kentucky. Morale is high in Newtown District, but the widespread lack of enthusiasm for KERA, coupled with the perception that the district does not need reform, may create problems in implementing the reform law. Malen and Ogawa's study of site-based governance councils in Utah suggests that traditional decision-making structures are unlikely to be challenged in school districts characterized by a "stable and congenial" environment (1988: 265). Teachers and administrators generally expressed satisfaction with the current district structure and performance, which may make it difficult to institute the major *philosophical* changes required by KERA, though the district will undoubtedly obey the letter of the law.

Humphrey County School District

> It's always been a political ring and I think it will continue to be, because the board members—now I'm not saying all the board members, but some of the board members—they want political power. The teachers and parents feel like they are not for . . . what's best for the children. In fact, a study was done last year, an audit by the state department, and it found that all of the board meetings that they attended, hardly ever a reference was made to the benefit of the children. It was, like, hiring and firing this person, this bus driver, this cook, this teacher—whatever.
>
> A Humphrey County teacher

The District

The Humphrey County School District is located on the western edge of the Appalachian Mountains in eastern Kentucky. There is little industry in the county, and much of the mountainous terrain is unsuitable for farming or located within the boundaries of a national forest. As a result, the economy is depressed, the tax base poor, and the school system is the largest employer in the county. About 70 percent of Humphrey County students are classified as economically deprived, and the assessed property value per pupil in the district is just over $56,000 (among the lowest districts in the state).

The district contains six schools that serve a student population of less than 3,000. Academic achievement in the county has historically been quite low. The district had the highest dropout rate, the lowest attendance rate, and some of the lowest student test scores of the six districts originally studied. Statistics for the 1989–90 school year indicate that only about half of all Humphrey County students who begin the ninth grade graduate from high school, compared to a state average of 67 percent (Kentucky Department of Education, personal communication, 1991).

Because the economy of Humphrey County is depressed and the school district is the largest employer in the county, a system of political cronyism has developed within the school district, in which school board members win election by promising school district jobs to supporters. These jobs are usually noncertified, but teachers and other professionals have also found themselves demoted, transferred, or threatened for not having supported the proper school board member. The local board and superintendent have traditionally not worked well together, and the district has gone through several superintendents in the past few years. In addition, relations between the district leadership (central office and the school board) and school personnel appear to be tense and distrustful.

Responses to KERA

Thirty-four persons in Humphrey County were interviewed for the study. Perhaps because of the plethora of problems facing the school district at the time KERA was passed into law, some Humphrey County respondents displayed ambivalence toward the legislated reforms. This ambivalence stemmed chiefly from a fear that the KERA measures designed to eliminate political abuses would be ineffective and that the problems facing the district are so entrenched that they will be difficult to overcome. In spite of these misgivings, half of the people interviewed in the fall of 1990 were judged to be more positive than negative about the law, and another third appeared to be neutral or ambivalent. Many respondents commented that KERA had given them hope for the first time in years that Humphrey County's plight might be improved, even though they were fearful that the law might not be as successful as they hoped. Only a few respondents were reacting to KERA in a primarily negative way.

The level of awareness about the reform law appeared to be somewhat lower in Humphrey County than in the other three districts. In Humphrey County, just over half of the respondents felt themselves to be adequately informed or as well informed as possible (compared with 70 percent in all districts), while slightly less than half described their level of information as inadequate. Some respondents commented that staff development activities and the dissemination of information by the administration had left something to be desired. One individual commented: "There is a lack of communication between the central office and each school. . . . It seems to me that they expect us to just know these things—'Do this'—and they expect us to do it without explaining what it is they want. . . . I feel like they are just sitting back and letting it happen instead of making it happen."

The perception that the district leadership was not doing enough to inform and prepare staff appeared to center primarily on staff development and awareness activities. The administration was clearly moving forward with the implementation of other components of KERA, and no complaints were heard about their handling of them. The extended school services program was being offered after school five days a week, the preschool program was available to all four-year-olds in the county (not just to at-risk children), and the district was making plans for family resource and youth services centers for the fall of 1991.

The school board, by contrast, moved quite slowly in raising the local tax rate and only increased the rate to the minimum level required to qualify for school construction funds. Even so, the district received the maximum 25 percent increase in state funding allowed under the basic funding formula, and this was reported as a major effect of the law by several respondents.

As in the other three districts, SBDM (along with increased funding of education) was the most frequently identified strong point of KERA in Humphrey County. Frustrated over having had little voice in decision making in the past, many teachers remarked that the sheer scope and ambitious nature of KERA had energized them. One teacher remarked, "[KERA has] given me hope that things will change, and it's kind of given me . . . a new life. This year I feel more energetic. I don't know if it is related to the raise, the site-based decision making coming in. We started some new programs at our school, got involved in a lot of new things."

Humphrey County teachers reported feeling empowered by other aspects of the law as well. Some teachers reported that during the summer's salary negotiations they had had an opportunity for the first time to examine the district budget. Their eventual success in negotiating a substantial salary increase had raised morale and enthusiasm throughout the district.

Another feature of KERA that over half of Humphrey County respondents (compared to 33 percent across the four districts) identified as a strength was increased funding to education. This was also the only district where a substantial number of respondents (about one-fourth) identified the preschool for at-risk four-year-olds as a strength.

Even though many Humphrey County respondents reported that KERA had had a significant financial effect on the district, they reported that the KERA governance measures designed to eliminate political machinations on the part of the school board had made little difference. When asked to identify the weak points of KERA, 50 percent of Humphrey County respondents (compared to only 15 percent overall) listed these governance measures, chiefly because they believed the measures would be ineffective. Respondents cited three major flaws in the measures. One is that KERA focuses on eliminating nepotism, but the problem in Humphrey County has been one of cronyism. In fact, not a single Humphrey County board member lost his seat as a result of the nepotism measures.

The second flaw, according to Humphrey County respondents, is that KERA attempts to eliminate cronyism by transferring all hiring and firing authority from the school board to the superintendent. Respondents were not confident, however, that the superintendent would be willing or able to resist making political appointments himself, given the long tradition of such activity in the district.

A final flaw was identified by some respondents in all eastern Kentucky districts, not just Humphrey County. This is that educators in eastern Kentucky tend to come from a few "education families." When relatives are prohibited from working in the same system, the job pool is severely restricted. A Humphrey County administrator explained the problem:

> Eastern Kentucky is being depleted of its population, and I feel like the people that are leaving are the quality people. The people that are educated are going to find better jobs, and when you restrict and say that a superintendent's relatives cannot work in the system and a principal's relatives cannot work in a certain school, then you are discouraging them from bringing their skills back home. . . . Many times those of us who are in education and those of us who are in vital roles are the ones who see the importance of sending our children off to college and getting them an education.

Many respondents in the district (about one-third), however, identified the *attempt* to eliminate political abuses by school boards as a strength of the reform law (compared to less than 17 percent in any other district).

General Prognosis for Successful Implementation of KERA

When respondents were asked to give a general prognosis for the prospects of successful education reform in their own districts, the majority of respondents felt that the reform would be more difficult for their district than most. Many respondents said reform would be difficult because of the long-standing tradition of cronyism on the part of the board and the lack of communication between the schools and the district leadership. An administrator reported that the current administration is working to overcome the political problems but is finding that many district employees harbor deep-seated bitterness toward the administration. Some respondents also commented that the citizenry of the county has little appreciation for education and that this will make improving education especially difficult. One respondent remarked:

> I really can't see anything that would be easy. . . . We have people who grew up around here—some people didn't get to go to school or they quit school when they were in the third grade or fourth grade. They have done well, they've raised their kids, and they don't see any value in [formal] education. They say, "I've done good with a fifth-grade education, and my kids should be able to, too." . . . It's not that they don't love their kids; it's just that they don't see why their kids should have to have an education.

Thus it appears in the early stages of restructuring that Humphrey County schools had many obstacles to overcome to achieve the high ideals set forth by KERA. A return visit in the spring of 1991, however, revealed that some positive changes had occurred. In the fall, school board members appeared to have limited awareness of the reform law and appeared unwilling to pull together for the betterment of the students. A spring trip revealed that board members had begun to accept their new role and had improved their relationships with school personnel. In addition, one administrator expressed the view that with continued assistance from the state department of education, the district would be able to pull away from its troubled past and make real improvements in educational services. Teachers and principals also felt that KERA offers the district the first opportunity it has had in years to make real changes.

Unfortunately, there still appears to be a severe communications gap between the central office staff and school personnel. Even though both camps professed some optimism about the district's future, each continued to question the behavior and motives of the other.

Lamont County School District

> We're not a rich county; we're a rural county. Our people are not rich; we don't have much, if any, industry, and our tax base, we really couldn't raise it. We tried it a few years ago and put it on the ballot, and the voters turned down a tax increase. So our students were suffering some because we didn't have enough money to have some extra things that a lot of other schools did have. Then, when all the revenue and funding came through the legislature, they ended up actually just telling us, "If you want more money, you're going to have to raise it yourself." . . . I'm disappointed in that because if we had been able to raise the money ourselves to do all these things that we need to do, we wouldn't have needed to ask the state for more money, for more help. We wouldn't even have joined that lawsuit.
>
> A Lamont County board member

The District

The Lamont County School District is a small district located in an agricultural area in western Kentucky. There is very little industry in the county, and one is struck when driving through the countryside by the acres and acres of fertile farmland that line the highways. The primary crops appear to be corn, soybeans, and tobacco. Because of this agricultural economy, Lamont County is not a wealthy district, but it is above the state median. The assessed property value per pupil for the 1989–90 school year was just under $141,000—about the same as Newtown Independent's average. About 30 percent of the Lamont County student body is classified as economically deprived, again about the same as Newtown Independent's percentage and much lower than those of Orange County and Humphrey County. Lamont County can best be described as a working-class farming region whose citizens are getting by through farming and traveling to larger communities in other counties to work.

The five schools in Lamont County serve fewer than 2,000 students, and student achievement in the district has been relatively high. Students at the fifth-, seventh-, and tenth-grade levels scored in the top 40 percent statewide on the 1989–90 standardized test, and the district ranks in the top 40 percent statewide on attendance rate and has a lower than average dropout rate. About 65 percent of Lamont County ninth-graders end up graduating, but slightly fewer than half of the graduates attend college (Kentucky Department of Education, personal communication, 1991).

While the Lamont County School District—as in Orange County and Humphrey County—is the largest employer in the county, many Lamont County citizens are employed on their own farms and thus are not so desperate for employment as are, for example, the citizens of Humphrey County. As a result, political cronyism and nepotism do not appear to be problems in Lamont County.

Responses to KERA

Thirty-seven persons were interviewed in Lamont County for this study, and many of them were reacting to KERA with some ambivalence, primarily because of dissatisfaction with the funding formula. Because of the higher level of Lamont County's recorded property wealth, the district did not receive the windfall in state funds that went to many eastern Kentucky districts as a result of KERA. While Orange County and Humphrey County had received the full 25 percent increase in state funding, Lamont County received just above the minimum 8 percent. Most of this went to salary increases and increased transportation costs for the mandated every day kindergarten program.

Because of the perceived lack of financial benefits from KERA, the largest number of Lamont County respondents (32 percent) were judged to be ambivalent about the law. However, a nearly equal proportion were primarily positive (30 percent). The most positive reactions came from teachers, while administrators and school board members were more negative. Those teachers who expressed positive feelings toward KERA tended to focus on teacher empowerment. One teacher reported in the fall of 1990 that she had already begun to feel empowered by KERA:

> I'm beginning to feel like there are some people who will respect my opinion as an educator, as a professional, [some people] who feel . . . I can make certain decisions. . . . In fact, I went to a board meeting last night for the first time in thirty years. I could see the board working with our local [teacher] association on the guidelines for our local site-based management policy, and it really was impressive to me, because for years this is something we have wanted, and I actually got to see it come to pass.

Board members, however, were less enthused about KERA, because of both the funding formula and their own loss of authority. One board member commented:

> One of the biggest problems I see with it is that they've taken the public out of it. I don't think the public is going to have much say on what happens in education, because normally their voice is through the board members, and they've really lost that. You don't know

> where to go because you don't have any clout, and I think the public will suffer for that.

Administrators felt negative about the law primarily because of the funding formula and the fact that the district has a very small administrative staff to deal with reform implementation. Administrators reported that not only is it difficult for the few administrators to help the district prepare for implementation, but the district lacks sufficient resources (money and substitute teachers) to send classroom teachers out for training on the various aspects of KERA. This lack of resources was apparently affecting the ability of the district to inform personnel about the law. Lamont County (along with Humphrey County) had the highest proportion of respondents (35 percent) who described themselves as inadequately informed about the law.

In spite of the relatively few benefits from KERA reported by Lamont County respondents and the resulting ambivalence toward the law, the district was moving forward with implementation. The at-risk preschool was under way, and the superintendent reported that nearly all at-risk four-year-olds in the district were being served. In addition, the extended school services program had begun at all schools, and plans were under way to build a combination family resource center and preschool near one of the district's elementary schools. A teacher at one of the district schools reported that she had been hired during the summer after being interviewed by a committee of teachers at the school. Although SBDM had not yet been implemented, the school had been encouraged to experiment with this process of filling a teacher vacancy to prepare for future implementation of SBDM.

Apparently, it was most difficult for the district to implement the professional development component and to increase local taxes. The district provided only professional development offered through the state department of education, and many teachers and administrators reported dissatisfaction with the videotaped instruction that the state department had offered for the 1990–91 school year. In addition, the school board had raised the tax rate quite a bit just to reach the minimum level required under the law but had been unwilling to move very far into "Tier 1" and thus passed up an opportunity to receive a larger increase in funding.

When asked to identify the strong points of KERA, Lamont County respondents followed the general trend in identifying SBDM with the greatest frequency (65 percent). However, nearly half of the respondents also cited the feature as a weakness. (Some identified both strong and weak features of SBDM.) The majority of those who cited negative features were supportive of the concept of SBDM, but they were dissatisfied with the mandated composition of the school council, the rushed timelines for implementation, or the fact that SBDM is mandatory. A parent expressed the view that while teachers may be feeling empowered by SBDM, the implementation process is set up in a way that disempowers parents:

> I do have a problem with this: two-thirds of the faculty have to vote if they want [SBDM] or not. Where's the parent part? . . . If you have a school full of teachers who say, "Why should we fool with this now? Let's wait until the very last," and the PTA feeling is, "Let's start now and by 1996 it will be working and we'll have the bugs all worked out and we'll be doing good. . . . " To my understanding . . . the state rewards schools that are making achievements in this, and we feel if we go on and get a good start on it and work out the bugs—so I do disagree with the two-thirds of the faculty approving.

A noncertified employee (who is also a parent) reported that the newly adopted board policy on SBDM—which prohibits all school employees from serving as parent members of school councils—had made her, too, feel disempowered.

> On this site-based management deal, they decided to put all employees—which includes bus drivers, janitors, lunchroom aides, instructional aides, secretaries—with the teachers, where no employee of Lamont County [is eligible to be] a parent representative [on the school council]. If I can't be voted for as a teacher, which I can't, why can't I be voted in as a parent?

About one-third of the Lamont County respondents identified the KERA funding formula as a weakness, while very few identified it as a strength. Lamont County was one of the sixty-six litigants in the lawsuit that resulted in the passage of KERA, and many respondents remarked that the law had really not helped the district financially. They were especially dissatisfied with the local tax burden mandated by the law. Most Lamont County respondents believed that the unwillingness of the school board to set a higher tax rate is justified when one considers the agricultural economy (i.e., the farmers of the area own valuable property, but their farms produce low incomes). A school board member explained, "We still have several [full-time farmers] here, and several of them just operate on a shoestring, and you throw another couple thousand dollars a year—maybe more—taxes on them, sometimes that could be enough to break them. When people are on a tight budget and you have a bad year cropwise, that's scary."

Lamont County respondents also expressed ambivalence about various aspects of the new student assessment program mandated by KERA, and a majority of all comments about this (both positive and negative) came from principals and teachers. Those respondents who identified the program as a strong point of KERA tended to focus on performance-based assessment and the *concept* of accountability. One teacher commented, "We can walk around, even in our building, and see there are people who don't put forth all the effort they should with the student. . . . It seems to me they sit and let the students do, and maybe this will help. Maybe this will light a fire under them. They'll find out they have got to do a little something."

Those who identified the assessment program as a weak point of KERA focused on the random sampling of students or took issue with the fact that schools must take total responsibility for student learning.

General Prognosis for Successful Implementation of KERA

The Lamont County School District is characterized by an agrarian economy and philosophy, which has made and will continue to make it difficult for the district to advance economically. When asked if there was anything about the district that will make reform implementation especially easy or difficult, the largest number of respondents (about one-third) cited the agricultural economy as a major limitation. About one-fourth identified the inadequate size of the administrative staff as a limitation, and an equal number commented that the community and/or administration is traditional and resistant to change. Within individual schools, however, teachers and principals alike felt confident that they have the ability to change and benefit from KERA if they are given adequate resources, training, and support.

It is not clear whether Lamont County's lack of resources will impede the implementation of reform, but the prognosis appears better than in Humphrey County—which is plagued by political and attitudinal problems—and no worse than in Newtown Independent District, where respondents feel they have neither needed nor benefited from KERA. Lamont County administrators are pushing forward as best they can with reform implementation, and most respondents expressed a willingness to make a good-faith effort to implement the law as intended, even though they are frustrated by the lack of major financial benefits.

The fact that KERA calls for radical changes in the organizational and decision-making structure of school districts—with a strong emphasis on teacher empowerment—may, in the long run, present more of a sticking point than any of the issues that Lamont County respondents mentioned in the initial stages of restructuring. Lamont County was one of the most traditional and homogeneous of the districts studied. Leadership is male-dominated, and there appeared to be a clear gender-based division of responsibility that all role groups understood and had grown accustomed to. Thomas Timar, in his study of the implementation of a career ladder program in Utah, postulates that "in small, rural, culturally homogeneous communities that are rigidly stratified by gender roles and authority relationships . . . changes in organizational behavior that depend on disturbing those relationships are unlikely" (1989: 336).

At the time of this study, it was too early to tell if Timar's assertion would prove true in Lamont County. By the spring of 1991, however, one school had voted to implement SBDM, had elected a school council, and had begun holding meetings. In addition, the superintendent had announced his retirement, and the district had formed a committee of two teachers, a principal, a parent, and a board member (as mandated by KERA) to screen applicants for superintendent. Thus the time is at hand when the teacher and client empowerment aspects of reform implementation will be put to the test in Lamont County.

CONCLUSION

Interviews with respondents in four rural Kentucky school districts indicate that, overall, the reception of the new reform law in these districts is more positive than negative, although many people expressed ambivalence about KERA. Teachers and school counselors were among the most avid supporters of KERA, along with central office administrators other than superintendents. In addition, enthusiasm was highest both among those who felt best informed about KERA and in the one district (Orange County) where the leadership was very positive about reform and had taken the initiative to provide additional training beyond that mandated by the law.

Although most professional-level respondents said they were adequately informed about KERA, their responses as a whole indicated a need for increased information about the changes, particularly those in the curriculum section of the law. Although respondents were not asked to describe the philosophy behind any section of KERA, their general discussion of the law indicated that they understood more clearly the *intent* of the governance and finance measures (i.e., ridding the system of political influence and equalizing funding) than the *intent* of the curriculum measures. When respondents cited any aspect of the governance and finance measures as a weak point of KERA, they tended to do so based on a perception that the measures would not achieve their intent. In discussing the curriculum measures, on the other hand, they tended to focus on individual components of the section and displayed little tendency to view these measures as a cohesive whole, with all the component parts aimed at achieving a single goal.

A few respondents discussed the need to prepare for the massive changes in assessment and instructional strategies required by the new focus on student outcomes and emphasis on problem-solving and critical-thinking skills. Overall, however, it appeared that respondents were struggling to understand the law and implement the most immediate requirements, rather than planning for the major changes in professional behavior and attitudes toward student learning that KERA will require. Their preoccupation with immediate requirements of the law is consistent with the "Concerns-Based Adoption Model" (CBAM) postulated by Gene Hall and his colleagues (1975), which sets forth seven levels of use of the innovation. When CBAM is applied to respondents who participated in this study, it appears that few district-level respondents have advanced beyond the Level II, preparation, stage. Most noncertified employees appeared to be at Level 0: nonuse of the innovation, a state described by Hall, et al., as one "in which the user has little or no knowledge of the innovation" (1975: 8). During the fall of 1990, most teachers and principals were at the Level I, orientation, stage, in which they had acquired information about KERA and were seeking to learn more about it.

Return trips in the spring of 1991 revealed that some teachers and most principals had joined district administrators at the Level II, preparation, stage and were participating in activities preparatory to implementing various aspects of the law. If the concerns-based adoption model retains its applicability over the next five years, respondents can be expected to achieve greater understanding of KERA innovations as they begin to apply them.

Regarding the governance measures, most respondents who mentioned this aspect of KERA believed that the attempt to eliminate political abuse is a positive move, but were not enthusiastic about the manner in which the reform law attempts to do this. Respondents reported that the nepotism provisions fail to address the real political problem—cronyism and patronage—and expressed concerns that superintendents are frequently just as guilty of perpetrating these offenses as are school boards. In the two districts that had lost board members or school staff because of the nepotism provisions, no reports were heard that these individuals had been guilty of favoritism and most respondents expressed sorrow at losing these individuals. In addition, many respondents in the eastern Kentucky districts expressed concern that school-based councils would be subject to the same political temptations as school boards. If the same criticisms are common in other districts around the state, the 1992 legislature may come under pressure to revise the governance section of KERA.

The financial equalization aspect of KERA has apparently already brought about greater equalization in educational funding, at least on paper. Figures released by the state department of education in September 1990 revealed that most school districts in the state were grouped together at about the same funding level, with a per pupil funding range of about $3,000 to $3,500 in all but twenty-six school districts (*Courier-Journal*, September 13, 1990).

Attitudes toward KERA's method of equalization, however, were presenting problems not only in two of the districts included in this study, but in other districts around Kentucky. The Council for Better Education, Inc., the organization of school districts that initiated the lawsuit that led to KERA, released a position paper in February 1991 calling for changes in the new funding formula. The paper included demands that funding should not be left up to the "whims of local citizens" and that the legislature should fully fund the "Tier 1" program (*Courier-Journal*, February 19, 1991).

In Newtown Independent District, respondents reported that their past high taxation for education had resulted in a relatively small increase in state funding under KERA, and they viewed the reform law as penalizing the district for past efforts to fully fund education. This perception has created an ambivalence toward the law. The agricultural economy of Lamont County was also creating problems in moving forward with reform implementation, and it appears that farmland assessment may be leading to a misreading of a school district's real wealth—the district may be property-rich but income-poor.

The Orange County and Humphrey County districts, however, had received the full 25 percent increase in state funding, with only modest increases in local taxation. The finance portion of KERA appeared to be working well in these places and, by all accounts, was doing exactly what it was supposed to do (although a few respondents in both areas reported that the funding continued to be *inadequate*, even if it is more nearly equalized). It appears, then, that the KERA finance component has been greeted differentially in various parts of the state and has not yet succeeded in fully solving the funding problems that have plagued the state for years.

The reform law includes a provision requiring the newly formed Office of Education Accountability to conduct an ongoing review of the finance system, however, so a mechanism is in place for refining and improving this component of KERA.

One factor that may assist with successful education reform is the fact that school districts have been attempting to improve educational services since 1984, when reform-minded governor Martha Layne Collins instituted a number of reform initiatives consistent with "wave one" (or top down) reform efforts. (Some of these reforms, which emphasize professionalization—internship years for new teachers and principals—have not been affected by KERA.) In addition, a highly visible "wave two" restructuring effort has been underway in the state's largest school district, Jefferson County, since 1985 (Schlechty, Ingwerson & Brooks, 1988). Thus the need for reform has been well recognized, and most respondents interviewed for the study accepted the inevitability of change. Whether or not local districts will be willing or able to seize this unique opportunity to restructure education—and whether or not the legislature will be willing to enforce sanctions on those schools and districts that fail to improve—remain to be seen.

II Empowering Parents

7 The Case for Parent and Community Involvement

Donald R. Moore

Research and experience over the past twenty years have provided compelling evidence that some strategies for parent and community involvement in the educational process substantially improve the quality of students' educational experiences and their achievement in elementary and secondary schools. For example, Anne Henderson (1987: 1) summarizes a review of forty-nine research studies of the relationship between parent involvement and student achievement by concluding: "The evidence is now beyond dispute: parent involvement improves student achievement. When parents are involved, children do better in school, and they go to better schools." The task now confronting educational reformers and researchers is to refine our understanding of the characteristics of effective parent and community involvement and of the related conditions in educational systems and communities under which such involvement has the most beneficial impact. In assessing what forms of parent and community involvement are beneficial, this chapter is concerned especially with educational improvement for those students most at risk of school failure in major urban school systems (i.e., the contribution of involvement to increasing educational equity in urban schools).

With this focus, this chapter addresses the following issues:

- The varieties of parent and community involvement in schools.
- A conceptual model of the educational process that aids our understanding of the contribution that parent and community involvement can make to improving students' educational experiences and performance.
- An analysis of the characteristics of parent and community involvement that can have a beneficial impact and of related

conditions in educational systems and communities under which such involvement has the most positive impact.

- The potential for orchestrating productive forms of parent and community involvement.

As this chapter will repeatedly stress, careful analysis of the specific nature of involvement is essential, and broad generalizations about the impact of "parent involvement" are misleading. One implication of this need to be specific is that the present analysis, which is focused on urban school systems, may have less relevance for suburban and rural settings. Since the author was centrally involved in restructuring the Chicago Public Schools (Moore, 1991a; O'Connell, 1991), Chicago's restructuring experience is drawn on for examples.

VARIETIES OF PARENT AND COMMUNITY INVOLVEMENT

Parents and community residents can be involved in education in a wide range of ways. By way of introduction, some major types of involvement are described below, moving from the less controversial to the more controversial forms of involvement.

Parents and Schools Maintain Regular Contact

Fulfilling the traditional expectations that most schools have for parents, parents can attend orientation sessions and parent-teacher conferences, respond to communications from the school, appear at school when their children have problems, and the like. Establishing and maintaining this communication is a two-way street; as discussed below, however, schools vary significantly in the extent to which they systematically attempt to communicate with parents, even in these basic ways.

Parents Help Their Children at Home

Parents can aid their children's formal education at home through such activities as providing children with proper nutrition and rest, talking with them, playing learning games with them, and establishing favorable conditions and regular times for homework. Some parents, of course, carry out these activities on their own initiative without any encouragement from the school. During the past two decades, there have been increased efforts to foster such supportive parent activities among a higher percentage of parents through parent education classes and school outreach workers.

Parents and Community Residents Volunteer at School

Parents and community residents can come to school to tutor students, organize safety patrols on the playground and the routes to school, perform routine tasks to free up teachers, lead classes at their school for parents who want to learn how to help their children at home, accompany students on trips, organize special school events, and so on.

Community Agencies Provide Educational and Social Services

Community agencies can provide a range of educational and social services with potential to improve students' school performance, such as tutoring, structured after-school care, counseling, and medical care.

Parent and Community Involvement in Decision Making

In the area of decision making, a range of different types of involvement are possible. Of course, a long-standing avenue for such involvement is service on boards of education. A more recent form of involvement in policy making comes through school-site councils of the type, for example, that have been established in Chicago. Such parent and community involvement in decision making varies widely from school district to school district in terms of the issues that parents and community are permitted to address and the extent to which parents and community participate in clear decision-making roles, rather than merely giving advice. This latter type of advisory role is exemplified, for example, by parent involvement on parent advisory councils that has been part of the federal Chapter 1 program (Keesling, 1980).

Another variety of decision-making involvement focuses not on educational policy affecting schools or school districts, but rather on the individual child. The legally mandated role of parents in developing and approving individual educational plans for their handicapped children is the most widespread current example of such involvement. Of course, procedures for parent involvement in decision making about individual children can give parents clear decision-making powers (as in the case of special education), or such involvement can be advisory.

Advocacy by Parent and Community Groups

Independent parent and community groups press for educational change in many school districts across the country (Moore, et al., 1983). In major cities, such groups include, for example, Advocates for Children of New York, Philadelphia Parents Union, and Massachusetts Advocacy Center in Boston. The methods that such advocacy groups employ include preparing reports on educational problems, testifying before school boards and other public bodies, calling media attention to issues and solutions, litigation, and lobbying.

Parent Choice

Parents can participate in the education of their children by choosing the school or the educational program within a school that their child will attend. Traditionally, many parents have chosen their child's school by deciding to reside in a particular school's attendance area or by enrolling their child in a private school. Over the past twenty years, a major new avenue for parent choice has evolved, in which public school systems have given parents the right to choose among public schools, usually within their own school system (Moore & Davenport, 1990). Proposed but not yet tried in U.S. elementary and secondary schools is some form of voucher system that would allow families to choose among both public and private schools (Coons & Sugarman, 1978).

Proponents of expanded family choice argue that it will not only benefit the family that actively chooses a school, but also function as an overall spur to improved education, as schools respond to competition by improving their educational programs to retain their students (Nathan, 1989).

GETTING THE CONCEPTUAL MODEL RIGHT

Efforts to assess the potential impact of this menu of possibilities for parent and community involvement have been undermined by the simplistic models of the educational process that have frequently dominated educational research and policy making. One widely used input-output model, represented in Figure 7.1, envisions the educational process as consisting of:

- Educational inputs (for example, per pupil expenditures, teachers' verbal abilities, students' socioeconomic status).
- Students' educational experiences (particularly in the classroom).
- Educational outputs (for example, students' achievement test scores and graduation rates).

As has been recently pointed out (see, for example, Bryk, Lee & Smith, 1990), many researchers have focused largely on measuring easily quantifiable educational inputs (such as teachers' educational degrees) and outputs (such as student test scores). However, few have paid attention to analyzing the *educational experiences* that mediate between inputs and outputs, leaving them as a largely unexplored "black box." When researchers *have* analyzed the nature of students' educational experiences, many researchers have focused primarily on the classroom teaching process. They have not analyzed other key determinants of the nature of students' educational experiences pertinent to understanding potentially productive strategies for parent and community involvement, including the following:

- How students' educational experiences *outside the school* affect student performance and how these experiences in the family, peer group, and neighborhood can be altered to improve educational results. Characteristics of families and communities (as represented, for example, by parents' socioeconomic status) have often been conceptualized as input variables over which little control can be exercised by those working for educational improvement.
- How the social organization and functioning of the *total school* shape students' classroom experiences, including such schoolwide practices as tracking, labeling, discipline, and counseling.

Figure 7.1
Traditional Input-Output Model of the Educational Process

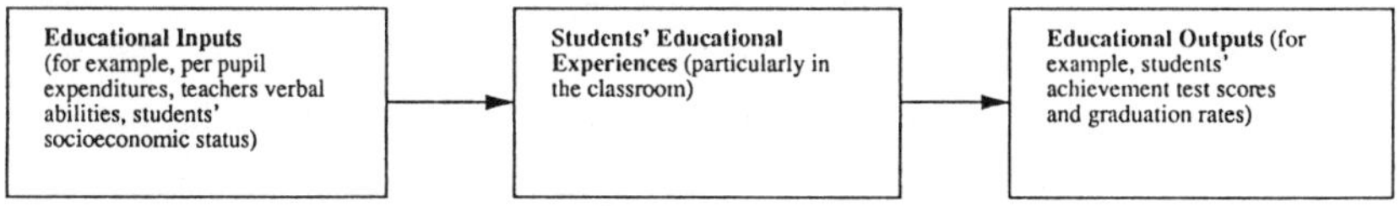

- How practices at the school level are shaped by policies, resource allocations, and practices at *higher levels of the educational system.*

In contrast, much recent educational research, including research by Designs for Change with which the author is associated, suggests more complex models of the educational process that allow us to sharpen issues pertinent to the contribution of parent and community involvement. Based on research about a range of strategies for improving big city schools (Moore & Hyde, 1979; Moore & Hyde, 1981; Moore, et al., 1983; Moore & Davenport, 1990), Designs for Change has developed a "Quality of Experience Model" that places a central focus on analyzing the most neglected box in the diagram in Figure 7.1: Students' Educational Experiences. This model, which calls attention to determinants of educational quality beyond the classroom, provides a more adequate basis for conceptualizing the potential contribution of parent and community involvement to improving the quality of schooling.

We have concluded that the most productive focus for analyzing educational improvement is a focus on analyzing the nature and quality of students' day-to-day educational experiences, not only in the classroom, but also in the school and the larger school community (including the family, peer group, and neighborhood). As one analyzes the quality of students' educational experiences, one then can ask what set of practices, policies, and resource allocations at all levels of the educational and social system are most critical in determining the quality of students' educational experiences and, through these experiences, educational results.

Note that emphasizing the importance of analyzing students' educational experiences in no way diminishes the need for the valid and reliable measurement of student outcomes. However, there has been a long history of manipulation of student outcome results in public education. An exclusive focus on outcome measurement that is not closely tied to analyzing the nature of students' educational experiences carries numerous risks:

- Exclusive focus on boosting numerical outcomes leads to cheating. Successful cheaters demoralize others who are trying to improve results through making real changes in educational quality.
- Exclusive focus on outcomes distorts educational practice, for example, by encouraging teachers to spend much of their time drilling students on narrowly focused test preparation exercises.
- When outcomes are measured without also looking at the nature of related educational experiences, it is unclear what practices

caused the improvements in outcomes and thus what can be learned from this apparent success.

Therefore, the Quality of Experience Model emphasizes the need to analyze student outcomes and students' educational experiences in close interconnection.

The Quality of Experience Model, depicted in Figure 7.2, has been described in some detail elsewhere (Moore, 1991b). Below, three elements of the model are briefly highlighted that aid the analysis of parent and community involvement.

First, the Quality of Experience Model focuses on the range of educational practices, *not only in the classroom, but also in the family, peer group, and neighborhood*, that make up the child's educational experience. The model reflects the reality that the children encounter "teachers" not only in the classroom, but also in the overall "school community" of which they are a part. While this point of view about the range of individuals who educate the child has often been acknowledged in principle, it has seldom been systematically applied in educational research as a way to understand and improve the quality of students' educational experiences.

Second, the Quality of Experience Model emphasizes that many practices, policies, and resource allocations of *the school as a social institution* shape the quality of students' classroom learning experiences. Through closely analyzing the nature of students' educational experiences in urban schools, Designs for Change has identified five major aspects of the student's educational experience that strongly affect educational outputs. These five aspects of the school as a social system have been restated as standards for judging the quality and equity of students' educational experiences in the Quality of Experience Model. As reflected in Figure 7.3, these five standards are as follows:

1. Enabling and encouraging student attendance and graduation.
2. Minimizing student sorting within and among schools.
3. Creating a decent, humane school environment.
4. Creating school environments that facilitate effective instruction.
5. Providing high quality instruction.

Figure 7.3 reflects the fact that the five areas of student experience that are the focus of these standards are interrelated and mutually reinforcing in complex ways. For example, lack of effective instruction in elementary

Figure 7.2
A Quality of Experience Model for Analyzing Chicago School Reform

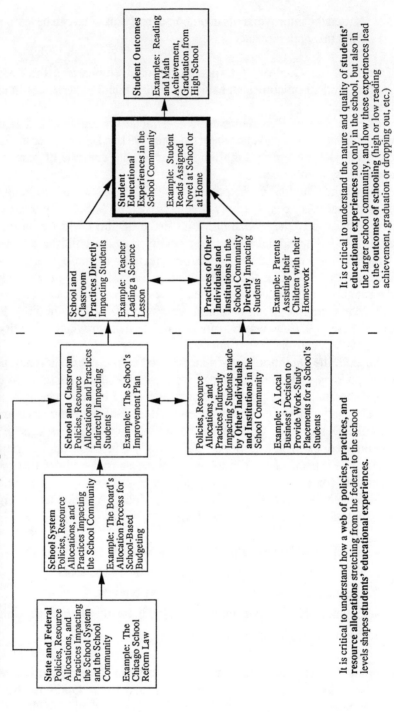

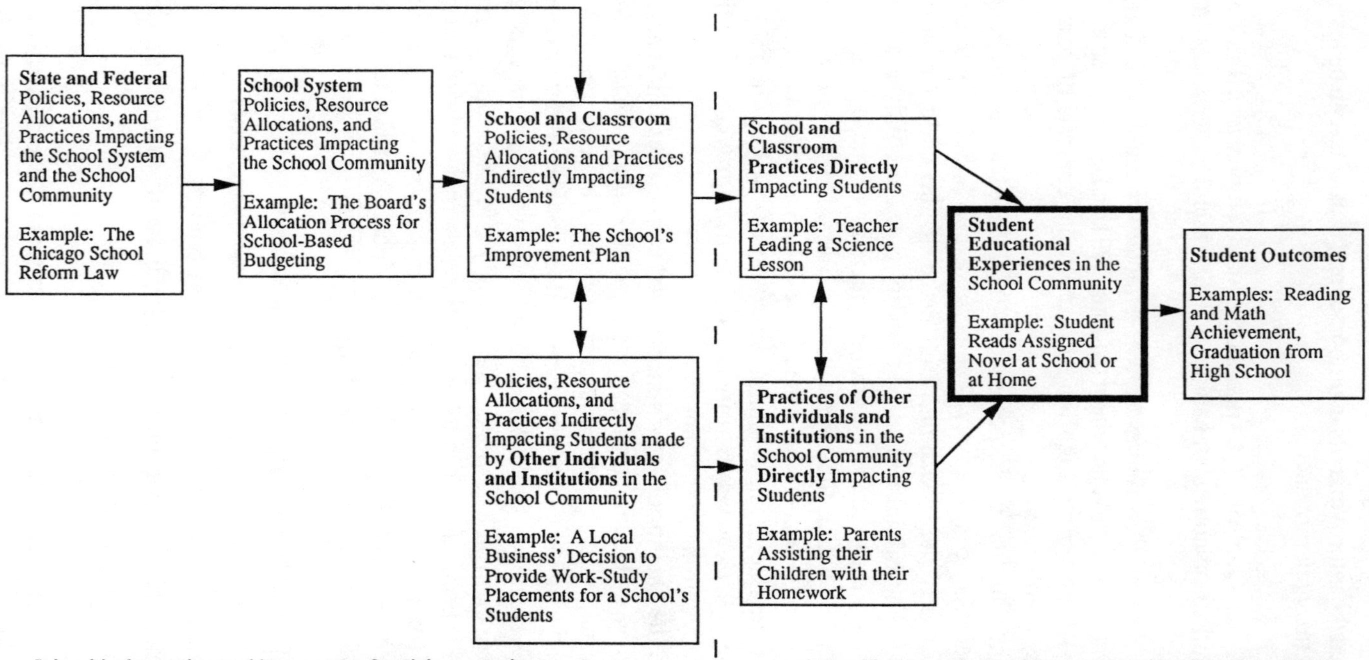

It is critical to understand how a **web of policies, practices, and resource allocations** stretching from the federal to the school levels shapes **students' educational experiences.**

It is critical to understand the nature and quality of **students' educational experiences** not only in the school, but also in the larger school community, and how these experiences lead to the **outcomes of schooling** (high or low reading achievement, graduation or dropping out, etc.)

Figure 7.3
Five Standards for Judging the Quality of Students' Educational Experiences

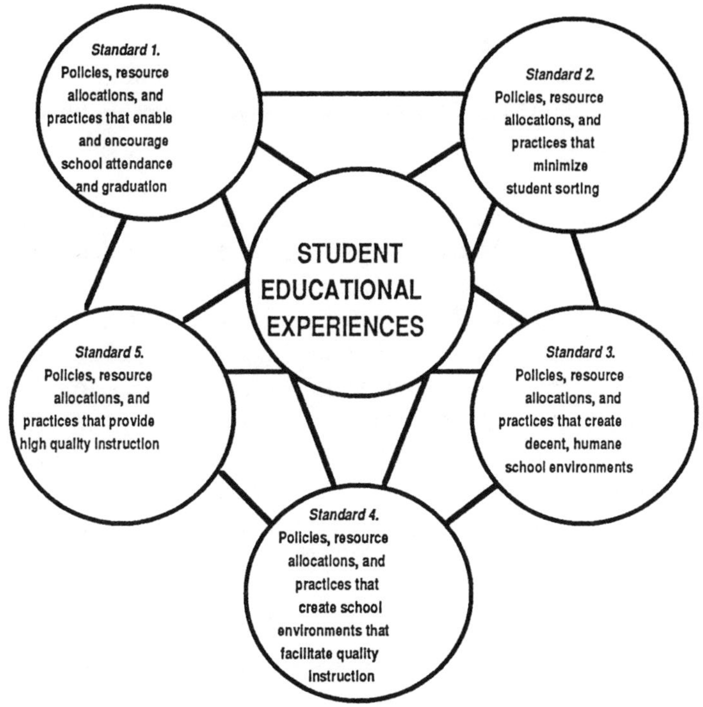

schools (Standard 5) leads to retention in grade (Standard 2), which contributes to the likelihood that students will drop out of high school (Standard 1). As presented in Figure 7.3, the five standards do, in some respects, constitute a hierarchy. For instance:

- If educational policy and practice systematically discourage students from attending school and students therefore do not attend school (Standard 1), students are unable to benefit from the quality of the instructional program (Standard 5), whatever that quality may be.
- If the school system is highly stratified into selective schools and tracks (Standard 2), this stratification spawns pervasive low expectations about the capabilities of students in the lower reaches of the system. These low expectations then make it very unlikely that these low-status students will be offered an educationally effective school experience that employs challenging educational materials and methods (Standard 5).

- If the school environment is overcrowded, shows obvious signs of physical neglect, and is characterized by physical and verbal abuse of students (Standard 3), it similarly makes an educationally effective experience unlikely. For example, teachers who believe that students can only be controlled through corporal punishment are unlikely to embrace an instructional strategy centering on student inquiry and challenging academic content.

This expanded view of the range of educational practices, policies, and resource allocations that shape student outcomes has important implications for analyzing the potential contribution of parent and community involvement. When the educational process is viewed narrowly as consisting only of classroom instruction, parent and community involvement might appear to have little relevance to improving students' educational experiences and thus their achievement. However, when researchers and policymakers begin to appreciate the range of school-level policies, resource allocations, and practices that structure students' educational experiences, the areas in which productive parent and community involvement might have a beneficial impact expand dramatically. Parent and community efforts to encourage students to attend school, to eliminate rigid tracking systems, to press for improved school upkeep, to improve school discipline can all be seen as relevant to improving student performance.

Third, the Quality of Experience Model underscores that the school is not a separate island, but that the policies, resource allocations, and practices of schools and classrooms are shaped by a web of policies, resource allocations, and practices at the school district, state, and federal levels. For example:

- Schools seldom offer bilingual education unless they are required to do so by school district, state, or federal policy and unless these higher levels of the system provide resources for bilingual programs.
- Schools are dependent on school districts and states for the resources to improve substandard physical plants, correcting such demoralizing conditions as leaky roofs, faulty heating systems, and the like.
- The nature and specificity of school district and state curriculum objectives and standards shape classroom instruction, as does the nature of student tests mandated by the school district and state.

The fact that the classroom and school are interdependent with the school district, state, and federal levels of the educational system highlights additional arenas in which parent and community involvement has the potential to affect the quality of education and educational outcomes.

Moving from simplistic input-output models of education to more complex analyses of students' educational experiences and the practices of educators, school board members, state legislators, parents, and community members who create these experiences highlights questions about (1) the ways in which various forms of parent and community involvement listed earlier might positively impact on students' educational experiences and thus on the outcomes of their educational experiences and (2) the conditions under which this involvement might have beneficial impact.

THE CHARACTERISTICS OF EFFECTIVE PARENT AND COMMUNITY INVOLVEMENT

While the recent research literature about the impacts of parent and community involvement has grown rapidly, parent and community involvement is still a relatively neglected area of research. However, the available research indicates a number of clear patterns that constitute a strong case for the virtues of parent and community involvement, both as a benefit to the child of the specific parent who becomes involved and as a benefit in improving a school's overall effectiveness.

Spokes in a Wheel

While evidence about each of the specific types of parent involvement described in the initial section of this chapter will be discussed below, one general finding of the research on parent involvement is that various forms of parent involvement tend to be mutually supportive — like spokes in a wheel (Gordon, 1978; Henderson, 1987). Researchers have found that combinations of good home-school communications, home-based parental support for student learning, and parent involvement in decision making produce the largest gains in student performance. What matters most is that the parent involvement strategy allows for varied forms of involvement, is well planned, and is carried out over an extended period of time.

Thus, those attempting to improve schools do not have to pick and choose among various types of involvement, but rather to orchestrate a number of them effectively. Having pointed out the benefits of comprehensive involvement programs, evidence about the effectiveness of specific types of parent and community involvement is described below.

Parents and Schools Maintain Regular Contact

This basic level of parent involvement is a necessary precondition for all the rest. If schools and parents are not in regular contact, parent education programs, parent involvement in decision making, and other forms of parent involvement cannot occur. Yet research about the frequency of such basic contact in one statewide survey indicates that 16 percent of parents reported they had never received a memo from their child's teacher, over 35 percent had never had a parent-teacher conference, about 60 percent had never spoken to their child's teacher on the phone, and 96 percent had never been visited at home by their child's teacher (Epstein, 1986). While some of this lack of involvement is due to an absence of parent initiative, schools serving similar student populations can differ significantly in the extent to which the schools facilitate such basic levels of home-school communication (Epstein & Becker, 1982a; Epstein, 1986).

Further, while it is often difficult to separate out the effect of this rudimentary form of parent involvement from other forms, several research studies indicate that frequent home-school communication is one aspect of a parent involvement program associated with higher levels of student achievement and more positive attitudes about school staff (Herman & Yeh, 1980; Becker, 1984; Dornbusch, 1986).

Parents Help Their Children at Home

A wide range of careful research indicates that variations in certain child-rearing practices are associated with higher levels of student achievement. Helpful family practices include, for example, communicating high academic expectations to children, holding regular conversations with children, and encouraging children to complete homework (Clark,1983; Dornbusch, et al., 1987, as cited in Henderson, 1987). In the relevant group of studies, researchers analyzed variations in parent practices that occurred independent of the school's effort to encourage such parent behaviors.

These studies indicate that parents who employ such practices can eliminate or greatly reduce the correlation between family Socioeconomic Status (SES) and student achievement (Henderson, 1987). With respect to the Quality of Experience Model, this line of research reinforces the view that the family's contribution to education should not be thought of as an immutable "input variable." Instead, families should be viewed as an additional set of teachers who can be helped to carry out practices at home that aid student achievement in school.

This is precisely the strategy that many early childhood education programs have implemented over the past two decades, and with uniformly positive results. Research about early childhood education programs that help parents to teach their children at home has documented significant improvements in school achievement and behavior (Bronfenbrenner, 1974; Barth, 1979).

Similar interventions with elementary school children have yielded positive results in reading, but not in math (Olmsted & Rubin, 1982; Epstein, 1988). Joyce Epstein, a leader in studying the impact of parent involvement, has concluded that parent education activities at home that boost academic achievement in specific subjects must be tailored to specific academic areas (math, social studies, art, etc.) if they are going to bring about significant gains (1987).

Evidence about the early childhood interventions summarized above suggests that *low-income children* can benefit significantly from parent assistance in learning at home. While teachers who do not actively encourage home-based parent involvement tend to believe that low-income parents are less capable of providing such support than middle-income parents, those who actively encourage such involvement report no differences in the cooperation that they obtain from low-income and middle-income parents (Epstein & Becker, 1982a).

Research concerning teachers' attitudes toward parent assistance at home indicates that many teachers do not make significant sustained efforts to involve parents, although they may agree in principle that parental involvement is important (Epstein & Becker, 1982a). Further, principals exert a strong influence on the extent of this form of parent involvement, with some actively encouraging it, some indifferent, and some actively discouraging it (Epstein, 1987).

Parents and Community Residents Volunteer at School

Epstein's research about the nature of parent volunteering at school shows that only a minority of parents are typically involved in such activities. Seventy percent of parents have never helped the teacher in the classroom or on trips. Eighty-eight percent have never assisted in the library, cafeteria, or other school areas. Even fewer are involved frequently; only 4 percent spent more than twenty-five days per year at the school.

However, as is the case with parents helping their children at home, teacher and principal commitment to foster volunteer involvement at school can significantly increase its frequency. For example, substantial percentages of low-income parents have become involved in preschools that hold strong expectations for such involvement (Henderson, 1987).

High levels of parent volunteer involvement as part of an overall parent involvement strategy have been associated with higher levels of overall school achievement (Henderson, 1987). Further, there is evidence that specific children whose parents are active as volunteers achieve better (Revicki, 1981), although it may be that this correlation reflects the tendency of parents whose children are already high achievers to become more involved.

Community Agencies Provide Educational and Social Services

Almost no one would dispute the general proposition that some types of educational and social services can enhance student achievement, graduation, and other desired educational outcomes when they are coordinated with the education program of the school. Indeed, a major current public policy focus in education is the coordination of the often-disjointed educational and social services that are supposed to benefit children and youth, especially at-risk children and youth. The mechanisms for achieving service coordination include better citywide or countywide coordination among service providers, making the school the major site for providing a range of services, and parent or neighborhood boards that are granted some authority to establish mechanisms for coordinating services for their children.

By employing the Quality of Experience Model, one can spell out sets of hypotheses about how the provision of such services might enhance desired educational outcomes. For example, availability of preventive health care could be expected to reduce student absenteeism, contributing to more time spent learning and thus to higher achievement.

However promising the provision of coordinated services appears to be, hypotheses about the benefits of particular approaches merit careful empirical study. In particular, some educational interventions by community agencies take the form of add-ons to the regular school program (for example, after-school tutoring). Such add-on programs are subject to all the questions that have been raised about the benefits of add-on programs offered by the schools themselves, such as pullout compensatory education programs (National Institute of Education, 1977). In many instances, such supplementary programs, which may leave a fundamentally inadequate basic school program undisturbed, provide little or no benefit for students and thus should be the focus of careful analysis before one assumes that they are promoting better student performance.

A final point to be made about the involvement of community agencies with schools is that schools in similar neighborhoods and in the same school system often vary significantly in the extent to which the school has developed strong working relationships with such agencies. The leadership of the school's principal is typically pivotal in determining whether the school has built a network of ties with community agencies or operates in relative isolation.

Parent and Community Involvement in Decision Making

While the forms of parent and community involvement discussed above typically meet with wide acceptance in principle (although they are frequently not carried out in practice), parent and community involvement in decision making is far more controversial. The present discussion of this form of involvement focuses particularly on a relatively recent involvement strategy that tends to invoke the strongest reactions, that is, involvement in policy making *at the school level* in which parents and community members are given *real decision-making authority* and not merely permitted to give advice that can then be ignored by school authorities. As noted earlier, Chicago's school-site councils are an example of this strategy for major parent and community involvement in school decision making.

Although parent and community involvement in decision making has not been studied frequently in the past, some previous research about decision-making involvement has concluded that such involvement does not have a positive impact on student achievement, while other studies have indicated that it does (Henderson, 1987). Further examination of this research indicates that in several of the situations studied in which parents were counted as having a decision-making role, their role was in fact advisory. Yet there is abundant evidence from studies of federal Chapter 1 advisory councils and other parent involvement programs that when parents are given such advisory roles, their advice is typically ignored (Gittell, et al., 1979; Keesling, 1980). Thus, it is critical to identify the specific nature of involvement in decision making in the specific situation being studied and to limit conclusions about effectiveness to this particular form of involvement.

The restructuring of the Chicago Public Schools represents the first large-scale urban reform effort in which school-site councils with a majority of parent and community members have been given clear decision-making authority concerning issues that fundamentally shape the school's educational program. This restructuring was accomplished through rewriting the special section of state law that governs the operations of the Chicago Public Schools. It will be several years before evidence from the Chicago experience will begin to indicate whether the Chicago strategy is improving the quality of students' educational experiences and the performance of Chicago's students (see Hess & Easton in this volume). However, the Chicago reform strategy is based on a careful analysis of past research and experience that suggest the necessary features of an effective plan for school improvement through strong parental and community involvement in decision making, and these features have general relevance for other urban settings.

Critical Conditions for Effective Decision-Making Involvement

Key hypotheses on which the Chicago reform plan is based, which are spelled out below, specify conditions that must be present if parent and community involvement is to significantly improve student performance.

First, *the school must be the key unit* over which the decision-making councils have control. The much-discussed New York City decentralization program broke the school system into community school districts with an average of 20,000 students, which were still larger than 98 percent of the school districts in the United States (Moore, 1991b). Few parents had the resources to run for office in districts of this size, and these community school board elections have typically been dominated by established political interest groups (Manhattan Borough President's Task Force on Education and Decentralization, 1987). In contrast, the Chicago plan creates a separate governing council at each school. More parents and community residents find it possible to run in an election carried out in a much smaller district (over 15,000 parent and community candidates ran in the 1989 school-site council election, and candidate turnout was consistent across schools with varying racial and economic compositions

[Designs for Change, 1989]). And parent candidates are motivated by the fact that their potential authority is over the individual school that their child attends.

Second, school-site councils must include *all key stakeholders* in the school, with *parents in the majority*. In Chicago, the school-site councils are composed of six parents, two community residents, two teachers, and the school's principal. This composition was selected based on evidence about school-site councils where parents and community either are in a minority or have numerical parity with educators (e.g., Berman & Gjelten, 1983). Because school staff are more assertive and more familiar with educational issues, parents and community must have a numerical majority of council seats to hold a rough equivalence of power with school staff in actual fact. While some predicted that such a scheme would heighten conflicts between parents and educators, 65 percent of teachers on Chicago's school-site councils report that staff-parent relationships have improved since these councils were elected (Richard Day Associates, 1990).

Third, school-site councils must have *significant decision-making authority* in areas critical for school improvement, including staffing, priorities, and budget. Further, the council's focus must be on *setting policy* and not on running the school day-to-day. Under the Chicago plan, school-site councils have the authority to select their principal for a four-year performance contract, to help develop and approve a school improvement plan, and to help develop and approve a school budget tied to the priorities of the improvement plan. Control over budget is meaningless unless the school-site council has some significant discretionary funds available; in Chicago these discretionary funds averaged $250,000 per school in the 1990–91 school year. However, while Chicago councils set key policies, the law gives the principal the authority to manage the school day-to-day and, for example, gives the principal the right to select educational staff for open positions without regard to seniority.

Fourth, incentives must be put in place that *focus the council's priorities on improving the quality of students' educational experiences and their performance*. In the case of Chicago, the reform law spells out targets for improving graduation rates, achievement, and successful transition to college and further education. The school improvement plan, the principal's performance contract, and the school's budget must be focused on improving educational practice to achieve these improved results.

Fifth, school-site councils and school staff must have *ongoing training and assistance* to help them carry out their responsibilities and to improve their schools. Merely shifting the balance of authority to give parents and community more of a decision-making voice can, by itself, bring some benefits, as will be discussed below. However, significant widespread improvement in student performance requires long-term help. Elsewhere, Designs for Change has described the features of a decentralized support system for school improvement through which this help can be effectively provided (Moore, 1991a).

Sixth, to allow the school-site council to exercise its decision-making authority, the *authority of the central administration and board of education must be decreased* and these entities must be restructured in light of their changed responsibilities. Without such a restructuring of the role of central authority, the initiative of school-site councils will typically be thwarted. For Chicago, the reform law formally alters the authority of the central board and administration, making them responsible for supplying specific services that can be provided more efficiently through centralized action (such as transportation and school construction) and for ensuring that schools operate within basic ground rules in such areas as nondiscrimination. However, the law takes from the central administration the responsibility for the day-to-day operation of the schools, which now lies with the school-site councils and the principals. Further, the Chicago law has reduced the size of the central administration by limiting the amount of the total school system budget that can be spent on central administration.

Benefits of a Potent Decision-Making Role

Why should one believe that a strategy for parent and community involvement through school-site decision making that incorporates these features will significantly improve the quality of students' educational experiences and their performance? Many have argued that educational reform should move in exactly the opposite direction, giving more authority and discretion to "professionals" and further insulating educators from "political" influence (Carnegie Forum on Education and the Economy, 1986). Again, the Chicago experience is just beginning, but there are substantial reasons for believing that increased parent and community involvement within the framework outlined above will improve educational results.

School-site management schemes dominated by educators have, to this point, typically brought about very limited changes in educational practices (Malen, Ogawa & Kranz, 1991). Based on our own analysis of the reform process in large school systems (Moore, et al., 1983), educators are typically too constrained by existing organizational routines, frames of reference, and political bargains to initiate basic changes in school policies, resource allocations, and practices on their own initiative.

The view that only "professionals" can contribute to solving educational problems flows from a misunderstanding of the problem-solving process that is needed to improve urban schools. One must carefully analyze the nature of each step in the problem-solving process that occurs in schools and other institutions through which:

- A problem is publicly identified and placed on the agenda for attention by the school.
- The specifics of the problem are defined.
- Steps for solving the problem are defined.
- Steps for solving the problem are implemented.

These problem-solving steps are not neutral and technical. For example, whether a problem is ever placed on a school's public agenda, as well as the way in which a particular problem is defined by the school, is shaped by existing organizational routines, frames of reference, and political bargains.

If one assesses the functioning of urban schools in light of the five standards for judging the quality of students' educational experience discussed earlier, one identifies a long list of deficiencies that are repeatedly observed in urban schools but are never publicly defined as problems in particular schools or are never made the subject of concerted corrective action. In Chicago's neighborhood high schools, for example, these can include such problems as disorganization during the critical first month of school, failure to follow up with absent students, misclassification of students into special education, suspension of students for being absent, neglected building repairs, shortages of supplies, failure of the principal to supervise staff, and persistent teacher turnover.

Principals and teachers typically avoid naming and acting on such problems, for example, when:

- These problems run counter to professional norms that make teachers reluctant to evaluate each other's performance (Weiss, 1990).
- An established practice that is harmful to students is viewed as helpful to teachers.
- The solution to a problem, such as getting neglected repairs completed, would require aggressive initiative by educators, whose

prevailing frame of reference is to "make do" (Lieberman & Miller, 1978).

A related aspect of the urban school problems highlighted by the Quality of Experience Model is that the nature of the problem or the nature of its solution is often fairly straightforward. It does not take an advanced degree in education to recognize, for example, that a school cannot follow up on absent students if it doesn't have an accurate attendance-taking system, that outsiders roaming the halls without challenge pose a threat to student safety, that late buses rob children of learning time, and that leaky roofs and long delays in the arrival of textbooks make it difficult to teach.

Even issues that relate to instructional quality are often not difficult for noneducators to understand, given some training. For example, Designs for Change parent training activities indicate that parents can readily accept, understand, and act on the proposition that children learn to read better if they do substantial self-selected reading of good literature. The changes needed to encourage such independent reading at school and at home are reasonably straightforward, and a parent member of a school-site council can both suggest that the school encourage independent reading and analyze what would be needed to encourage independent reading both at school and at home. Chicago parents, for example, can and have pointed out that the common practice in low-income schools of prohibiting children from taking their books home is an obvious barrier to independent student reading.

When one analyzes the problem-solving process in this manner, it becomes apparent what kinds of resources a strong parent and community voice in decision making and problem solving can bring to an urban school. Because parents typically speak from the perspective of students' needs, because they are not bound up in the school's existing frames of reference and organizational routines, and because they are not a part of past political bargains internal to the school system, these "outsiders" can, as we have repeatedly observed in the first few years of Chicago school reform:

- Place new problems on the school's agenda that were not previously acknowledged (for example, persistent teacher absence and the lack of sufficient substitute teachers; students' fears of physical attack in bathrooms, on playgrounds, and on the way to and from school).

- Suggest and act on new ways of solving problems (for example, locating space that can be rented in the neighborhood to reduce overcrowding).
- Draw on their own political and organizational networks to get the problems solved (for example, making a major public issue of late bus arrivals through appeals to the media and to elected officials; getting their employer to donate management consulting help to the Local School Council).
- Bring to bear supportive parent and community resources that were not previously available (for example, recruiting community agencies to counsel students and families; organizing parent safety patrols).

While the reform process in Chicago is only beginning and it is premature to evaluate the Chicago strategy's impact on student performance, we can point to hundreds of individual examples in which tangible improvements in the five areas identified in the Quality of Experience Model have already occurred in particular schools (see, for example, Illinois Bell, 1990; Richard Day Associates, 1990).

One critical change that substantial involvement in decision making can facilitate is to increase the likelihood that other beneficial forms of parent and community involvement are implemented. In the earlier analysis of the benefits of home-school communication, home-based parent involvement in helping children to learn, parent and community volunteerism at school, and the involvement of community agencies in aiding the school, we consistently noted that the priority given to these initiatives by principals and teachers is decisive in determining the extent to which they are implemented. In schools where parents and community members have a major voice in decision making and where school-site councils are educated concerning the practical ways in which they can act to increase parent and community involvement through these other avenues, it is much more likely that the school will implement the kind of multipronged long-term effort to involve parents and the community that has been shown through past research to improve the quality of education and its results.

Advocacy by Parent and Community Groups

Independent advocacy by parent and community groups employs such methods as preparing reports on educational problems, testifying before school boards and other public bodies, calling media attention to issues and solutions, litigation, and lobbying. Like involvement in decision making, advocacy often focuses on changing basic power relations and raising sensitive issues, and thus it has been highly controversial.

At the request of the Carnegie Corporation of New York (Moore, et al., 1983), Designs for Change conducted one of the few systematic studies of the methods of education advocates and of the impact of such advocacy efforts on the quality of education. Based on an analysis of fifty-two state and local advocacy projects aimed at improving the quality of education for children at risk, Designs for Change identified twenty-two of them that brought about significant or highly significant improvements in the quality of education for children at risk. Further, this analysis indicated that the methods employed in effective advocacy projects differed from those employed in ineffective projects. This analysis yielded twenty-one methods that characterized effective advocacy projects, such as the following:

- The group develops an increasingly precise understanding of what specific changes in children's school experiences would address the problem they are concerned about and then presses for these changes.
- The group brings about or capitalizes on a major policy change supportive of the improvements in children's educational experiences that they are pursuing.
- The group vigorously monitors the implementation of promised changes in practice to make sure that improvements actually take place in children's day-to-day school experiences.
- The group develops an accurate "map" of the educational system, including its formal and informal aspects.
- The group builds a well-organized, committed constituency that is capable of mobilizing substantial political power.
- The group intervenes at multiple levels of the educational system in pursuing its objectives in the project.
- The group uses multiple intervention tactics (e.g., face-to-face negotiations, filing complaints with government agencies, commenting on regulations) in pursuing project objectives.

One way of describing effective advocacy is that good advocates focus on the concepts highlighted by the Quality of Experience Model, that is, that improvements in the educational experiences of children are vital in improving the results of education and that interventions to change policies, resource allocations, and practices at multiple levels of the educational and social system are vital to improving children's educational experiences.

As is the case with other forms of parent and community involvement, then, one cannot make the unqualified statement that parent and community advocacy is consistently ineffective or effective. For example, advocacy groups are quite capable of pushing for changes that are irrelevant to or harmful to improving the quality of students' educational experiences. However, as is the case with other forms of parent and community involvement, one can identify a set of features of effective advocacy that can form the basis for expanding its productive use in improving educational quality.

The campaign to pass the Chicago reform law and the ongoing campaign for its appropriate implementation provide multiple examples of effective advocacy initiatives (O'Connell, 1991). Without sophisticated parent and community advocacy, there would never have been a Chicago reform law in the first place. Without advocacy, the implementation of the reform law would have been blunted at a number of points after the law was passed. For example, in the 1990–91 school year, advocacy initiatives kept the superintendent of schools from reinflating the size of the central administration, taking $80 million in discretionary funds from the schools for use by the central board of education, and weakening the authority of the school-site councils.

Parent Choice

A final avenue for increasing parent involvement is to allow parents to choose the school or educational program within a school that their child will attend. As noted earlier, proponents of expanded family choice argue that it will not only benefit the family that actively chooses a school, but also will function as an overall spur to improved education, as schools respond to competition by improving their educational programs.

Public opinion polls show substantial support for the proposition that families should have the right to choose their child's school, and family choice among both public and private schools is being strongly advocated by President George Bush (*New York Times*, 1991). Further, substantial choice is already a reality. For example, in Chicago, more than 50 percent of African-American high school students do not attend their neighborhood high school (Hess, 1990a).

At least two questions need systematic analysis concerning the usefulness of the parental choice strategy, particularly in urban school systems:

- Does choice increase the quality of students' educational experiences and performance?
- Are students at risk being given an equitable chance to participate in the school choice process, and is choice resulting in improved performance for these students?

To this point, there is no consistent evidence that choice, in and of itself, leads to consistently better student outcomes in U.S. elementary and secondary schools. Since choice programs are often formally or informally selective in their entrance requirements, those who have studied the choice process have not successfully separated the benefits of participating in choice programs from the initial achievement levels of the participating students (see, for example, a review of research about magnet school achievement by Blank, 1990). Further, reforms that entail choice often involve a complex combination of school improvement and staff development, so it is not clear whether observed changes can be attributed to the choice component of the change strategy (Fliegel, 1990; see also Harrington & Cookson in this volume). The most highly publicized urban choice program (the East Harlem program) has never been systematically evaluated, and data about gains in student achievement in East Harlem over time indicate that achievement scores in East Harlem improved no more than the achievement scores of the New York City schools as a whole (Moore & Davenport, 1989).

Further, existing evidence about school choice raises major concerns about whether those students most at risk of school failure can gain access to desirable educational options. A study of high school choice in Chicago, New York, Boston, and Philadelphia indicated that students at risk were largely being excluded from high status schools of choice and that school choice in these cities was creating a multitiered educational system in which the schools attended by the students most at risk of failure were characterized by high dropout rates and extremely low achievement levels (Moore & Davenport, 1989).

However, it is also true that some of the country's best urban public schools that accept a broad spectrum of students, such as Central Park East in New York City, have grown up, in part, because of educational choice. And it is possible to identify a set of procedural safeguards that might potentially address the equity concerns that are raised by current choice systems, although it may not be politically feasible to put them in place (Moore & Davenport, 1989).

Considering both the promises and pitfalls of school choice, particularly in urban settings, choice can best be seen as a secondary strategy for educational improvement that can be effective in combination with other strategies. For example, the Chicago school reform plan places primary emphasis on improving every school in the system through the new accountability structure described above. Then, after schools have had the opportunity to improve for several years, increased family choice, with safeguards for equitable admissions practices, will be implemented as a further spur toward improvement.

ORCHESTRATING EFFECTIVE PARENT AND COMMUNITY INVOLVEMENT

Certain themes recur in analyzing the existing evidence about the effectiveness of parent and community involvement.

First, a number of types of parent and community involvement have proven to be effective in improving the quality of students' educational experiences and student outcomes. However, it is essential for researchers and reformers to delve behind the catchphrases that identify particular types of involvement and ferret out the specific practices for carrying out this general approach that are effective and the particular conditions under which this approach is effective.

Second, the most effective overall approach to implementing parent and community involvement is to carry out a long-term comprehensive strategy that employs a number of different types of involvement, rather than to pick and choose among them. As we learn more about the characteristics of particular types of involvement and the circumstances under which each is effective, we can become increasingly sophisticated in determining how best to orchestrate specific types of involvement into an overall strategy.

Third, prevailing conceptual models of the educational process hamper the ability of researchers and reformers to think productively about the role of parent and community involvement in improving educational quality. The Quality of Experience Model described briefly in this chapter and elaborated elsewhere provides the basis for a more productive approach for thinking about the potential and problems of increased parent and community involvement.

8 Who's Making What Decisions: Monitoring Authority Shifts in Chicago School Reform

G. Alfred Hess, Jr. and John Q. Easton

In December 1988, Chicago embarked upon a grand experiment to improve the quality of its public schools when Governor James R. Thompson signed the Chicago School Reform Act (P.A. 85-1418).[1] The legislation contained three major elements: a list of goals that emphasize that Chicago students should be achieving at the national norms within five years, a limitation on noninstructional costs and a reallocation of funds toward the local school level, and the institution of school-based management through the establishment of parent-dominated Local School Councils at every school. The act explicitly states that it is the General Assembly's intent

> to make the individual local school the essential unit for educational governance and improvement and to establish a process for placing the primary responsibility for school governance and improvement in furtherance of such goals in the hands of parents, community residents, teachers, and the school principal at the school level. (P.A. 84-1418, Sec. 34-1.01.B)

To foster that intent, the General Assembly devolved to the school level a number of powers previously exercised solely at the central administration or board level. The Local School Councils (LSCs) were given three major powers: to adopt a school improvement plan, to adopt a school budget, and to select (and terminate) the principal to serve

The authors would like to acknowledge the contributions of their colleagues to the research that is summarized here: Hilary Addington, Darryl J. Ford, Cheryl Johnson, Jesse Qualls, Susan Ryan, and Sandra L. Storey.

under a four-year performance contract. In addition, principals were given the right to select all new educational staff who were to be employed in their schools without concern for seniority. The procedure for terminating unsatisfactory staff was eased. A number of other related decisions were also shifted to the school level. A Professional Personnel Advisory Committee (PPAC) of teachers was mandated to advise the principal and the LSC.

However, a number of powers were explicitly reserved for centralized decision making, decisions that in other school-based management systems, such as in Great Britain (cf. Hess, 1991a), were also delegated to the school level. Many of these reserved decisions have direct impact upon decisions that might be made at the school level. Among the reserved decisions are the responsibility to negotiate and sign contracts with employee unions, to adopt a systemwide budget, to adopt a systemwide school reform plan, to determine enrollment patterns across the system, and to assure the continued implementation of desegregation programs operating under a consent decree with the federal government. In addition to all applicable local, state, and federal laws and regulations, LSCs are required to act within the constraints of contracts signed by the central board and within the policies established on the basis of these various reserved powers. Thus it is clear that local schools are not entirely free to do as they please in deciding how to manage their educational programs and facilities.

In this chapter, we will attempt to describe the shifts in authority that occurred under the initial implementation of the Chicago School Reform Act and will point to areas in which the locus of authority was still in dispute. In addition, we will describe some decisions for which authority is not contested, but the impacts of which are seen by LSC members to be unfair and inappropriate.[2]

MONITORING AND RESEARCHING THE EFFECTS OF SCHOOL REFORM IN CHICAGO

In early 1989 the Chicago Panel on Public School Policy and Finance designed a five-year project to monitor the implementation of the Chicago School Reform Act and to do research on its impact on the public education available to the city's students. Some of the subprojects entail huge systemwide statistical analyses while others augment those more comprehensive approaches with more intensive, site-level qualitative studies of a limited number of schools.

AUTHORITY SHIFTS UNDER CHICAGO SCHOOL REFORM

Under the Chicago School Reform Act, Local School Councils were to become the primary site of school governance in Chicago. There has been considerable disagreement in the city, however, about what that entails. In addition, there are some, both within the school system and outside it, who believe this central aspect of the Chicago School Reform Act is a fundamental error that should be undermined, if not reversed. Thus the first year of school reform could be described as a set of informal negotiations about how much authority LSCs now have and how much authority the central board and administration retain. These negotiations have not been conducted in comfortable conference rooms with representatives of the contestants gathered around tables. These negotiations have taken place in decisions of councils and of the board, in memos from the superintendent, and in court decisions. Several of these major decisions need to be examined before proceeding to an analysis of how authority was exercised at the local school level.

One central element of the reform act required the board of education to reallocate its resources in two ways. First, a cap was placed on administrative spending. An interim board was installed to initiate reform. Its first act was to rewrite the superintendent's proposed budget to eliminate 550 central office staff positions and shift $40 million to local school budgets. This shift funded the first-year effort in the other reallocation requirement, that funding to schools with high numbers of low-income students be progressively increased and that the use of those compensatory funds become, over five years, completely discretionary at the local school level (for a fuller description of this funding shift, see Hess & Addington, 1991). As a result of these requirements, the average elementary school received $90,000 in new discretionary resources in the first year of school reform, and that figure was projected to increase to $450,000 in the fifth year. However, the interim board also entered into contracts with its employee unions, totaling 26 percent increases over four years, for which new resources were not available. This forced the board to cut the base level of funding for all schools, undermining much of the new discretionary budget power of the LSCs.

Two other sets of related decisions impinged upon LSCs as they were first getting started. The very first decision LSCs faced, before they even elected officers, was where to meet. While this decision seems to have an obvious answer, in fact this was not the case. The law requires LSCs to meet in a public place where their meetings can be observed by the public.

However, custodians refused to open school buildings at night without overtime pay, and the board refused to fund that cost. Thus LSCs were required to scramble just to find places to meet. After several months, a compromise with the engineers' union allowed LSCs to use schools two nights per month.

Similarly, within weeks of their election, LSCs were informed that they had to adopt spending plans for the current year's compensatory (State Chapter I) funds by December 1. This meant that, just as they were getting organized and before the members had had a chance to get to know one another, LSCs had to devote several meetings to deciding upon the best use of fairly sizable amounts of money. This was a considerable disruption in the intended pattern of reform in the first year, that LSCs would spend their initial months getting training and then doing an assessment of the needs of their school prior to exercising their three major responsibilities: adopting an improvement plan, adopting a budget, and selecting a principal. Instead, they were forced to make important budget decisions prior to receiving training and prior to conducting a needs assessment.

Two important decisions were made in court. On November 30, 1990, the Illinois Supreme Court announced its decision on a suit brought by the Chicago Principals Association. The suit had claimed that LSCs should not have the power to terminate any principals, because to do so would be to violate their rights of tenure, which had been extended under previous legislation and rules and regulations of the Chicago Board of Education. In addition, the suit charged, LSCs were not properly elected under the requirements of the federal constitution's one person, one vote requirements; therefore, LSCs could not constitutionally act to strip principals of their employment or take any other significant action. This suit challenged one of the primary authority shifts mandated by the Chicago School Reform Act.

The Supreme Court rejected the principals' claims about their tenure rights but agreed with them that LSCs were unconstitutionally elected. Since the LSCs were the core of the reform legislation, the Court declared the whole act unconstitutional. Thus the right of LSCs to terminate principals was upheld, if their own status could be corrected. On January 8, 1991, the Illinois General Assembly reenacted the Chicago School Reform Act (P.A. 86-1477) but excluded an election procedure for the October 1991 elections. A new election procedure was adopted during July of 1991. Thus school reform in Chicago proceeded, after a brief diversion, as originally intended.

LSC OPERATIONS DURING THE FIRST YEAR OF SCHOOL REFORM

LSCs are to be the essential unit of school governance and improvement under the Chicago School Reform Act. They are given broad powers to adopt a school improvement plan, to adopt a budget, and to select the school's principal. They are also charged to advise the principal and staff on curriculum, textbook selection, discipline, and attendance. We found that at various schools these powers were exercised in different ways. In some schools, LSCs formally acted to make decisions that were not strictly within their purview under the law. In other schools, LSC decisions were hard to discern and frequently were little more than agreements with reports from the principal. In this section, we will analyze the shift in authority as our staff observed it in LSCs across the city.

During the first year of school reform, we set out to enlist a representative group of schools whose councils would allow themselves to be studied throughout the school reform effort. We wanted to be able to describe the dynamic of reform implementation at the local school level as well as to analyze changes in quantifiable measures of school resources and performance. We were able to secure the cooperation of twelve such schools during 1989–90 and have added two more during the second year (cf. Easton, et al., 1990).

Staff from the Chicago Panel observed council meetings for the second half of the school year in these fourteen schools—ten elementary and four high schools. Two of these schools did not formally agree to participate in the observational study until the second year, and they are not included in much of the ensuing analysis. These fourteen schools are representative of the school system as a whole in terms of racial characteristics, size, and geographic location, but we do not claim that our observations can be automatically generalized to the system as a whole. We do hope that our data will illustrate the distinctive ways that different LSCs operated. We also hoped that the report on which much of this section is based (Easton & Storey, 1990) would help council members evaluate the effectiveness of their own councils through a stimulated process of self-analysis.

We examined *who* attended LSC meetings and who participated in the discussions of issues. We examined *what* issues were discussed and with what frequency. We looked at the school improvement plans that were adopted to examine the extent of authority LSCs were appropriating for themselves. And we examined *how* participants in this process, particularly principals, saw their roles changing under school reform.

Who Attended LSC Meetings?

As school reform was being debated in Chicago, there was some concern expressed that LSCs would not be able to function at many schools, particularly those in areas with many low-income families. There have been some reports of LSCs that have not been able to maintain a quorum at their meetings. None of the LSCs in our sample had this problem, though several did deal with the issue of nonattending members. In the elementary schools, the average attendance rate for LSC members was 70 percent. This translates into an average attendance of eight of the eleven members.[3] In the high schools, attendance was somewhat higher at 78 percent, or eight or nine members per council. High schools also had nonvoting student members elected by the student body. These students only attended about half the high school LSC meetings.

Attendance varied greatly from council to council, ranging from a high of 9.6 in average attendance to a low of 6.8 (6 members present represented a quorum for most matters). Nine of the twelve LSCs had a core of at least half of the members who could be counted upon to be present at most meetings. Thus, at these schools, there was a continuity of discussion from meeting to meeting. Attendance also varied from member to member and among types of members. Principals attended nearly all meetings (97.3 percent—two of the twelve principals each missed one meeting). The chairpersons, who were all parents, and the teacher members attended 88 percent of the time. Community members (67.1 percent) and other parents (61.7 percent) averaged attending more than three out of five meetings.

Several LSCs were concerned about the lack of attendance of some of their members. About 10 percent of parents who were not chairpersons and 21 percent of community members attended less than a quarter of all LSC meetings (most LSCs conducted regular monthly meetings, with several additional special meetings). One LSC discussed the nonattendance of two of their members at nearly every meeting. Finally, after repeated failed efforts to reach these members, the LSC voted to ask the principal to write to these members to request their resignation. They also voted in support of an effort to amend the reform act to allow LSCs to remove nonattending members. One other LSC also wrote requesting the resignation of a nonattending member.[4]

Members exercised their authority in different ways. Acting together, LSCs adopted school improvement plans, adopted budgets, and selected principals. Across the system, all but eighty-one schools had adopted school improvement plans by the end of June 1990 and all but forty had submitted budgets for 1990–91, according to the superintendent of schools

(*Chicago Tribune*, August 15, 1990). By mid-February of 1991, 324 principals who were serving schools when the reform act was signed into law had been selected by their LSCs to continue in that role. That means some 203 schools (38.5 percent) were being served by principals who had come to their schools since reform was enacted. Only one of the schools in our sample selected a new principal. Systemwide, this was a significant change in the persons exercising newly expanded authority at the local school level.

Different members had different degrees of influence on decisions made by the LSCs, and different members participated more frequently on some topics than on others. As might be expected, principals participated more frequently than any other LSC members. Together, they addressed nearly two-thirds (66.3 percent) of all items discussed at LSC meetings during their first year. (See Table 8.1.) The chairpersons participated next most frequently (43.4 percent). Teachers participated 31.6 percent of the time, community members at 27.5 percent, and other parents spoke least frequently, to only 17.0 percent of discussed topics.

Not only did different members participate in discussions at different rates, they participated on some topics more than on others, as might be expected. Principals spoke more frequently (more than 74 percent of the times these items were discussed) about the school program, building and safety matters, and issues of finance and budgeting. They infrequently spoke on parent and community involvement and participated less often on the range of other topics that we did not classify. Participating at a generally lower level, LSC chairs spoke to about half the discussions of LSC organization and procedures, building and safety, and personnel. Other parents rarely spoke to any of the issues, though, on average, at least one other parent spoke each time school programs, building and safety, and personnel were discussed. Teachers and community members spread their participation fairly evenly across all subjects.

Our analysis of these participation rates, when combined with our firsthand observation, led us to the conclusion that principals frequently played the role of *information provider* to the LSC. Frequently, the items principals participated in started as items in the regular principal's report, an agenda item for virtually all regular LSC meetings. The chairpersons, who participated more evenly on the range of topics discussed, more frequently played the role of *facilitator*, helping the LSC to understand an issue or come to a decision. It is worth noting that the chairperson participated least frequently in school program issues, the arena in which the principal participated most frequently. Other parents and teachers participated most often on personnel and building and safety issues.

Table 8.1
Percent Participation in Topics Discussed

Topic category	Principal	Chair	Other Parents	Teachers	Community Members
School Program	82.0	33.8	18.8	28.9	25.2
LSC Organization & Procedures	58.3	51.2	14.6	33.6	28.3
Building & Safety	74.2	51.6	20.3	34.7	34.4
Finance & Budget	76.5	37.3	13.8	31.0	27.5
Personnel	52.1	50.0	21.4	38.9	26.0
Parent & Community	25.0	40.0	14.0	22.5	20.5
Other	40.9	36.4	10.9	15.9	27.3
ALL TOPICS	66.3	43.4	17.0	31.6	27.5

Interestingly, teachers made fewer comments on school program items than did these parents. Community members were most likely to be heard on building and safety issues and on LSC organizational matters and less frequently on school programs.

How Principals View Their Roles

In addition to noting who participated on what items during LSC meetings, we wanted to analyze how principals saw changes in their own roles. The Chicago School Reform Act was built upon the conviction that an effective school would be led by an effective principal (Edmonds, 1979; Brookover & Lezotte, 1979; Purkey & Smith, 1983). Still, it is obvious from the filing of the suit by the Chicago Principals Association that not all principals approached school reform enthusiastically. In fact, only six of the eleven retained principals in our original school sample identified changes in their role that they characterized as positive.[5]

Two principals cited the increased discretion/flexibility that they have as a result of school reform. One principal noted that she could get things done more quickly because she did not need approval from various layers of the bureaucracy. She also noted she could acquire better teachers for the school by conducting her own interviews and making her own selection based on merit, not seniority. She also liked the discretionary funds now available at her school. She put it this way:

> We were able to take State Chapter I money and allocate more money for books and supplies. We were able to allocate where we felt our needs were. And I've also written in four positions for summer school. We always have far more kids wanting to go to summer school than the board ever let us have.

Several principals commented on the additional assistance they receive under school reform. One commended the additional wisdom brought by LSC members and the advantage of making decisions collaboratively. He commented, "It's inconceivable to me that a lot of people are going to come together and agree on something that isn't for the benefit of the children." Another principal commented that reform had given him ten potential allies but noted that the potential "ain't happened yet." Other principals commented upon the new assistance they were receiving from professionals and universities. Yet another principal commented upon the higher level of communication required by working with her LSC. She noted that she had always been a planner but realized now that she had not always let others know what those plans were. She saw the new need to communicate as increasing the involvement of others.

Principals also appreciated the power they had to select staff. One commented:

> You might say that students have been better served because for the first time this year, when I had a vacancy, I didn't have to take the teacher [that] the Personnel Department sent me. I had a choice. I know of one case, . . . who I would have gotten, and I know that I made a better choice because this [other] teacher, the last seven schools he was in, every principal closed the whole . . . program just to get rid of him. That's how bad he was, and nobody wanted to go through due process [to terminate him] because it was easier to close the program for a year and later reopen it.

Interestingly, there was no evidence in our sample schools of principals seeking to use the relaxed procedures for remediation and dismissal of unsatisfactory teachers. This is a new power principals had not begun to utilize.

Some principals felt school reform had brought an increase in total power at the local school level. While others saw the power equation more as a zero sum game, one saw it somewhat differently:

> One of the things about the school reform act is that it stresses a sharing of power and hopefully we will be able to illustrate that through sharing, we all have more power. Rather than diminishing power that we all have, we increase it. We increase our ability to accomplish by sharing power. That's the great hope of reform.

However, overall, principals were more prone to make negative comments about changes in their roles under reform. The most common complaint was about time. One principal said:

> The only thing I worry about is time: time, time, time. It's amazing, these people get on one small topic and you can spend an hour on it. Then, when you think about the many things that we have to cover, it adds up. But the one thing I am fully committed to is spending all the time that I am asked to spend.

Another principal echoed that complaint and reinforced the image of the principal as the information provider:

> The downside of school reform is that I just don't have enough time in my day. It's taken far more time. First of all, I'm spending a lot of time explaining to people who have no background knowledge. It's just time-consuming. I'm not decrying it; it's just time-consuming.

Other principals noted that the time demanded by the LSC elections and new activities related to council operations have entailed certain opportunity costs, particularly related to supervision and contact with other members of the faculty.

Another principal noted that she had taken on three new roles that she did not think appropriate. The first was that of being a public relations figure. She complained about the time she had to spend with parents on PR instead of doing her job. She suggested that if she did not spend a lot of time smiling at parents, her contract would not be renewed. Several other principals also mentioned the fears they had about LSCs misusing their powers to fire principals without good reason. This principal also complained that she had to spend time being a referee, trying to bring together two different factions in her school community. Finally, she was frustrated in that she felt like her post-reform role was primarily clerical:

> But you know, this is becoming very frustrating because it seems like everything is falling on my shoulders—dealing with the parents, dealing with the local school council, dealing with the teachers, getting all of the reports done—and it's very frustrating. . . . You know, I feel like a glorified clerk. You see what I'm saying, why I'm so frustrated—because that's all that I am, a glorified clerk.

One other principal, in commenting negatively about the way his council was operating, unknowingly revealed how some councils infringed upon the powers legally mandated to the principal. He complained:

> Here we are, we're interviewing four persons for the position of child welfare attendant. *We* are interviewing. Now, I have to adjust to that. That is my problem with it. I just honestly feel that I'm in the better position to know which of those four should be in that position.

Interestingly, this principal is uncomfortable with the LSC being involved in personnel selection but is apparently unaware that this function is really his prerogative, not the LSC's. However, it may be that this principal has been intimidated by the other members of the LSC. Other principals were worried about LSC members exceeding their authority. One was particularly concerned that LSC members would not stick to policy issues, as board of education members are supposed to do, but would try to circumvent the principal to be directly involved in issues such as teacher evaluation, another responsibility clearly delegated to principals under the reform act.

Several principals commented on the new demands on them to work collaboratively with new groups of people, whether it be the LSC on budgeting or the Professional Personnel Advisory Committee on instructional matters. These cooperative efforts provide increased involvement but are not as efficient as when the principals did things by themselves.

But some principals saw this expansion of authority at the local level less charitably. One principal complained that she possessed more responsibility for education but had less help, the same salary, and her job on the line. She commented, "[We] have all this power, but on the other hand, we have a sword hanging over our heads." Another principal commented that she did not like the fact that two teachers would help to decide whether her contract would be renewed.

Nearly half of the principals echoed the concern about ultimate responsibility lying with the principal. Principals commented that "the final burden is on the principal" or "the ultimate responsibility is mine" or "let's face it; responsibility for this stuff really comes back basically to the principal." Still one principal expressed the relationship between the principal and the LSC a bit differently: "The local school council is an oversight [authority] for the school—who operates through the principal. That's the kind of relationship we have—oversight committees or as liaisons, and they work through, not with."

What LSCs Discussed and Decided

On an average evening (LSCs usually met at night), six topics would be discussed. The most frequently discussed topics were those related to school programs. For those who were worried that LSCs would simply concern themselves with political wrangling and maneuvering to get relatives hired at the school, this finding gives reassurance about the forces set loose at the local school level and how the newly granted authority will be used. School program topics included issues of curriculum and instruction, school improvement planning, school administration, and overcrowding. The next most frequently discussed issues related to the LSC's own organization, its procedures and training. Relatively equal amounts of time were spent discussing building and safety topics, finance, and personnel. Least frequently discussed was the matter of parent involvement, and when it was, it was often in the form of an announcement about an upcoming event for parents. There were a number of other miscellaneous matters that came before LSCs infrequently. (See Table 8.2.)

Different councils focused on different issues, as might be expected. Some councils spent a great deal of time on school program issues, while others spent almost no time on these central school concerns. Some councils were consumed with their own procedures and organization, while others operated with accepted routines that needed little discussion. Councils with low attendance tended to spend more time on organizational issues, including nonattending members. Councils with higher attendance tended to focus more directly on school program issues.

Some issues dominated the attention of some councils. One council focused on the fact that its school was severely overcrowded and discussed the issue at every one of its meetings. These meetings were well attended and had extensive participation among the LSC members and frequently included extensive participation by members of the

Table 8.2
Topics Discussed at LSC Meetings

Categories and Sub-topics	Percent of All Topics	Members Participating
School Program Topics	**28.5**	**3.2**
Curriculum and Instruction	12.4	3.1
School Improvement Planning	6.2	4.2
School Administration	7.3	2.2
Overcrowding	2.6	4.3
LSC Organizational Topics	**27.5**	**3.1**
LSC Procedures	19.3	3.1
LSC Training	8.2	3.0
Building, Security, & Safety Topics	**13.3**	**3.6**
School Infrastructure	3.4	2.8
Security, Safety & Discipline	9.9	3.8
Finance Topics	**10.9**	**3.0**
Finance and Budgeting	7.3	2.9
School Fund Raising	3.6	3.1
Personnel Topics	**10.7**	**3.4**
Principal Selection and Contract	6.0	3.9
Other Personnel	4.7	2.6
Parent and Community Involvement	**4.3**	**2.2**
Other	**4.7**	**2.2**

audience. The council members took a very active role in looking for new space and developing alternative plans to relieve the overcrowding. They were constantly frustrated by the difficulty they had in working with, and coming to agreement with, central office staff assigned to help solve this problem.

Another council focused on gang problems and eventually developed a dress code for students to try to overcome gang identification in clothing. When students at the school requested a meeting to discuss the issue, the LSC cooperated. Council members discussed their plans and then received comments from parents and students; they discussed with them the positive and negative aspects of adopting a school dress code.

The decision-making process of councils was more difficult to analyze. In most cases, decisions were made by votes, which were the culmination of preceding discussion. Sometimes the discussions were very brief, followed by a quick, routine approval (for example, transferring funds from one line in the budget to another). On other occasions, such as when the school improvement plan was to be adopted, the discussions were long and protracted and the vote was far from routine.

But decisions were not always easy to determine. Councils used a range of procedures when they made decisions. Some councils did not require that motions be seconded. Voting mechanisms often varied, from roll call votes, to show of hands, to voice vote. Frequently it was difficult for our observers to tell how individual members had voted on particular issues. In a few instances, the only way an observer knew a decision had been made was the announcement of the chair that the motion had passed. In some cases, councils had a strong enough sense of consensus that they did not bother to formally vote. Interestingly, very few motions were defeated and most votes were very one-sided.

A little more than a quarter of all items discussed came to a vote. Since discussion topics included announcements and reports, this proportion seems appropriate. Budget items were more likely to culminate in a vote, while those dealing with miscellaneous topics, parent and community involvement, and the school program were the least likely to have culminated in council decisions. (See Table 8.3.)

What Improvements Are Planned?

Each of the fourteen schools we were observing adopted a school improvement plan during the spring of 1990. Panel staff have undertaken an analysis of these plans to understand what schools intended to do to improve the quality of education they were offering their students.

The Chicago School Reform Act mandates that each LSC create a three-year school improvement plan that would lift student achievement,

Table 8.3
LSC Topics Culminating in Decisions

Topic Category	Number Discussed	Number Voted Upon	Percent Voted Upon
School Program	133	29	21.8
LSC Organization	128	43	33.6
Building, Security, Safety	62	16	25.8
Budget	51	21	41.2
Personnel	50	18	36.0
Parent/Community Involvement	20	4	20.0
Other	22	3	13.6
TOTAL ALL TOPICS	466	134	28.8

attendance, and graduation rates to the level of national norms, while providing "a common learning experience that is of high academic quality and that reflects high expectations for all students' capacities to learn" (P.A. 85-1418, Sec. 34-2.4).

The legislation then provides a list of important components that should be included in school improvement plans, including a needs assessment, a list of objectives, the activities, staffing patterns, and training needed to reach the objectives, and a process for monitoring whether the objectives are being achieved.

School improvement plans in the fourteen studied schools varied widely. In three of the schools, the plans were rather cursory, with fewer than ten objectives set forth. None of these three schools made any plans to address the curriculum or instructional program of the school. The only schoolwide programs they addressed were related to improving attendance and student discipline. Only one sought to improve on the educational resource centers available to students (a high school seeking to open a math lab). About school organization they made only minor suggestions, which were essentially focused on adding time for students to work rather than any form of reorganization of their current resources.

By contrast, three other schools addressed changes in virtually every aspect of their curriculum, intended to create new learning resource centers for students, and envisioned rather extensive reorganization in the ways teachers interact with students, including team teaching and regrouping to foster cooperative learning. It is apparent, from reading these plans, that these school councils had much more extensive ideas about changes they wanted to see happen in their schools. It also seems obvious that, in these schools, teachers took a more active role in proposing changes that they thought would be beneficial to their students. Two of these schools had been involved in a year-long staff training and planning process under the system's desegregation programs. The third had employed professional, nonprofit planning facilitators to assist them in creating their plan. The remaining eight schools in our sample seem to fall somewhere in between these extremes.

When we looked at the relationship between the needs assessments conducted by schools and the school improvement plans LSCs adopted, we again discovered great variance. In a number of schools, the needs assessments were quite detailed and carefully pointed out specific problems that needed to be remedied. Frequently, the school improvement plans then included quite specific approaches to attack those problems. However, in other schools virtually no needs assessment was completed. In several, the needs statements seemed to be simply a restatement of the goal arenas incorporated in the school reform act (the central office had supplied all LSCs with a school improvement planning guide that included planning pages for each arena included in the legislation). In these latter schools, the improvement steps were more cursory and seemed less likely to be realized.

As might be expected from Chicago style restructuring, there were many different approaches adopted in the fourteen schools in our sample. One school decided to focus on boosting the self-esteem of its students as its major focus for improvement and therefore adopted an Afro-centric curriculum as the centerpiece of its reform. It intends to integrate that curriculum approach in all classrooms in the school. Other schools identified particular parts of their school program that were weak or in which students were not achieving as well as needed to meet national norms. They designed programs aimed at those specific problem areas. Still other schools saw their major problem in increasing attendance and focused on ways to get kids into school, while paying little attention to improving what these students would encounter when they did attend.

We were pleasantly surprised to discover that, with one exception, virtually all of the initiatives included within the fourteen school improvement plans were well supported by current research on school improvement. There was some interest, in some schools, in moving toward cooperative learning and the general approaches included under the heading "Student as Learner." In many schools there was a focus on increasing time on task. There was an attention to moving beyond simply using basal readers to include literature and, in several schools, the Junior Great Books approach, to move students toward an enjoyment of reading. It must be remembered that it has only been a few years since all Chicago classrooms were forced to use Chicago's peculiar form of mastery learning that concentrated almost exclusively on subcomponents of reading and the use of workbooks, so that the movement back to basal readers in 1985 was a major step. Many schools now seem ready to take the next step. The major exception to this alignment with current theories in school improvement was one school that unapologetically decided to adopt homogeneous grouping of students to facilitate instruction. This unabashed tracking plan flies in the face of most recent research demonstrating the harmful effects it has on students labeled as the slow learners (Oakes, 1985; Rosenbaum, 1980; Slavin, 1988).

When we move back from the specific analysis of individual school plans, we must concur with staff from the school system's central office that most of these plans are not likely to create radical change in the schools we studied. They rely more upon adding on small increments than upon making radical changes. Central office staff who analyzed plans from across the system put their assessment this way:

> Most school improvement plans stick to traditional methods of instruction, relying on a good basal reader or textbook supplemented by workbooks and seat work. More than one-fourth of the schools place major emphasis on remediation, extra study, or tutorial time for students below grade level or identified as at risk of failure.
>
> Evidence of innovation, in the sense of a sharp change of direction or the adoption of a wholly new approach, is rare in the plans. Far more of the schools, it seems, prefer to do more of what they are already doing or to do that better. Incremental change is what is seen, not uprooting and replanting.
>
> Nevertheless, the plans promise more change in the 1990–1991 school year than Chicago's public schools have seen in a long time. (Chicago Public Schools, 1990: 2)

On the basis of our examination of school improvement plans adopted at fourteen schools, we have a similar concern. In three of the schools, fairly significant changes have been planned. In three others, the plans seem pedestrian exercises. In the majority of schools, the plans call for more of the same, in educational programming. That is probably not radical enough to create the kind of change many national critics of schools think is necessary. But it may be the necessary developmental step to later plans that are more radical. Only time and further observation will determine if that potential is realized.

DISCUSSION

The Chicago School Reform Act is a major effort to realign authority and decision making in a major urban school system. An explicit goal of the act is "to make the individual local school the essential unit for educational governance and improvement" (P.A. 85-1418, Sec. 34-1.01.B). The first year of implementation was the year in which most of the shifts in authority were to take place. We have tried to present an accurate picture of the new decision-making pattern that is now in place.

There are undeniable new arenas for decision making being exercised at the local school level. Schools have chosen their educational leaders and signed them to four-year performance contracts. In the process, they have chosen to dismiss some principals or to encourage others to retire. It is this latter aspect of the principal selection process that is really new to Chicago school communities. In the past, when a new principal was to be appointed to a local school, a search committee, composed of parents and teachers, was created, which interviewed candidates and chose three in rank order of preference. Though it was not always the case that schools got their choice, in most cases the first choice was appointed to the school by the general superintendent. It was the ability to change principals that was the new authority being exercised by LSCs. The fact that LSCs could make their own choice is an important element in the new process, but represents a smaller increase in authority than the ability to change principals.

Similarly, the ability of local school personnel to select teachers and other educational staff on the basis of merit rather than seniority was a welcome change for school principals. However, as we have demonstrated, in some schools there were some differences in who exercised that authority at the local level. The legislation indicates that staff selection is a responsibility of the principal. Whether through the desire for broader participation by the principal or through intimidation by the council, in some schools, LSC members were participating in the staff hiring process.

It is also undeniable that there is a new outpouring of energy and enthusiasm directed toward planning for school improvement among the members of the local school communities. Whether exercised perfunctorily or engaged in with extensive training over a prolonged period of time, the process of creating a local school improvement plan has mobilized more intense involvement in trying to change Chicago public schools than at any time in the system's postwar history. Sustaining that interest and involvement will be a major challenge for reform activists during the next several years of implementing the legislation. Similarly, enabling local school improvement planners to envision scenarios for more radical educational change will be an important component of efforts to translate authority shifts into improved educational opportunities for the city's schoolchildren.

However, it must be noted that LSCs are experiencing frustrations in exercising their new authority because of decisions being made by the board of education and the school system's administration. Decisions about the system's budget and its contracts with its employee unions are properly the responsibility of the board of education under the reform act. But major changes in the terms of those contracts and in elements in the budget during the first year of implementation have changed the conditions under which LSCs were planning. Dramatically increasing the compensation of teachers and other personnel has forced the system to reduce the number of employees employed at local schools to be able to fund the raises. The decision to reduce the number of employees, rather than to redistribute them equitably as the legislation had anticipated, has forced LSCs to divert their projected discretionary spending to maintain program efforts they had considered as part of their basic program.

Similarly, the central administration's refusal to reexamine the functions of central office personnel in any significant fashion has left LSC members frustrated with the inadequate level of support they are receiving as they seek to deal with difficult problems such as overcrowding. The board of education's compromise decision to experiment with three different sub-district arrangements in order to provide support services to schools has further complicated the decision making at the school level. A whole set of specific problems has arisen over which the central administration and individual LSCs disagree as to who has the authority to determine a resolution. These tussles developed over regulations that were imposed without prior notice and spawned calls for establishing a formal rule-making procedure similar to that utilized by the state board of education when it seeks to create rules and regulations that have an impact upon local school districts.

Still, with all the uncertainty and continued "negotiation" on some issues, it is clear that major new decision-making authority has been devolved from the central office and board, authority that is now being exercised at the local school level. Similarly, it is clear that many new actors are now participating in exercising that local authority. In the schools we studied, the primary participants in most of the discussions leading up to local decisions were the principal, the LSC chair, the two teacher representatives, and the two community representatives. Other parents on the LSC participated less frequently, yet it seems obvious, from the fact that most votes were nearly unanimous, this does not mean those parents were uninvolved or ignored. It is, perhaps, important to note that the near unanimity on most matters is an indication that the various constituencies on the Local School Councils are working collaboratively on behalf of their schools, at least at the schools we have been studying. Since the willingness of parents and teachers to work collaboratively was one of the major concerns expressed by some critics of the Chicago reform effort, that is a significant finding for the first year of implementation.

NOTES

1. This act was declared unconstitutional by the Illinois Supreme Court on November 30, 1990, because the method of electing members to Local School Councils violated the

one person, one vote provisions of the federal constitution. On January 8, 1991, the Illinois General Assembly reenacted the legislation's main provisions (P.A. 86-1477) and in July adopted a new LSC election mechanism.

2. For a fuller description of the Chicago School Reform Act, its history, and initial implementation, see Hess, 1991b.

3. LSC membership includes six parents, two community representatives, two teachers, and the principal. In high schools, a nonvoting student member was also elected. The 1991 amendments gave the student member a vote on most matters. The reform act required that the chairperson be one of the parent members.

4. The July 1991 amendments to the reform act created procedures for removing nonperforming LSC members.

5. Principal interviews were conducted during the spring of 1990. The analysis of those interviews, which forms the basis of this section of this chapter, was conducted by Darryl J. Ford (1991).

9 School Reform in East Harlem: Alternative Schools vs. "Schools of Choice"

Diane Harrington and Peter W. Cookson, Jr.

THE CONTEXT

If one were to describe the landscape of urban education in the United States today, what would be the most salient features? To begin with, we would probably be struck by the number of poor children who attend inner-city public schools. By now, most of us know the profoundly disquieting statistics: whether we examine housing, health, safety, or education, it is undeniable that the children of the urban poor are generally ill-housed, undernourished, habitually victimized, and poorly educated. Sometimes the impression is created that poor urban families are indolent and in need of moral uplift. In fact, most of the poor are rightly thought of as members of the working class, who labor long hours and receive meager compensation.

Another key demographic feature of the inner-city public school population is that it is increasingly multicultural, multilingual, and often defined by the dominant culture as "learning handicapped." It is not terribly surprising, then, to discover that many inner-city students are functionally illiterate, liable to drop out of school before high school graduation and engage in "antisocial behavior" with such consistency that it amounts to a kind of rebellion (cf. Williams, 1981).

If we turned our attention to the schools themselves, we would most likely witness a system in disrepair, physically, academically, and spiritually. Not that all urban educators are dispirited; on the contrary, given the conditions in which they work, we would have to count many public educators among the heroic. Very often, they teach, and teach well, in spite of the educational bureaucracy and the social problems facing their students. Yet the odds are against most of their students succeeding.

In the last ten years, educators and policymakers have been searching for models of educational reform that appear to be effective within the inner city. In this chapter we examine an important educational reform that began in the mid-1970s in Community School District 4 in New York City, in an area of Manhattan known as East (or Spanish) Harlem.[1] In 1973, when this experiment began, the schools of District 4 were failing: only 15 percent of their students were able to score at grade level on standardized reading tests, and overall the district ranked thirty-second out of the thirty-two community school districts in the city (Domanico, 1989).

The East Harlem public schools, then and now, serve a particularly poor and isolated community, even for New York City. Roughly two-thirds of their students are Latino; most of the rest are African-American. Half of them live in families headed by a single female, over one-third are supported by welfare, and more than three-quarters of them qualify for a free or reduced-price lunch, meaning that they meet the federal guidelines defining poverty (Domanico, 1989; Kutner & Salganik, 1987).

The educational experiment in District 4 is heralded by many school choice advocates, who argue that choice was the engine that drove the reforms (Domanico, 1989; Fliegel, 1990). As we show, this argument is fundamentally incorrect. One of the authors of this chapter (Harrington) had the opportunity to work in District 4 shortly after the experiment was initiated by Anthony Alvarado, who became superintendent in 1973. She was witness to the reforms, and her account refutes those choice advocates who point to District 4 as an example of how choice can reform urban schools. In fact, these advocates have put the conceptual cart before the empirical horse. Alternative schools of quality make choice work; the innovation precedes the mechanism of selecting students.

In the last five years, school choice has become the reform of choice for a wide variety of educators and policymakers. The underlying assumptions of many choice advocates is that simply allowing greater flexibility in student assignment to schools will somehow—almost magically—lead to schools that are innovative and educationally exciting. Some recent work, by John Chubb and Terry Moe (1990), would have us believe that market mechanisms, in and of themselves, will lead to a renaissance in American education. We believe that before a market-oriented view of educational reform is accepted, we ought to examine how effective educational reforms actually begin and are sustained.

One of the values of participant observation and qualitative research is that they ground our observations and analyses in events as they actually transpire. To understand the effects of school choice, we need studies that clarify the relationship between choice and innovation. This is important, because subsequent histories of "school choice experiments" tend to attribute virtually every success to choice. In time, the collective power of these histories creates the impression that by simply letting parents, students, and teachers choose schools, we will experience dramatic educational improvements. To our way of thinking, these histories overlook the true chronology of reform and ignore the structural problems facing education in the inner city and in our society in general.

Thus this chapter might be thought of as a form of revisionist history. Based on Harrington's observations, we argue that innovation precedes choice and that it requires spirited leadership that has very little to do with market models of human behavior. Later on in the chapter, we explicate those elements of District 4's experiment that we think are useful in understanding how reforms can lead to better schools. But we begin by looking at the experiment itself.

THE EXPERIMENT

Anthony Alvarado believed that education could make a difference for the kids of East Harlem. It wasn't doing much for them in 1973, but he believed that it could make more options possible for their futures. He had energy and vision, something that had been lacking in district leadership for years.

He searched through the schools and found others—mostly teachers—who shared that belief and brought them to the district office to help him. He also hired a lot of new people, mostly outsiders without city teaching licenses, nearly all young, energetic, and idealistic. The sense of mission in the district office in those days was palpable.

Alvarado himself was quite young—barely thirty years old when he became superintendent of District 4. Certainly, he was much younger than many longtime East Harlem principals. He had been a teacher and then a school administrator for just a few years in public schools in the Bronx before this meteoric rise (as some saw it) to head up a district.

It was not Alvarado's style to tell people what he wanted them to do. Rather, he created a climate encouraging risk taking and innovation, tossed in a bit of competitiveness, and waited for new ideas to rise to the surface. The word was out—informally—that Alvarado wanted to hear about new ideas, good ideas, that he would support the best of them, and that he especially wanted to hear from teachers.

One teacher tells the story of going to him with her idea for starting a school based on what she and a colleague were doing, together, with their sixth-grade classes. It was Alvarado's first year on the job. She had rehearsed, over and over again, her answers to all the objections she knew this new superintendent, whom she hadn't met, would raise. When, instead, he said, "Sure. Go ahead and try it," she found *herself* raising all those objections. (She did, by the way, go ahead and try it: East Harlem Performing Arts School was one of the first three alternative schools begun in 1974—along with the BETA School, for "acting-out" youngsters, and Central Park East, East Harlem's most famous nontraditional school.)

What happened in District 4 over the next ten years was the gradual development of a new definition of "school" as separate from "building." A system of schools within schools was created. East Harlem Performing Arts School, for example, operated at first out of a church basement. As it gained stature and students, however, the district had to find the school more "legitimate" space. But the school was not big enough—nor did it intend ever to be big enough—to fill a whole school building. Alvarado's solution was to put the school on the top floor of P.S. 50, a relatively new elementary school overlooking the East River.

Thus overnight P.S. 50 became home to two schools. One, the "regular" elementary school, had a principal, while the alternative school (East Harlem Performing Arts) was run by a teacher-director, the same woman who had proposed the idea. Alvarado put P.S. 50's principal in charge of the building, giving him authority over all building-related decisions (getting extra power up to the third floor for the lights needed for performances, for example) as well as continued authority over the elementary school on the first two floors. East Harlem Performing Arts School's teacher-director, on the other hand, was in charge of curriculum, programming, and student-related decisions within the alternative school.

Virtually all of the new schools in District 4, like East Harlem Performing Arts School, ended up occupying a floor or two of an existing building. Ultimately, some "schools" (like P.S. 50) came to house three or four or five schools.

Most of these new schools were begun by teachers who became their "teacher-directors." Like East Harlem Performing Arts School, they too were small, theme-centered, and staffed mostly by people who opted to work there.

Money was needed to support the new schools and new ideas, so the district went after federal dollars and managed to bring in several million over the next few years. Most of this came through the Emergency School Aid Act (ESAA), which funded desegregation efforts. This money provided the "extras" that helped the fledgling schools get going—extra people, extra supplies, extra time. It also supported some innovative programs within the mainstream, such as the Open City Project, which created monthly basic skills curricula focused on special events like field trips, workshops, and assemblies.

Alvarado did not believe in rules. So people in his new programs and schools were allowed, sometimes even expected, to break the rules. For example, in East Harlem Performing Arts School every student took classes in music, dance, and drama as part of the school's program. To tie everything together, the school developed a "Humanities Institute," whose monthly themes became the focus of work in other classes. Exciting as this was, something had to go; there are only so many hours in the school day. With Alvarado's permission the Humanities Institute became the social studies curriculum—an educationally sound decision, but not bureaucratically justifiable. As another example, in Central Park East, truly pioneering forms of assessing student progress resulted from Alvarado's willingness to bend or break the rules.

For staff, breaking the rules wasn't always an advantage, however. A number of new employees had to wait months to get paid because the district didn't fill out or process papers appropriately.

On balance, though, the cavalier attitude about rules helped to create a sense of adventure and camaraderie: us against them. "They" included all the bureaucracies: the federal funders, who changed the funding rules every year; the central board of education at 110 Livingston Street, which controlled the purse strings; and the United Federation of Teachers, the teachers' union, which limited the hiring and firing practices through its contract. "They" didn't care about kids; "we" did.

THE RESULTS

By 1983, nine years after the first three opened their doors, there were more than twenty alternative schools—and District 4 had choice. From the vantage point of the present, it's hard to remember how difficult it was for the first few schools to get going. Parents and students didn't line up outside the doors to get in. The schools were an experiment, and in a poor community where education was seen as just about the last legitimate way out, parents didn't want their kids to be guinea pigs. Only those whose children weren't making it in traditional schools or who knew the teacher-directors well were willing to take the risk. The first schools succeeded and built their reputations with these brave kids.

And they did succeed. In terms of reading scores, the district moved up to about the middle of all the districts in the city, where it has remained (Domanico, 1989). Given the fact that most of the district's students were not only poor, minority inner-city students, but also spoke English as their second language (even though they did not necessarily qualify for bilingual instruction), this accomplishment was impressive indeed.

For parents, however, success was often measured in high school placements. For years only a handful of East Harlem youngsters had been accepted to New York City's elite, selective high schools.[2] Suddenly, this began to change; by 1987, the rate of acceptance from District 4 was double that of the rest of the city (Domanico, 1989). Some students were also accepted into prestigious private schools, such as Andover, Brooklyn Friends, and Dalton.

As this trend became apparent, the schools began to attract more applicants and to have the luxury of selecting from among them. Even students from outside the district applied. And, in the end, District 4 became nationally known as a symbol of successful reform and hope for inner-city education.

THE KEY INGREDIENTS

Was school choice responsible for creating the innovative and effective schools in East Harlem, as some analysts now claim? Or would it be more accurate to pose the question in reverse: were the innovative and effective schools created in East Harlem responsible for the system of choice that evolved there?

Deborah Meier, founder and director of the Central Park East Schools,[3] argues that the District 4 success story could not have happened without choice. Choice, she writes,

> was an enabling strategy for a District Superintendent, Anthony Alvarado, who wanted to get rid of the tradition of zoned, factory-style, bureaucratically controlled schools that has long been synonymous with urban public schooling and replace it with a different image of what "public" could mean. The District 4 way was deceptively simple; it required no vast blueprint, just a new mindset. (Meier, 1991: 266)

This is an appealing argument from the standpoint of the 1990s restructuring movement. But Meier's terms, including "choice," were not around in the 1970s; and the language we use is a critical filter for how we look at the world. At the time, Alvarado and his colleagues were trying to establish new models of schools that worked. They were looking for practices, structures, and curriculum that would educate District 4's students.

And they called these "alternative schools," *not* "schools of choice." There is a subtle but important distinction between the two.

By definition, an alternative school is not just chosen; more important, it is a *nontraditional school* in its educational values and teaching methods. It provides an alternative (for teachers, students, and parents) to the "regular" neighborhood public schools. A school of choice is only chosen. It is not necessarily different in any way from the regular schools—in fact, it usually is a regular school. So what was being attempted in District 4 in the 1970s went far beyond what is being touted by many choice advocates in the 1990s.

That is not to say that choice didn't play a role in District 4's success; it did. It just wasn't the most important or the determining ingredient of that success. The fact that parents, students, and teachers *chose* these schools was important. Because of this, all of them had a sense of ownership in the schools, a stake in their success.

But probably the most important ingredient was school size. Every one of the alternative schools was small; East Harlem Performing Arts School included only about 150 seventh- through ninth-graders, for example. This meant that each child was known by the adults and other children there; each child was connected to the school community. The difficulties they brought to school with them daily were known and taken into consideration by their teachers, many of whom taught them every year. Problems didn't fall between the cracks.[4]

Size alone made these alternative schools nontraditional in New York City, where public schools are about as large and impersonal as you can get, even at the elementary level. In addition, small and personal school communities were particularly important in the East Harlem community, whose youngsters had not been well served by their public schools and whose lives exemplified urban dangers.

Other ingredients also contributed to the success of the East Harlem experiment. Certainly, the climate in which innovation was expected, not just encouraged, was a critical factor. Alvarado, for example, constantly reminded his staff that they had a mission: to create better schools for children. He reinforced the sense of mission by regularly visiting and teaching in schools and classrooms throughout the district. Working with him wasn't just a job; it was a *calling*.

In addition, people's imaginations were liberated because they were not bound by the bureaucratic limits, the standardization that defined schools in other parts of the city. This is how Alvarado encouraged people to take the risks associated with innovation. No one expected every experiment to succeed; failure was something to learn from, not something to avoid, as it is for far too many school people.

Within the schools, the extra funding helped make it possible for staff to try out their new ideas. The school themes—performing arts, marine biology, visual arts, and sports, for example—helped to create excitement and motivation for students and teachers alike. Teachers could teach subjects that they loved, that they knew a lot about, and that, for the most part, they previously had held separate from their teaching. Students could choose to explore subjects that interested them or that they thought might interest them.

For the first time, in addition, high expectations for student achievement were held by whole schools; previously, this had varied from teacher to teacher. When Maxine Greene from Columbia Teachers College lectured to seventh-, eighth-, and ninth-graders at the East Harlem Performing Arts School, for example, she spoke not much differently than she would have to a college audience—and they handled it. They took notes, asked intelligent questions, and were fascinated (they said later) by her way of looking at the world.

Another important ingredient was time—time to try out ideas, carry them through, see whether they worked. In this forgotten corner of Manhattan, where students had done so poorly for so long, no one was looking over teachers' shoulders for instant success. It was several years, in fact, before much notice was taken of the success that was happening there.

Finally, Alvarado was practicing and nurturing teacher professionalism—long before this term was even used, much less popularized. He trusted, encouraged, and pushed the teachers of District 4. In enabling them to put their ideas and dreams to the test of real inner-city classrooms, he also gave them responsibilities far beyond what most New York City public school teachers had. Virtually every alternative school was the idea of a teacher who then usually ended up running it. These teachers truly "owned" their schools.

WEAKNESSES

When Alvarado left District 4 in 1983 to become, briefly, chancellor of the entire New York City public school system and then, a few years later, superintendent of another district, most of the creative energy left East Harlem, too. All too often, this is a pattern in educational reform: it is too closely tied to particular individuals, and when they leave, the reform dies.

One reason for this is the failure to make changes permanent, to "institutionalize" them. In District 4, for example, most of the teacher-directors were not principals. Usually they were "teachers assigned," meaning that they were working under their teachers' licenses and were not permanently appointed to their jobs. This left them very vulnerable, both to manipulations by sometimes resentful "regular" principals and to dismissal at the whim of the administrators who followed Alvarado. Since so many of these teacher-directors had begun their schools, without them some essential ingredients and vision were lost.

This vulnerability was characteristic of Alvarado's style in other ways. Like too many school leaders, he was a visionary often bogged down in fighting fires, meeting deadlines, just getting by. This "seat of the pants" mentality doesn't facilitate long-range planning or institutionalization.

Finally, these weaknesses, taken together, meant that the District 4 experiment was tremendously demanding of the time and energy of a relatively small number of people—a circumstance that can, and often did, in this case, lead to burnout.

CONCLUSIONS AND IMPLICATIONS

As this case study demonstrates, successful educational reforms can act as magnets to those who are in search of evidence to support their reform agendas. In particular, District 4 in Manhattan has been held up by many school choice advocates as a clear example that choice can lead to improved schools in the inner city. We have argued, however, that while choice was an important aspect of the East Harlem experiment, it was far from the driving engine of change. In fact, it was the vision of Anthony Alvarado and the teachers of the district that brought about change. They believed in the children, themselves, and the possibilities inherent in risk taking. Abstract arguments about the reputed benefits of "the market" ring a little hollow when placed beside what actually happened in District 4. Market mechanisms are not substitutes for imagination, intelligence, daring, and collective efforts.

We believe that this case study also should serve as a warning to those pragmatists who sincerely believe that school choice is *the* way to reform schools. Alvarado (1991), himself, recently wrote:

> Much of the literature on school choice cites the experience of New York City's community School District 4, where I was Superintendent for ten years, as evidence that choice can improve schools. But I espoused choice in District 4, as I have in District 2, where I have served since 1987, out of pragmatism, not ideology. . . . Promoting choice as the primary method of educational change is like rearranging the deck chairs on the *Titanic*.

First and foremost we suggest that the "evidence" that choice "works" must be examined very closely. Second, school reform researchers should take considerable care to establish the relationship between a reform and its antecedents. Third, we have indicated that good ideas alone are subject to great danger if not supported by appropriate institutionalization, including permanent appointments and appropriate teacher empowerment. Last, we urge reformers to keep faith with the power of collective effort and vision and not to be beguiled into accepting unproven theories of the marketplace as guidelines for educational reform.

NOTES

1. The New York City public school system is divided into thirty-two community school districts that administer the elementary and junior high or middle schools. The high schools are run by a division of the central bureaucracy. The community school boards choose their own superintendents and principals but have limited authority over teacher hiring and firing and over their budgets.

2. Four high schools—Stuyvesant, Bronx Science, Brooklyn Tech, and the LaGuardia School of Music and Performing Arts—are highly selective and often are considered among the finest high schools in the country. A second tier of high schools, called "education option" schools, is also selective. Students who do not get into these schools generally attend their neighborhood zoned high schools.

3. Four schools are now part of the Central Park East "family" of schools, each with its own director and separate identity but linked by common philosophies and practices. Three are elementary schools: Central Park East I, begun in 1974; Central Park East II, begun in 1980; and River East, begun in 1982. The fourth is Central Park East Secondary School, grades 7–12, begun in 1985.

4. William Fowler and Herbert Walberg (1991) have reviewed the extensive literature that confirms that school size is the most significant characteristic, after the social and educational status (SES) of students and schools, associated with student achievement levels. Fowler and Walberg direct their readers to qualitative studies such as this one to explain why size is important.

III Anthropological Perspectives

10 The Role of Anthropologists in Restructuring Schools

Thomas G. Carroll

Anthropologists can make important contributions to school improvement as well as to the ethnography of education, if they recognize that school restructuring is a significant response to social changes that are raising fundamental questions about the purpose and organization of schooling in this country. On a smaller scale, in *The Face of the Fox*, Frederick Gearing (1970) demonstrated that anthropologists could contribute as well as learn by actively working with a culture confronted by dramatic change. As the Fox Indians worked to respond to a host of legal, demographic, and economic forces impinging on their survival, traditional roles and rules governing day-to-day activities were called into question. When members of the tribe struggled to deal with these questions, some fundamental values and relationships of their culture that were normally never discussed were brought to the surface. The anthropologists, in turn, grappled to understand what they were learning from these discussions by asking questions and seeking additional information. As they did, the anthropologists became, in effect, a sounding board for various members of the community to reflect on their situation. In the end, the decisions about what to do were the tribe's, but these decisions were informed by insights into tribal values that were gained through extended exchanges with the anthropologists.

As educators struggle to change our schools in response to the new conditions we face as we enter the twenty-first century, they have similarly become engaged in a national debate about the underlying values and

This chapter represents the personal views of the author; it is not a policy statement of the U.S. Department of Education, where he is employed.

purposes of schooling. Anthropologists have much to learn from this debate, and in turn they have much to contribute by becoming actively involved in the exchange of ideas about how to restructure schools.

The restructuring movement is important because, in contrast to other reform initiatives, it is school-based. Most school change initiatives in this country are driven by agendas initiated by reformers or social critics from outside the school system who have little political power to bring about change. When these initiatives confront large, bureaucratically organized school systems that perceive no need for change, they are defeated, isolated, or diluted. In the end, the fundamental purpose and organization of schooling are rarely brought into question, and real change fails to occur. In the case of the restructuring movement, however, those who have political power and responsibility for schools are themselves confronting the fact that these institutions are not working. They are not all in agreement about why schools are not working or what should be done about it, but the debate is under way, and we are witnessing a number of fascinating experiments in school-based change.

Educators in such places as Miami-Dade, Florida; Hammond, Indiana; Jefferson County, Kentucky; and Rochester, New York are actively working to decentralize the management of their schools by supporting new leadership roles for their administrators, enhanced professional roles for their teachers, and more active participation by parents. Similarly, dozens of school districts are working to adopt new expectations for student learning that are central to James Comer's School Development Program, Henry Levin's Accelerated Schools, and Ted Sizer's Coalition of Essential Schools. In addition, court orders and subsequent legislation in Kentucky are transforming that state's entire education system, and legislation in Illinois is leading to radical change in the Chicago Public Schools.

But school-based change is not without problems. In *The Culture of the School and the Problem of Change*, Seymour Sarason observed:

> [A]ny attempt to introduce a change into the school involves some existing regularity, behavioral or programmatic. . . . It is a characteristic of the modal process of change in the school culture that the intended outcome (the change in the regularity) is rarely stated clearly, and if it is stated clearly, by the end of the change process it has managed to get lost. It certainly was not an intended outcome of the introduction of the new math that it should be taught precisely the way the old math was taught. But that has been the outcome, and it would be surprising if it were otherwise. (1971: 3)

He further observes that the

> existing structure of a setting or culture defines the permissible ways in which goals and problems will be approached. Not so obvious, particularly to those who comprise the structure, is that the existing structure is but one of many alternative structures possible in that setting and that the existing one is a barrier to recognition and experimentation with alternative ones. (1971: 12)

It is in respect to this problem of recognition and experimentation with alternative structures that anthropologists can be most helpful. Anthropologists, with their training in the study of culturally patterned behavior, can serve as effective outside resources to educators as they work in their schools to identify existing roles, rules, relationships, and expectations that must be changed to achieve new results. Following this initial step, anthropologists can continue to provide useful feedback to educators on the extent to which their efforts to make these changes and restructure their organizations have been successful, as measured by observable changes in roles, relationships, and outcomes.

THE HISTORICAL PURPOSES OF SCHOOLING

But since we have seen that operating from within the perspective of an existing structure can limit our ability to understand it, where are we to begin? Phillip Schlechty suggests that we must step outside the structure to consider its purpose. Form follows function, purpose shapes structure, and "any reasonable effort to restructure schools must begin with a serious consideration of the purposes of education" (Schlechty, 1990: xx). Schools serve a purpose by responding to the perceived needs of their community. To serve a given purpose or to meet a specific need, educational resources and the roles, rules, relationships, and expectations that govern behavior in schools will be structured in specific ways. If we conclude that we want our schools to serve different purposes and meet different needs than they have in the past, we will begin to see where we must restructure those aspects of the schools' organization to achieve new purposes.

The Common School

Examined from this perspective it becomes apparent that our schools are nineteenth-century institutions designed to serve purposes that are in conflict with twenty-first-century needs. Based in small agrarian communities with homogenous populations, the "common schools" of New England during the early 1800s had as their first purpose to serve the needs of a newly emerging republic by developing a strong foundation for its experiment in constitutional democracy. To provide a secure footing for this new venture the curriculum focused on the study of values embodied in ancient cultures and classical literature. By reaching into antiquity, a young nation could establish a secure underpinning and a sense of timeless authority for its new undertaking, and the schools were among the central institutions of the community organized to express and transmit these civic values. Schlechty is among those who point out that there was an almost religious reverence associated with the mission of schools to preserve and transmit these core values:

> Indeed, much of the mythology of America is tied to the view that education is not only liberating but essential for liberty. Thus the survival of the republic depended on the young coming to understand and respect the traditions upon which the republic was based. . . . It is not surprising that the study of ancient cultures, especially those in Greece and Rome, was the central feature in the education of the young, for it was to these cultures that educated Americans looked for guidance in the republican experiment. (1990: 18)

Schlechty goes on to point out that an emphasis on the classics of English literature and on Protestant morality tales also fit the cultural context of the early years of the American republic, with its Anglo-Saxon, Protestant heritage. He continues:

> If the curriculum is viewed as the lore of the tribe, then there is a certain logic to the assumption that teaching is a sacred profession; for those who hold and transmit the traditions of the tribe have a sacred role. (1990: 19)

To serve their purpose as institutions charged with preserving and transmitting the fundamental truths governing affairs in the republic, the common schools became agencies of socialization with all the qualities associated with such institutions in small-scale, traditional cultures that derive authority from the past (see Carroll, 1990). Traditional cultures develop a communal consensus about core values and important knowledge. To maintain the continuity of this consensus over generations, the knowledge held in common is transmitted as a set of immutable truths by the elders of the community to their children as their heritage ("We hold these truths to be self-evident"). Children in such cultures are expected to develop unquestioned commitments to these values. Indeed, the set of beliefs that constitute knowledge in such cultures can take on the character of a religious canon. The role of the teacher is to serve as an authority who is to convey the canon to the children, who are to receive the knowledge as truths, to be acquired by rote as a catechism. Because the common school's purpose was to express and preserve a common consensus about important beliefs and values, the elders of the community maintained active control over what was taught in schools and who taught it.

The role of the teacher as an authority responsible for conveying immutable truths to students expected to be passive learners and the status of the curriculum as a sacred canon central to the preservation of the republic were firmly established in the common schools during the first half of the nineteenth century. They still stand as barriers to the perception of alternatives for anyone working to restructure schools in response to today's needs.

The Melting Pot School

During the latter half of the nineteenth century, public schools were called on to serve a second national purpose. Successive waves of immigrants and the end of slavery were swelling the population of young people in need of schooling. But the different cultural backgrounds of these students and their families, with their diverse languages and historical experiences, were viewed as divisive forces that could erode the underpinnings of the republic by challenging fundamental truths. In response, educational reformers of the time, such as James Carter, Horace Mann, and Henry Barnard, came upon the idea that the common schools, which had been effective in expressing and preserving the existing community consensus about important beliefs and values, could be used to forge a new community consensus that would reduce these differences and the threat they posed. Until then the community had shaped the school; now the school would be used to shape the community.

The canon of thought that was at the center of the curriculum in the small New England common schools was extended to the new public school systems that were developing in urban areas and the South, with the hope that these large schools would become a melting pot for the formation of a homogenous, common culture in America. The curriculum of the common school, with its roots in classical Western thought, was the only ingredient in the pot, however, and there was little room for inclusion of the diverse perspectives of the newly arrived immigrants. Since the purpose was to shape the community around the particular beliefs and values represented in the common school curriculum, these large public school systems could not be as responsive or as accountable to the diverse urban communities of the latter half of the nineteenth century as the common schools had been in the smaller and more homogenous communities of earlier times. The melting pot assimilated those who chose to give up their languages and customs to enjoy the benefits of participation in mainstream American life; it marginalized those who did not, and it excluded some who never had a real opportunity to choose whether they would participate to begin with.

A considerable body of literature has addressed the effects of the melting pot policy on the participation of various minority groups in U.S. education and society. From the perspective of restructuring schools for today's needs, however, what was most significant about this policy was its underlying assumption that public schools could be used by policymakers to shape the community and that a common culture could be fabricated, as it were, from whole cloth. The adoption of the melting pot policy marked the beginning of a loss of community control over what is taught and who teaches in public schools that continues to this day.

In those cases where the curriculum was in conflict with community perspectives the schools began to buffer themselves from community influence. As a sacred canon, the curriculum was preserved, but accountability for educational outcomes was lost. When students from different backgrounds did not succeed in this curriculum, the failure was attributed to their differences and not to the school's lack of responsiveness to the community's needs. Perhaps the most extreme instances in which differences in culture or historical background disenfranchised communities occurred in the education of Native Americans on reservations and black Americans in the South:

> Through most of American history, missionaries and government officials took it as their duty to civilize and Christianize the Indians; usually this meant that Indian culture and language and folkways had to be eliminated. While some were "weaned away from the blanket," as the saying went, most simply developed a strong internal resistance to the new behavior. Forced efforts at assimilation tended to produce precisely the opposite of what was intended . . . across the South in the two decades after 1890; loss of the ballot through such devices as

> poll taxes and literacy tests assured the Negro's political impotence. A disenfranchised people could have no influence in the shaping of educational policy, no voice when school funds were unfairly apportioned. It was a classically vicious circle: Illiteracy was the justification given for excluding blacks from the polls (though equally illiterate whites could vote by grace of grandfather clauses); their exclusion left them powerless to contest for educational facilities with which to remedy their illiteracy. (Ravitch, 1985: 192–193 and 200)

Diane Ravitch is careful to caution that the effects of the melting pot varied greatly from one minority community to another. As an alternative, some turned to the formation of private schools in which they could continue to exert control over their education:

> During the second half of the nineteenth century, public schools were firmly established throughout the country; the New England ideology, which asserted that the survival of the American republic was dependent on the common schools, became widespread. The ideology seems to have been more a selling point for public support than an article of faith, however. If Americans really believed that their nation's institutions and freedom depended on the strength of the common schools, they would have prohibited nonpublic education. But Americans apparently respected freedom of choice more than the common school ideology, for private schools abounded. Many minorities took full advantage of the freedom to maintain their own schools, and there were Catholic schools, Jewish schools, German schools, French schools, Polish schools, and numerous other schools run by benevolent agencies and small sects. (Ravitch, 1985: 186–187)

Today we are still dealing with public school systems that are unable to restructure their curriculum to include the diverse perspectives represented in their communities, and these systems continue to be characterized by limited accountability, poor academic performance, and high dropout rates.

The Factory School

Closely coupled with demographic changes in the latter half of the nineteenth century was the industrialization of the U.S. economy. Employers managing large manufacturing enterprises needed employees with a wide range of skills, and they looked to the schools to provide them. As Schlechty (1990: 21) points out, this multiracial, multiethnic urban world was far different from the small New England village with its assumed consensus of values. And the shift in the role of the school in the new urban economy forced educators to begin to think differently about themselves.

The small agrarian village was a typical face-to-face community in which almost everyone knew everyone else and they could be expected to encounter one another on a weekly, if not daily, basis. There was ample opportunity to observe the skills, knowledge, and ability of each member of the community, and when someone was needed for a specific job it was not difficult to know to whom to go. In contrast, large, urban, industrialized communities were populated by strangers with diverse backgrounds, who had limited contact with each other and little direct opportunity to know about each other's skills or abilities. It fell to the schools, with their common curriculum, to develop a system of standards to sort, select, and certify individuals for participation in the larger society.

The melting pot policy had already laid the groundwork for differential treatment and success in school. But public schools were becoming large organizations with hundreds or thousands of teachers and tens of thousands of students from different backgrounds. If the common curriculum was to be preserved as the standard for assessing an individual's knowledge or skills, decisions about what to teach and judgments about who had learned it could not be left to every teacher responding to the diverse needs and abilities of the particular students in her classroom. As large public institutions responsible for maintaining standards in the community, the schools required effective management, and school leaders, along with industrial leaders of the time, looked to the concepts of scientific management and industrial efficiency to organize their enterprises. The principles of standardization and assembly-line mass production were adopted, and the graded school, organized as a factory, became the model for public education.

To maintain standards and to achieve efficiency, all decisions about what to teach in the graded school were centrally controlled. Teachers became technicians responsible for implementing a uniform curriculum that was not of their making, and the principals became their supervisors. All children at a given age were grouped in the same grade and taught from a set of standard materials on the same schedule. Since children vary in the background and knowledge they bring to school, however, many of them experienced remarkable failure in this system. But in public schools, where it had become important to sort, select, and certify students, this outcome was acceptable: "[A] new concept was introduced to American education: the concept of school failure. . . . Indeed, educators who insisted that children should not fail were viewed as 'soft' and were later seen as the culprits who caused the supposed erosion of standards in America's schools. 'How' it was asked 'could schools have standards if no one failed?' " (Schlechty, 1990: 22).

At the turn of the century, the expectation of school failure for some students was reinforced by the work of psychologists who developed the early concepts of intelligence and norm-referenced testing. In the factory model of schooling, students became the raw material, and it was clear from available tests that the quality of this material varied, or so it seemed (Schlechty, 1990: 22). Thus even if the schools made an effort to expose all children to the best curriculum and instruction available, some children would still be expected to fail. It was assumed that some children lacked the ability to benefit from education and the school therefore could not be held accountable for the result. Many of the failures were children of the poor, those who had limited expectations for full participation in society, and those whose cultural backgrounds and experiences differed greatly from the core curriculum of the school. In the context of the common school curriculum and norm-referenced tests, their differences became deficits. When they left schools at an early age, it was taken as further evidence that they did not value learning.

Educators soon concluded that if children did vary in their ability to benefit from schooling, it was not efficient to continue investing the same resources in every student. Consistent with the factory model, children with different abilities could be presorted into different assembly lines, or curriculum tracks, with appropriate resources allocated to each track. Children with high ability were on the fast track to college, those with moderate abilities on the general education track, and those with low abilities on the vocational track. Some children were simply not good raw material for the educational enterprise, and they were allowed to drop out of the system entirely.

Tracking, of course, became a system of self-fulfilling prophecies. Where schools had high expectations for children in the fast track, they allocated ample resources to support their success. For middle-range students the school's investment was more restrained:

> With the sanction of the prevailing sentiment that in a democratic society, ability and hard work should determine a person's fate, failure was expected and accepted. Education was laissez-faire in its conception of the student's role in the learning process. Students could work or not as they saw fit, and if they didn't work and failed, the failure was their fault. (Tomlinson, 1981: 49G)

For the remainder of the students, however, the expectations were so low that many schools planned their allocation of resources around the assumption that adequate teachers, classrooms, and textbooks did not have to be devoted to them, because they were certain to fail or leave the system. Indeed, school systems that planned their budgets, year after year, around the expectation of a high dropout rate soon were committed in a very real sense to the failure of a significant portion of their students. If those students did not leave the system there would be no classrooms, teachers, or books available to serve them.

This factory model of schooling, with various approaches to tracking, has served as the dominant mode of schooling in the United States for most of this century. Between the end of the Civil War and the end of World War I, schooling had been transformed from the common school model to the factory model by the convergence of three forces: demographic change, new industrial theories for the organization of work, and theories about the psychology of learning. By the turn of the century, the common school curriculum, which still had the residual trappings of a religious canon, had taken on scientific authority as the normative standard against which all learning was to be measured. Large urban school systems managed as factories were no longer accountable to their communities; in fact, in most cases the teachers and administrators of the schools were strangers to their students and their families. Schools were responsible instead for maintaining a set of educational standards and allocating resources to produce students who could meet them.

The Information Age School

But as we enter the last decade of this century demographic and social changes are again converging with new theories of work and learning to challenge the prevailing structure of schooling. In response, educators and policymakers are calling for a fundamental restructuring of the educational enterprise. Three forces are converging to drive these changes: the social justice movement, the shift to a postindustrial economy, and the significant growth of demographic diversity in the United States.

Almost from the outset, the factory model of schooling, with its hierarchical structure of central control and inequitable allocation of resources, has been attacked as antidemocratic. John Dewey (1914) believed that democracy would thrive only when individuals were able to engage in a free exploration and exchange of ideas. He was frustrated by the standardized curriculum. Dewey felt that a standardized curriculum and instruction in the factory school seriously undermined any possibility of self-directed work and learning for either the teachers or the students. He thought that schools ought to be models of democracy, and he encouraged educators to support active learning and involvement in deliberations that would help all students develop the skills and knowledge needed to participate responsibly in the larger society. His was a curriculum that included, even encouraged, a diversity of viewpoints and the expectation that all children could learn. His approach was rejected by the public schools, which continued their practice of organizing resources and instruction around the standard curriculum and then electing to serve only those students who had the ability to benefit from it.

Up until the last two decades, subsequent proposals for school change were met and defeated by similar responses from the schools. But in 1966 this cycle was broken. James Coleman and his associates (1966) reported in a major federal study of urban schools that the only variable that consistently correlated with low student achievement was the social and economic status of the student's family. Inner-city educators once again began to use these results to absolve themselves of any accountability for the poor performance of students in their systems (see Hess, 1990b: 11). Here was more proof, it was said, that there are children who do not benefit from schooling because of their background and abilities and it was beyond the schools' resources to do anything about it. However, minority groups and immigrant communities that had been disenfranchised in earlier times were feeling increasingly entitled to voice their opinions and participate in society on their own terms. If the educators were to be believed, inner-city parents would have to accept an argument that the schools in their communities had high dropout rates because 60 or 70 percent of their children could not learn. These parents rejected this notion out of hand and began to demand that adequate educational resources be allocated to their children.

During the next decade a body of literature that became known as the "effective schools research" emerged. In response to the reports of Coleman and others, Ronald Edmonds and a number of other researchers found and documented the work of selected inner-city schools where students were meeting national norms and exceeding the traditional expectations for their performance. Edmonds was able to identify five characteristics of these effective schools, and three of these were in direct conflict with the structure of the factory school (Edmonds, 1979). Effective schools had principals (not supervisors) who provided strong instructional leadership in their schools, the teachers expressed high expectations for the achievement of all students, and the staff used frequent monitoring and assessments to tailor the school's instructional resources to the specific learning needs of students. From the perspective of the social justice movement, effective schools research demonstrated that if educational resources were equitably distributed to schools and appropriately allocated to each student, all children could learn.

Running parallel to the effective schools literature was a body of research in industry that found that decentralized organizations with participatory, site-based management were achieving higher quality and better productivity than the old factory model of production. When these findings were combined with the results of effective schools research a strong argument developed for decentralized, school-based management. Hess, in his discussion of Chicago school reform, has documented one of the most dramatic instances in which these forces combined to fundamentally restructure a large urban school system that had actively resisted change (1991b).

The adoption of participatory management in industry is linked to the shift to a postindustrial information economy, which is the second force driving restructuring of schools. During the height of the industrial era and rise of the factory school, manufacturers had a broad spectrum of low-skill jobs requiring little education, and they had a huge labor pool to draw from. In the manufacturing economy at the turn of the century there was no need for a highly educated labor force, and it made little economic sense for very many students to aspire to an education beyond elementary school. Over the last two decades, however, we have had a declining birthrate, which is shrinking the labor pool, and with the rise of the postindustrial economy based on information processing, the delivery of services, and international competition, employers have begun to echo the new slogan of the restructuring movement: "All children can learn." All children can learn, because all children must learn if we are to remain competitive. We can no longer afford high dropout rates and poor academic performance. In this new economy all students must learn at a higher level than they ever have before.

But this is not just a question of acquiring more of the content of the standard curriculum in the factory school. All children must still learn to read, write, add, and subtract, but in addition they must also learn to solve problems, integrate knowledge, and work in teams (Business Roundtable, 1991: 4). In Schlechty's view, children in an information-based economy will become knowledge workers, and this role is fundamentally at odds with school structures in which the teacher is an authority who conveys knowledge as a body of fixed truths to children as passive recipients:

> For many, the *teacher* is synonymous with instructor and conveyor of knowledge. In schools of the future, teachers will not be sources of information; they will be guides to information sources. Too often the word *student* stirs up the image of a child sitting passively, receiving instruction from an adult. In the school of the future, students will produce knowledge, not simply receive it. (Schlechty, 1990: 37, emphasis in original)

Complementing the transformation of the economy we have current research that provides new insights into learning in schools. Howard Gardner finds that children come to school with multiple abilities—"multiple intelligences"—which include seven modes of symbol use: logical-mathematical, linguistic, musical, spatial, bodily-kinesthetic, interpersonal, and intrapersonal. He finds that since the dominant modes of schooling and assessment focus only on the first two of these, they place restrictions on learning that are not "intelligence fair" or inclusive of all of a student's abilities (Gardner & Hatch, 1989). Lauren Resnick has amply documented the convergence of current cognitive theories about the child's active construction and invention of knowledge. She suggests that theories point toward the need for a psychology of instruction that places the learner's active mental construction of new knowledge at the heart of the instructional exchange (1985: 36). Finally, Lee Shulman's pedagogical content knowledge

> includes an understanding of what makes the learning of specific topics easy or difficult: the conceptions and preconceptions that students of different ages and backgrounds bring with them. . . . If those preconceptions are misconceptions, which they so often are, teachers need knowledge of the strategies most likely to be fruitful in reorganizing the understanding of learners, because those learners are unlikely to appear before them as blank slates. (1986: 11)

This is to say that all children can learn if we restructure schools to be responsive to what we know about cognition and learning. Children have multiple modes for learning, and educators must have multiple instructional responses. Children bring their existing perspectives to school, and they are actively interpreting events and constructing new knowledge while they are there. Effective curriculum and instruction cannot be centrally controlled or standardized; it must be responsive to this active learning. Children possess multiple intelligences and complex bodies of knowledge, which cannot be assessed using a single standardized test. If what we know about learning is combined with what we know about the organization of roles and expectations in effective schools, we should be able to serve all students. "When we fail with a single child or class or school, we must recognize we do not yet have the proper mix of how, where, when, and who" (Business Roundtable, 1991: 4).

Although the effective schools approach to restructuring derives its force from the social justice movement and the learning approach is driven by an information-based economy, it is clear that they mutually reinforce each other. As Dewey (1914) and many others have suggested, active inquiry and the open participation in the construction of new knowledge are essential conditions for a democracy to flourish. Schlechty observes:

> One need not be an admirer of America's corporate leaders (some of whom I admire, some of whom I find abhorrent) to understand that in the information-based society, commitment to human development and creating the conditions of freedom, growth, and respect in the workplace are not simply ethical choices. Investing in people is simply good business, for in the information society, knowledge and the ability to use it are power. And those who have knowledge are the employees. (1990: 40)

The principles of democratic participation, free inquiry, and active learning are also linked to the third force driving school restructuring—a new wave of immigration and increasing demographic diversity. As a consequence of the Immigration Act of 1965, we are now experiencing the largest influx of immigrants since the turn of the century. Sixty-eight percent of these immigrants have been from the Americas and Asia, 16 percent are from Europe, 10 percent are from the Caribbean, and 6 percent are from other continents and Canada. Hispanic-Americans number over 15 million, with communities in almost every major urban center in the country, and the Asian community has more than doubled in the last decade. By the year 2000, nearly one in three Americans will fall within the Census Bureau's designation of "Minority." This demographic shift has already occurred in twenty-one cities where African-Americans, Latinos, and Asians constitute an absolute majority of the local population. By the end of this decade California, Texas, Florida, and New York will become states with "minority-majority" school populations (see Schensul & Carroll, 1990: 341).

These new immigrants bring with them their languages and knowledge, their skills, their history, and their cultural wealth, values, and perspectives. Their children bring the potential for rich cultural and linguistic variation to the schools. Jean Schensul has observed that if this diversity is treated as a national resource, our schools and communities could respond by favoring use of first language in informal settings, teaching multiple languages, and establishing multilingual, multicultural schools. They could draw upon and enjoy the literary, media, and expressive traditions of most of the countries of the world, and they could promote multicultural perspectives in literature, music and the arts, history, philosophy, and the social sciences (Schensul & Carroll, 1990: 343). If this diversity and these ideas are perceived as threats, however, the schools can attempt to ignore all of this by reaffirming allegiance to the perspectives of the original common school curriculum and reembracing its classical intellectual tradition as a standard against which all other cultural traditions can be comfortably rejected as inadequate.

In the higher education community this has become the focus of a grand academic debate. There are those, echoing the concerns of an earlier era, who believe that all of this diversity has become a threat to the future of the republic. They argue that "we" must preserve *The Common Culture*, which turns out to be the classical Western "canon" of the common school. They are attacked, in this debate, by the "canon bashers" or "politically correct," who attribute all things bad in the world to the Western canon and who would replace it with third world perspectives and traditions.

But this is a debate that need not occur. A common culture grows out of the experiences its members share in common—all of its members. A culture is dynamic; its contours are shaped and reshaped by the contributions of all who live it. Contrary to what Eric Donald Hirsch (1987) suggests in *Cultural Literacy: What Every American Needs to Know* and contrary to what the adherents of an Afro-centric curriculum would advocate, a culture is not the static possession of a self-selected group with a particular perspective to be distilled and conveyed to others. If we adhere to the democratic principle that all are entitled to participate in the shaping of our culture—that no one is disenfranchised by differences in language or cultural background—we will learn, as Margaret Mead suggested, that it is possible "to incorporate in a society a very large number of adults, differently reared and with different expectations" (1969: 25–26). Given the range of diversity in this country, it is inevitable that our common culture will be multicultural (Ravitch, 1990: 339).

While the debate rages on the campuses, many public schools have already had to grapple with this issue by developing new programs. Recent immigrants and those who won the right to reclaim their identity through the social justice movement of the 1960s are the new majority, and they expect their perspectives and contributions to the culture to be included in their school's curriculum. Recognizing that it is possible for students to develop the tolerance and sound judgment needed to live in a more complicated world than the timeless social order envisioned in the common school, California has recently announced a statewide multicultural curriculum and dozens of local districts around the country are exploring more inclusive approaches to education. To this end, school-based management, with its participatory philosophy, is making it possible for educators to be much more responsive to their communities. The new learning theories of the restructuring movement make room for the inclusion of children's culturally rich perspectives in the instructional process.

We have seen that, just as they did a century ago, economic, demographic, and social forces are converging to bring about a fundamental restructuring of schools. The factory model of schooling, with its central control and standardization of instruction around a single intellectual tradition, will not meet the needs of the twenty-first century. In its place, we need a wide array of new forms of public schooling with new rules, roles, relationships, and expectations. We need schools in which children become active learners, skillful at constructing new knowledge. We need schools in which teachers will be responsible for orchestrating a wide array of instructional approaches and learning resources in response to the diverse needs of their students, schools where administrators become instructional leaders responsible for networking these resources to support their teachers. We need schools that use multiple forms of assessment to monitor and document student progress, schools that are held accountable for ensuring that all children learn. We need schools that become community centers for learning, where school boards become educational advocates and parents and community leaders become active partners in the educational enterprise because clear roles are defined for them and the necessary resources are made available. And ultimately, we need schools that become a vehicle for the ongoing construction and expression of an inclusive common culture in a multicultural society.

All of this may seem a bit utopian, but the first steps necessary to restructure schools in this direction are already being taken in Chicago, Kentucky, and the dozens of school districts that are working to adopt Comer's community-based school development program, Levin's Accelerated Schools approach, and the principles of Sizer's Coalition of Essential Schools. It took over fifty years to transform the common school into the factory school. Change happens more quickly these days, and the leaders of the restructuring movement have given themselves ten years to dismantle the factory school to make way for the new schools of the next century. It may take longer than they think, but given their commitment and the convergence of economic, social, and demographic forces driving these changes, it is inevitable that these changes should occur.

A ROLE FOR ANTHROPOLOGISTS

As these changes occur, anthropologists have an important role to play in the restructuring movement. Anthropologists are well suited to the study of changing expectations and relationships, and there is a significant need for them to use their expertise in action-oriented research to provide educators with constructive feedback on the quality of education and the progress of improvements in their schools. Without this feedback, it will be easy for some to accept the illusion of change as a substitute for the real changes in roles and rules that are necessary to restructure schools.

The change process is difficult, complex, and long-term. There will be many false starts and hard lessons learned. One-shot evaluation studies, with their focus on unexpected outcomes and embarrassing failures, won't do. Anthropologists should tell it like it is, but they must be prepared to work with educators over the long haul to document the successes as well as the failures. When failure is observed they must be prepared to assist educators as they seek explanations, explore alternatives, and consider new options.

Restructuring will result in widely varying approaches to the creation of new schools. As they study this process, anthropologists should expect this variation and should not apply a single model to determine success or failure. Each initiative should be understood in terms of its own goals, objectives, and setting.

The work of anthropologists in restructuring schools should include training teachers, parents, school administrators, and community leaders in techniques that empower them to analyze and manage the roles, rules, relationships, and expectations that shape their schools. This should include the expectation that significant changes in schooling are complex and will take time. There will be no quick fixes, and a long-term perspective must be established.

Multiple measures for monitoring student learning are essential to restructuring schools. Anthropologists should actively work with educators to develop qualitative assessments to complement the more quantitative techniques that will be in use. This should include observational techniques and descriptive reports that can be included in portfolios documenting student performance.

Finally, anthropologists should actively work with community leaders and educators in multicultural schools to support the construction of an inclusive curriculum that avoids replacing one ethnocentric perspective with another. They should help these schools become cultural democracies where diverse cultural perspectives are nurtured for their contribution to learning.

11 Critical Friends in the Fray: An Experiment in Applying Critical Ethnography to School Restructuring

John M. Watkins

In July of 1989, ten middle and high schools in the early stages of restructuring each sent a team of teachers and administrators to Providence to attend the first part of a year-long training run by the Coalition of Essential Schools (The Coalition, or CES). The Coalition designed the training program, called "The Trek: A Year Long Course of Study," to help teams learn to understand and manage the complex process that is restructuring.

Some assumptions that drove the Trek design were:

- Restructuring change could not be designed or managed from outside.
- The people in the school who were managing the change process would have to develop an approach that was driven by structured question asking and reflection about both the place their school was and the place they could envision it becoming.
- Eventually the team would have to orchestrate the involvement of the whole faculty, administration, and members of the community in a similar and ongoing reflective analysis.

CES also believed that, in the teams' initial stages of learning, to understand and manage that work the teams would need to learn and practice using a research-based framework for looking critically and reflectively at the place their school was and could be. However, CES believed the framework would not succeed unless it resulted in action steps for the school. Thus the framework included learning approaches to planning for and engaging in the complex process of restructuring based on the team's analysis. In addition, teams would need team-building exercises to help them create a setting where valid and effective collaborative inquiry and action could be accomplished.

Teams left the summer workshop with an initial understanding of this framework, with a first cut at plans to begin work in their schools, and with a commitment to visit each other during the year. CES believed those visits would provide an opportunity for the teams to observe each other's schools, interview each other about the work the team had done, and engage in a reflective critique of each other's work and underlying beliefs and attitudes about that work that either supported or impeded the team's progress.

This chapter is about the research strategy embodied in these Trek site visits and the resulting relationships among teams and CES. We have called the relationships "critical friends" and the setting "in the fray" because the work that happened at the site visits clearly demonstrated a powerful format for critical inquiry and collaborative action research, engaged in by insider-outsider teams, focused on beliefs, attitudes, and norms, as well as structural and procedural issues, that resulted in teams devising new theories about their work and their schools that they used to drive new actions in support of restructuring.

BACKGROUND: RESEARCH IN THE SERVICE OF CHANGE?

The research base on school improvement is broad and dismal. After more than a decade and a half of serious improvement effort, schools are pretty much the same places they have been for almost a century. Teachers struggle to engage in meaningful educational work with too many students to know their needs well, too fragmented a schedule to focus on sustained and serious work, and little time to engage in professional exchange about educational matters with their colleagues. Students' lives in school are segmented, chaotic, and unfocused. For the most part, they spend their time being shuffled and sorted; at best, some succeed in mastering the system. Competing priorities constrain budgets and district structures. Decisions about the direction of education are, as often as not, made with little reference to improving student learning. A century of unexamined beliefs about education and the role of schools in society has ossified into an ideology that defines teachers as task performers who are intellectually dependent upon others for their knowledge. Too often, schools turn out students who are systematically de-skilled and unable to ask their own questions or direct their own learning. Positive change under these circumstances is extremely difficult. Blaming one group for disempowering another in such a system is futile. Single-strategy solutions ignore the deep underlying structures of power, influence, and unexamined ideology that keep such a system in balance.

When we do ask about change to improve learning for all students, the research base tells us that we know more about what doesn't work to change schools than what does (cf. Cuban, 1990). The self-critical reflection that could stimulate change is not supported by the model of schools that makes teachers assembly-line workers unreflectively assembling students who are viewed as passive products. The school improvement movement only reinforced those beliefs by giving teachers new tasks to perform within the same structures and patterns of belief and insisting that change be viewed as an individual process rather than a redesign of the system. Because they have been thought of as receivers of tasks to perform in an organization where there was little need for collegial coordination, teachers have remained for the most part isolated. That isolation has made it even harder for the kind of dialogue to develop that would enable reflection and reflective change. And as workers in segmented organizations, school people have not been able to look systematically at their own school as a system, as it is now, as a way of understanding why it should change, how it could change, and what resources there are to support change. Finally, school people, community members, policymakers, and researchers alike have lacked a sense of the effect of their own personal unexamined beliefs and actions on the maintaining of the status quo.

The same ideology that makes teachers intellectually dependent has created an immense gulf between researchers and practitioners. That gulf has meant that people in the midst of the difficult work of change in schools have had little access to work of researchers that might help them. Researchers discuss why their research does not better help schools change. School people puzzle over why the research they do read seems so impenetrable and irrelevant, abstract and vague, or simplistic and out of touch with real school problems. Most research on school improvement has involved outside researchers looking at specific improvement projects in order to generalize to the larger education and policy community about the success of such efforts. What is generalizable is often unavailable to schools when they need it, for fear that reporting early results or emerging issues will contaminate the study or just because the traditional research process is slow to reach generalizable conclusions. When information is finally available, it is often too late.

Most research in schools continues to be structured around outside researchers looking in on improvement efforts or outside-inside partnerships looking at individual practice. There is very little research on large-scale or organizational change in schools that takes an action orientation, where a research partnership between outsiders and insiders looks at organizational as well as educational practices, beliefs, and structures with the intent that the research process itself would directly effect change. Over the past few years, a methodological and theoretical debate has grown about such research in education (Anderson, 1989), yet actual examples do not abound.

The ten schools that took part in the first Trek experimented with such an approach, derived from the methods of critical inquiry (Sirotnik, 1991), critical ethnography (Anderson, 1989), and collaborative action research (Whyte, 1984). This partnership brought school teams together with CES facilitators to use an action-oriented research framework to understand and manage the first stages of restructuring in the teams' schools and to critique each other's understandings and efforts by attending site visits held at each other's schools periodically throughout the year. Our use of critical inquiry, critical ethnography, or collaborative action research methods to inform and drive restructuring is in an early and experimental stage; however, the results are promising.

The Trek was based on acknowledging the limitations of an outside, non-school-based group (CES) in helping a school to manage its own change process. It emphasized the benefit of peer critique, feedback, and assistance in developing specific strategies for and an understanding of change (from other schools participating in the Trek). It included periodic checkpoints (through the use of site visits) during a year after a workshop to ensure that participants were able to use what they learned in the workshop to best advantage back in their schools. While CES could provide the school teams with general information about change and change management strategies, and could do so while attempting to create an atmosphere conducive to the teams becoming researchers into their own work and beliefs about it, CES could not predict beyond general categories what specific issues teams would need to address in order to be successful at understanding and managing the early stages of restructuring in their schools. Thus the Trek was also based on the idea that outsiders could provide general frameworks for change that, by being linked with insider knowledge of day-to-day details, understandings, personalities, and the anomalies of a particular school, could result in a significantly more powerful understanding of and ability to manage complex change.

The Research Base for the Trek and Its Consequences for the Trek Design

The Trek resulted from an analysis of the early experiences of Coalition schools with change, the analysis of the first CES workshop on change, "Facing the Essential Tensions: Restructuring from Where You Are," and an extensive review of the literature on school and organizational change, team building and teamwork, critical inquiry and action research, and outside assistance in change management (see Watkins & Lusi, 1989, for a more complete summary of this research).

Our design for the Trek would have to create a "curriculum and pedagogy of change" that fit the philosophy of the Coalition. Thus it would be inquiry-based, focusing on "essential questions" about both the status quo and the change process, require the "students" (in this case, the Trek teams) to be the workers, and be assessed through "authentic" means, in this case, the trial by fire of teams being the real managers of change in their schools and subjecting their work to critique in site visits from critical friends. Such a design would have to address the failures of the school improvement process to result in improved learning conditions and the failures of the research on improvement to result in action alternatives for both policymakers and school people. Yet the design would have to take advantage of what that research told us worked and didn't work to change schools and, as well, benefit from the identified conceptual frameworks to help begin focusing the inquiry process. The Trek would have to lead team members through activities that overcame the culture of isolation and silence in schools and create the possibility of real, substantive, and accurate communication. It would have to move beyond the orientation to change of innovation implementation to look at the whole organization and the cultural attitudes that bound activities in it and do so by moving teams beyond a task orientation to an inquiry approach. It would need to enable the teams to engage in the painful process of examining how their own attitudes kept real change from happening.

Our review of relevant literature to aid our design was thus necessarily action-oriented and for that reason not bounded by traditional disciplines and not exhaustive within disciplines. Our search took us through the literature on school improvement and the school improvement change process, the use of ethnographic methods to study school culture, the application of qualitative methods to the change process in schools and in industry, and more recent attempts to define strategic, conceptually focused, and flexible planning approaches to the complexity of restructuring. Certain of the studies we reviewed stood out.

A recent article revisiting the Rand study of school improvement efforts in the 1970s (McLaughlin, 1990), although unpublished at the time of our design work for the Trek, clearly summarizes many other studies' findings on the supports and constraints to school improvement. David Crandall, Jeff Eiseman, and Karen Seashore Louis (1986) serve to complete a picture of both the school improvement process and the situation of schools trying to change using it. Beverly Anderson and Pat Cox (1988) and a 1986 draft version of Louis and Matt Miles (1990) both expand upon the school improvement literature by generalizing from it to make recommendations for the success of larger-scale, more complex change efforts. Anderson and Cox present a model of cycles of diagnosis, visioning, and acting that fits with the older Kurt Lewin model of action research (1964) and modifies it to account for the need for a focusing vision and a flexible and participatory planning process to deal with the complexities of large-scale change. Louis and Miles describe categories that combine dynamically to affect a complex change effort and thus serve as guideposts or predictors for success. Together, these provide much of the basis for the Trek framework and analysis tools described below.

Because of their focus on describing change, the school improvement studies miss rich descriptions of the dynamic systems of structurally reinforced and communicated power, authority, values, and meaning making that define schools as cultures. Ethnographic studies of schools such as those reviewed in Kathleen Wilcox's 1982 work provide powerful reminders of what factors both inside schools and in the outside society keep schools the way they are. Critical theorists take the ethnographic process beyond interpreting meaning to look at the ideological determinants of culture and the possibility for communication that moves beyond the ideological. Eric Bredo and Walter Feinberg (1982), in their introduction to critical theory, helped us to rethink the change process from a critical perspective. Critical ethnographic approaches, again summarized in an article that was published after our design for the first Trek (Anderson, 1989), enlarge the scope and role of ethnography beyond description and into effecting change. Yet for the most part even the critical approaches do not describe a participant-driven research process. Critical ethnography, combined with participatory methods, would provide a powerful means to examine life as it is and could be in schools in ways that would directly effect change, we believed.

Thus we sought out methods that were more explicitly participant-driven. William Foote Whyte's 1984 work and, in particular, Whyte's references to the work of Max Elden describe an approach to participant-driven inquiry and change that strongly influenced our design. Thinking through the consequences for his own expertise and success as an outside researcher and consultant, Whyte realized that "[m]y success could deprive [participants] of opportunities to learn how to solve their own problems" (1984: 166). Both Whyte and Elden began to see the researcher as a colearner with participants who were capable of developing theories about their own organization, collecting and analyzing their own data, developing their own recommendations, implementing changes, and analyzing the results. Elden referred to this process as the "democratization of the change process" (1979: 249, in Whyte, 1984).

Whyte and Elden's work on workplace redesign and participatory action research as an approach to change led us to seek out methods being used by school people that were similar; hence our review of teacher research. Two studies will stand for that part of our review. One (Evans, et al., 1981) captures the critically important process that teachers must go through to make the shift from thinking of themselves as unskilled task performers to skilled inquirers and details the kind of setting that is necessary for that transformation to occur. The other (Miller, 1987) tells of a teacher-researcher group that resulted in clear insights into reflexive methods and emancipatory processes, both of which are crucial to the success of the Trek design.

Ken Sirotnik's 1991 work on critical inquiry in schools describes a process that parallels Whyte's and mirrors our own thinking about cycles of inquiry and action similar to Anderson and Cox's and Lewin's. Sirotnik uses cycles of questions to guide the inquiry process: What is currently the case in our school? How did it come to be that way? Whose interests are and are not being served by things being this way? What information do we have or need to get that bears on the situation? What are we going to do about it?

Sirotnik's work does not provide for the complexities of the planning and implementation process that the school improvement studies describe; both his and Whyte's work miss the organizational change perspective; Whyte's organizational change perspective doesn't capture the full dynamics of a strategic and aligned organizational change process. We found in Noel Tichy's 1983 work a more complete description of diagnostic procedures and approaches to managing an organizational as opposed to merely curricular change process.

The analysis of this research led the Trek designers to come to the conclusion that an outside-inside partnership involving peer teams and CES staff could best provide the settings for reflective change management. We drew conclusions from this work that suggested approaching restructuring by enhancing the ability of schools to become learning organizations. We characterized this approach as "action research" and "critical inquiry." Our conclusions showed us that collaboration was an important strand in effective reform. We attempted in the Trek to find specific and concrete approaches to learning about the complexities of schools and school change that acknowledge that complexity, but in such a way that it is the specifics of a particular school that need to be understood and it is the people in the school that need that understanding. Finally, we have realized from this work that what people engaged in change need and want is learning that grows out of and is oriented toward action. The characteristics of an approach that meets these criteria are:

- It is team-based, preferably composed of both insiders and outsiders, who help to provide perspective; teams also provide experiential settings for designing new systems of beliefs and ways of communicating.
- It makes purposeful and productive use of reactivity, designed feedback.
- It has developed reflexive processes, the reciprocal examination by both insiders and outsiders of their beliefs, habits of thought, values, and assumptions about their work and the structures of power and influence that surround and define the values at the base of that work.
- The participants learn from the process of designing the research agenda and gathering and analysis of data, as well as from the results of that analysis.
- The process of data collection, analysis, and action is iterative; successive stages increase the sophistication of grounded theory, thus the potential for contributing to change.
- Collaboratively built theory on actions, beliefs, and structures is collaboratively tested in action, by the researchers actually doing things differently in the research setting.
- Its main goal is understanding that aids action.

(cf. Watkins & Lusi, 1989: 35–37)

We cannot stress enough the interaction of research and action. In this approach, research is action, because by researching, we are doing something that changes us. Reciprocally, action is research, because as we build a learning community, we are experimenting with new ways of doing things and watching the process self-critically as it unfolds. We are engaging in a series of successive approximations, modifying our theories about our work as we go, and trying again. This is the same way a qualitative researcher develops grounded theory in the field, except that here the researchers are the participants and the grounded theory is tested by thinking about and doing things differently, rather than just thinking about things differently.

THE STRUCTURE OF THE TREK WORKSHOP AND SITE VISITS

The Trek consists of a summer workshop and three site visits throughout the school year. The five-day summer workshop is organized around an action research framework of structured activities to help teams ask, and explore possible answers to, questions about the place their school is and could be. The framework focuses on:

1. Diagnosing the organization of the school (e.g., examining its structures; educational goals; daily experience of students and staff; the school culture, including attitudes, beliefs, and habits that underlie its work; and the school's progress in articulating and implementing the nine Common Principles of thc Coalition).
2. Building a shared vision.
3. Developing, acting on, reflecting about, and modifying plans for change.
4. Team building.

The framework defined categories where the teams looked: their current school structures, school cultures, daily experience, and educational goals (diagnosis). Teams used the same categories to look at their ideal school (visioning). Finally, teams used the framework to plan coherent strategies to move from the diagnosed to the envisioned school (planning, acting, and reflecting). Besides categories to help teams focus their data collection, the framework provided two "lenses," structured ways of analyzing what they found in those categories. One lens enabled them to build conceptual maps by looking at the underlying logic (priorities, assumptions, and compromises) connecting all of these different parts of their school. The second approach helped teams examine the framework categories through the multifaceted lens of conditions, events, and processes that research on large-scale change has identified as necessary for success (e.g., active, positive principal support, existing or developed collegiality, shared vision, shared power, the use of teams, clear decision-making procedures), thus helping the teams to build causal maps of the change process. Teams practiced using this research framework, but CES facilitators asked them to examine their experience reflectively, because they would need to re-create the process with their school staffs in order to expand involvement and create ownership in their school and community. Repeating cycles of diagnosis, visioning, and planning/acting/reflecting would define the action research process.

Team building helped the team learn a set of norms, procedures, and processes for doing valid and efficient group work focused on inquiry. This type of validity was an essential component of site visits, enabling the teams truly to engage in critical inquiry and serve as "critical friends." We designed the team-building activities to mirror how teams work with real, day-to-day problems, focusing on developing an understanding of communication, decision making, and the ways groups assign roles for tasks.

Teams got to know each other through large group team-building activities, group discussions, critiquing each other's plans in smaller groups, and various other formal and informal activities. The teams left with a shared experience, a familiar framework, and a plan (that had been critiqued by other teams) to begin a reflective change process in their school. The team had itself become a tool for change because of the team-building work, such that when the complexity and turbulence of change assaulted them they could respond from a solid base. Combining the team-building experiences with the tool of the framework enabled the team to engage in structured reflection about their work and their own personal reactions to it. Thus they returned to their school with an approach to change that balanced using a framework and using the team, that focused on changing structures and actions but also on changing understandings. With this initial training and practice, we believed the teams would have less of a tendency to apply the framework in a mechanistic way.

Research on technical assistance (Center for New Schools, 1977) suggests that workshops alone have limited impact on the actual, day-to-day work of participants and thus on long-term change. Also, analysis by designers of the 1988 CES summer workshop on change, "Facing the Essential Tensions: Restructuring from Where You Are," suggested that the schools involved wanted and needed structures that would support ongoing feedback to school teams about their work from peers and CES staff (Watkins & Lusi, 1989). Thus to support continued development of the skills that teams practiced at the summer workshop and to encourage specific, concrete feedback, problem solving, and critique, CES asked teams participating in the Trek to host a site visit at their school and attend two site visits at other teams' schools. The site visits were structured to help the school teams and Coalition staff to serve as "critical friends" for each other, critiquing each other's work and the assumptions that either supported or impeded their effectiveness.

Site visits involving CES representatives and other Trek teams provided the setting for enacting the collaborative action research criteria described above. The school teams were able, because of their daily involvement with both the research process and the actions resulting from it, to look more closely at their experiences in trying to use an action research framework to aid their restructuring effort; visiting teams were able to view the host team's work from a critical perspective, experiencing the same issues, but not necessarily restricted by the same ideologies; CES representatives were able to look more broadly across schools to identify general themes, as well as differences among teams' approaches. Each critiqued the others' work.

At least two Trek teams from other schools attended each site visit, along with a CES representative and myself as a participant/observer. The teams examined the plan and the work of the host team and their theories about that work, as well as impressions and concerns from others in the host team's school and community. The assembled group analyzed what they had found, through reflection, feedback, critique, problem solving, developing new theories, and generating new plans for actions arising from those theories. Visiting teams returned to their schools with new perspective on their work and new strategies. The host teams went back to work with new understanding and plans for action.

Six of the ten schools held site visits; eight schools attended them. Held in November, January, February, April, and May of the 1989–90 academic year, the site visits averaged two and a half days. Each school designed its own format and schedule; however, most site visits included a dinner meeting the first night to review the host team's plan and set focus questions and agendas for the visit. A day was spent in the host team's school observing classes, talking to other teachers and students, meeting formally and informally with teachers, board members, and district personnel, collecting documents, and reviewing the team's and the school's progress. The final half day teams used for collective analysis, identifying and elaborating on themes or problems encountered, providing feedback, troubleshooting, and discussing strategies.

The Schools

The ten schools attending the first Trek came from Delaware, Pennsylvania, Illinois, and California. There were six high schools, three middle schools, and one junior-senior high school. Two high schools and one middle school were urban inner-city, zoned schools; the rest served suburban mixed socioeconomic, suburban white upper-middle-class, and rural mixed communities. Four had between 1,000 and 2,500 students; the rest had between 350 and 850 students. Some were considered successful schools by themselves and their districts; others were admittedly struggling with serious problems. All had decided by their vote that change related to the nine Common Principles was worth spending a few years actively considering.

Nine schools were members of Re:Learning, a collaboration between CES and the Education Commission of the States. Each school applied to join Re:Learning by a 75 percent vote of its faculty. The vote commits the school to a year of planning discussions and activities, followed by three to four years of work to begin restructuring the school, based on the nine Common Principles of the Coalition. Each school receives from $30,000 to $50,000 per year from the state to support its change work, attends Coalition workshops and institutes, and receives some support from the Coalition. Each state has a Re:Learning coordinator who oversees all Re:Learning schools in the state. Most Re:Learning schools have a coach to work directly with them.

The Teams

CES asked schools to send a team of at least three people, "represent[ing] different levels or functions within the school . . . [or] . . . district," at least one of them a teacher. Those people would "return . . . [with] concrete tasks to be carried out in your school" and should be "willing and able to engage in the work." The Trek brochure further stated: "The team should demonstrate leadership, energy, creativity, and commitment to change. They should begin the Trek with the understanding that there will be substantial work involved throughout the year. Your school should be willing to support this work." One school, which did not come as a full participant, sent only two people; five of the schools sent three people; one sent four; two sent five; one sent six. Eight schools sent their principal, one a school board member. Two sent an observer from a local university as part of their team. None included students.

METHODS FOR THE TREK TEAMS' CRITICAL INQUIRY AND MY STUDY OF THE SITE VISITS

How is it that the Trek teams were in fact part of a critical inquiry research team and not just superbly (or not so superbly) managed informants? The answer to that question lies in the answer to three other questions: Who did the work? Who owned the questions? What role did I play as an outside researcher? A description of the methods we used may answer all three.

This section of the chapter describes two levels of data collection and analysis and will suggest that there are significant role changes for outside researchers working with school teams who are doing collaborative critical inquiry. The teams, CES facilitators, and I took part in site visits where we collaboratively collected and analyzed data for the benefit of the teams and their schools to answer their action research questions with a critical inquiry approach. I attended all the site visits as a member of the larger critical friends team and thus in a role as outside coinquirer into the team's work, as a facilitator of conversations that centered around the sometimes painful and difficult issues that critical inquiry brings to the surface, and to gather data for this description and analysis of the Trek site visits and critical friends relationship. I gave my data and interim analytic memos to the teams to provide them with another external critique of their work, but that process also was designed to generate feedback to me about my evolving study. Teams then engaged with me in analysis and critique of transcripts from the site visits and my memos about them.

The primary sample for the teams' inquiry at site visits was the work of the team in its school, how that work was regarded by other people in the school and community, and the site visit discussions of the host team's attitudes and beliefs about their work. The teams gathered data that included interviews with team members and others (including students) in the host team's school, observation of the team during the site visit, observation of classes and other parts of the school, documents produced by the host team, documents about the school, such as master schedules and school improvement plans, and examples of curriculum design work and student work.

The primary sample for my study of the site visits was the school teams and the CES representatives who attended each site visit, although I did gather some data about each school for context and to be able to understand the work of the teams in their schools. My data collection included observation notes, documents, and transcripts from site visit meetings between teams and from meetings with other teachers, administrators, parents, and school board members in each school, observation notes from classroom visits, other school documents concerning the restructuring effort, responses to a questionnaire given to CES representatives who attended the site visits, and responses to a questionnaire circulated to team members at the end of their first year of work.

Site visits, analytic memos about them, and subsequent meetings scheduled to review transcripts from and the analytic memos about the site visits made it possible for me to feed these data back to the teams in a collaborative analysis process, thus aiding teams to revise their action plans based on a more thoroughly triangulated set of conclusions about their work. Acting on their plans, the teams were able to test their theories about what was going on and what would work and thus gather data for a new round of analysis. Thus the findings from the teams' collaborative critical inquiry process at site visits and from my early analytic memos were about the work of the teams in understanding and managing the change process and about their ability to engage in critique of each other's work at site visits and served to help them improve their work directly.

We developed questions collaboratively, with considerable overlap between what the teams wanted to know and what I needed to understand the site visits. We gathered data together and triangulated our analyses to answer questions both about the ongoing work of teams and about the general process and degree of success of the critical friend site visits. This process was neither as formal nor as explicitly framed in formal research language as one might assume. The self-consciousness of teams about their role as researchers varied considerably. If I could redesign one part of the process, it would be to emphasize more explicitly the formal inquiry aspect of the critical friend relationship.

The consequences of this approach for outside researchers are significant: they must reframe their thinking about researcher control and research design. Collaborative critical inquiry is messy at best. Researchers must become facilitators of others' question-asking process. They must be willing to engage in the political process of negotiation of the meaning of data, while also being willing to speak the unasked questions in ways that make it possible for teams to confront them. They must be willing and able to teach research design and methods while learning new and creative methods for doing inquiry from the teams. They must be willing to model reflexivity, step down from their traditional position of power and "objective" remove, and become part of the dialogue.

WHAT HAPPENED AT SITE VISITS: CRITICAL INQUIRY OR SCHOOL IMPROVEMENT?

In actual practice, there is a very fine line between the Trek approach and the traditional school improvement team approach. If teams or facilitators emphasize the framework and team-building process as a set of activities to be performed religiously by the team and repeated with their school staffs back home, then we are responsible for teams becoming de-skilled, as has traditionally been the case with teachers and students; they gain no insight into developing their own framework and question-asking process. They go home and assess the strengths and weaknesses and readiness to change of their schools, use the framework as a crutch to structure their tasks, take on a couple of the weaknesses as a focus for work in the first year, and fall into a school improvement mentality once again. The results are predictable. If, on the other hand, the facilitators and the teams can see the framework and team-building activities as a springboard, a scaffolding upon which to begin building their own question-asking process and change work structured by it, then true critical inquiry, a true curriculum of change, has begun, and it is self-sustaining and enlarges to meet the inquiry needs of the participants. Both of these alternatives happened with the first-year Trek teams. Most of the site visits represented excellent examples of critical inquiry at work, while the ongoing work of teams in their schools in between site visits looked less like critical inquiry and more like school improvement. In subsequent years, as the numbers of facilitators and schools involved have grown and the activities and rationale have been refined by CES and Re:Learning states, I am afraid that the number of Trek teams and facilitators who view the Trek as more similar to the familiar school improvement team process has increased.

During the first year, there were significant examples of teams developing questions and theories about those questions that were tested through data collection, analysis, and new actions. Teams were able to move their schools forward in various areas as a result of their involvement with the Trek, and in particular with the Trek site visits and the critical friend relationships that grew out of the Trek. Trek teams became effective at taking on the tasks of understanding and managing change through a process of inquiry. At site visits the conversation centered around these inquiry-oriented tasks, identifying problems in the work of the teams and theories about that work. One theory that emerged in the teams' thinking about their work as the year progressed was that there were overlapping or expanding phases in the growth of understanding and actions of the teams.

Those phases include the following eight arenas.

Becoming a Team and Making Mistakes

Most of the changes that occurred for Trek teams were the result of the team working to become an effective team that could then use the Trek framework to help it understand and manage change. Managing change created problems in the team's school (both from teams doing good work and from teams making mistakes), resulting in difficult situations that visiting teams diagnosed at site visits. The visits featured productive conversation among teams in which they developed strategies for overcoming the problems collaboratively. Trek teams and site visits provided settings for serious, experiential leadership development during the year. As one team member described the team-building process, "We had all 'worked together' for years, but we had not really ever worked *together*. The openness was not there before we went to the Trek. There we learned we could express ourselves, disagree, and not take it personally. We were able to deal with our emotions and our feelings and still keep on-track."

Early site visit conversations among teams centered on figuring out exactly what the role of the teams was in their schools and on figuring out what the purpose of the site visits was. "It's not a regional accreditation visit," said one participant. Another added, "I know we don't have a specific task here, and as teachers we are used to having a lesson plan, but I don't want Brown University telling me what to do; we have to figure this thing out on our own!" The teams became more visible in their schools as they developed various means of communicating better with (not to) their peers, orchestrated activities to involve people, and made decisions. They became more aware of the dynamics at work that make the larger school the place it is, including understanding the dynamics that keep the school from changing. They then examined ways to get around those dynamics to change things.

At the midpoint in the year, many team members expressed puzzlement about the difference between their own personal changing and the changing of the whole school as a synergistic system. They were beginning to become comfortable with their own personal change process, but the dynamics of managing change in the whole school created much discomfort for many. They were forced to move beyond thinking of change only in very individual and personal ways and into thinking about the whole. This change in their thinking did not negate their thinking about the need to support change in individuals but represented an enlarged conception of the requirements of complex change. At the same time (and not paradoxically), the team members became very aware of their own habits of thought that kept change from happening and thus were able to predict concerns in the rest of the school that the team would need to address.

Talking Together about Education

Teams convinced their faculties, principals, superintendents, school boards, and parents that providing time and monetary support for the faculty to get together to talk about educational goals, both formally and informally, either during or before or after school, was a worthwhile investment. Teams used the nine Common Principles of the Coalition as a vehicle for many of these early conversations, inquiring in depth into what the principles meant to all of the people assembled. These conversations generated awareness and stimulated people who had often had no opportunity to talk together professionally about matters of substance. They also created conflicts about what the educational goals of the school really were and how best to structure school life to achieve them. This new level of awareness resulted in some increase in tensions. As one teacher put it, "I know as teachers we are used to having a lesson plan. We want to know where we are going and when we are going to be there." Talking just to get at ideas without a clear task to accomplish or training to be done was a foreign experience in most of the teams' schools. The conversations resulted in people in the school and community having an increased need for information about CES and what "being an essential school" could mean for them.

Providing Information and Improving Two-Way Communication

One of the more complex issues that teams dealt with was understanding their role in providing information and improving communication. In part this problem centered around an old ideology that characterizes the teacher as the deliverer of instruction, standing in front of the class filling students with knowledge. The teams began their work in most cases with the assumption that it was their responsibility to be in charge of "getting all the information out to people." On two site visits, visiting teams identified situations where the host team was taking on too much responsibility for producing the ideas of the change project and then inventing a variety of ways to "disseminate" them. Visiting teams later heard that people felt purposely excluded, left out of the loop, uninformed, uninvolved, and fearful of what the future might hold.

Orchestrating Involvement—Inventing and Experimenting

When teams tried to start getting people in their schools into the loop of communication, one of the consequences was that people wanted to get involved. The teams had to orchestrate a variety of kinds of involvement. Much conversation at site visits centered on appropriate ways to get people thoughtfully involved without saying, "This is what IT is; now go do it." How to involve the community (and other groups) also became an issue for the teams. Some teams used Trek-like activities to get parents and faculty members involved in thinking about Coalition ideas, rather than just doing presentations. The teams have been extremely creative about developing and sharing strategies for increasing involvement; we as outsiders could not have predicted all of these strategies.

Decisions, Decisions

When people started to want to get involved, it forced the teams to make decisions about deploying their peers. Teams were initially extremely reluctant to make these decisions. Making decisions in an arena where there is high visibility and significant consequences for errors was frightening. One principal on a Trek team thought he was helping the team to become better at shared decision making by remaining silent when the team was having trouble with making decisions out of a lack of skills and fear of offending colleagues. As teams discussed this situation at a site visit it became clear to them that the skills and expertise of all the players were needed for the success of their shared decision-making venture, including those of principals.

The teams made mistakes in how to make decisions; visiting teams told this to host teams. Yet the teams were aware of how difficult this new responsibility was and talked openly about it at site visits:

> I'm scared. As a person who thought that she wanted change, now that we're making decisions about what it's really going to look like next year, I'm really scared. Are we moving too fast? It's a lot of

responsibility. Why am I taking all of this on? I'm just a teacher, and all of a sudden I'm making decisions about school structures that will affect my peers.

Redefining Implementation

Teams increasingly came to see implementation in a very different way from the traditional school improvement model. Implementation evolved into a coordinated set of experiments, individual, small group, and even "pilots," so long as this "pilot" was not the only show in town. They envisioned their role as keeping experiments consistent with the evolving shared vision and keeping communication going among the various experimenters and with the rest of the faculty. As one team member put it, "People in the school are talking about 'they' and it's got to be 'our.' You need interested parties watching how the pilot works. Instead, if they don't feel involved and interested, they will be looking for what's wrong with it, taking potshots. The team will be out on a limb." Representatives from this school discouraged other teams from designing an implementation plan that included only a pilot team. Such a plan puts too much pressure on a small group of people, they felt.

This communication across experiments and with people who may not be ready to dive into change but are possible to recruit as "critical observers" made possible the collecting of information, discussion, analysis, and reflection about what helps best to move the people in the school toward fully incorporating the nine Common Principles into their daily life. What really got implemented by Trek teams was a process for continued planning, experimentation, and analysis, driving new experimentation, with the evolving vision helping guide the effort.

On Being Reflective

One structure and norm that the Trek tried to inculcate in teams was to take time and create a team culture that encouraged critical reflection on both the process and the content of their work together. In fact, teams did reflect on their own work and beliefs more and more as the year progressed. They seemed to find understanding their own concerns helpful in figuring out how to help others in their schools deal with theirs. That is the case in this person's thoughts:

> I have tried to think back about what our mind-set was about CES and change before the Trek and how that has changed this year through the Trek. I wonder if that will help us to understand and empathize with the feelings and thinking of others who are uninvolved? Could we use that to understand the mind-set of the faculty? Can it help our work with our schools to think about how we have learned what we did and how we have changed?

Analysis of personal reflections helped teams to understand others, but analysis also provided the teams with some valuable insights into the change process. At one site visit, analysis by the teams of their own changes identified a key set of steps that the teams wanted to encourage in the faculties in their schools. Those steps were: openness to understanding, which leads to understanding, then to personal attempts to implement new ideas in the classroom (which someone called personal restructuring), then to experimentation, and then to structural or schoolwide restructuring.

The Role of Critical Friends

> I think having it happen with groups from other schools is important . . . because it is easier to take constructive criticism from outside than from your colleague, and then once you get open to this, then you take it back to your school and you work together.

That is a fair characterization of the role of critical friends, spoken by a team member during a site visit. Another person said:

> Part of the value for us in our school was to see the contrast between what we thought the teacher concerns were and what in fact the visiting teams discovered were really the teacher concerns. There were some surprising differences.

Second only to the question of whether the teams continued to engage in inquiry was the problem of the stubbornness that attaches itself to the fear of opening up the process to everyone in the school. Over and over again teams pointed out to each other the presence of rationalizations about not getting others involved. Over and over they fell prey to their own rationalizations about the same fear. In most of the schools, this fear impeded the team from seeking out people who were resisters and finding ways of engaging them and addressing their concerns. In some instances, this fear was disguised by concern for keeping the process manageable by keeping the numbers down. In one case, the fear was so strong that it kept a school from hosting a site visit with other Trek teams. In another case, this fear resulted in the team not involving the general faculty in thinking and making decisions about the direction of their essential school plans and in not involving key decision makers in the choices of who would be on a pilot team the coming fall and what the curriculum content of their work would be. The predictable result of this strategy was that people reported a general feeling of disempowerment (their word) in the school. Visiting teams identified all of these problems, and all of them became the focus of brainstorming sessions where teams developed strategies for overcoming them. In most cases, the teams seem to have adopted at least some of the proposed strategies, with increased success.

Over time, the visiting teams evolved a way of working together with the host team to discuss all issues as they arose. That meant that the eventual "critical friend presentations" emerged out of a common discussion and were framed within the host team's decisions about the focus of the visit, informed by the host team's contextual knowledge, and presented in such a way that they were not a surprise to anybody. However, at one site visit, the host team proposed a different structure: the visiting teams would deliberate privately before presenting their findings to the host team. This so unnerved the visitors that they did not know what to do. The force of their critique petered out in their own private discussions, and the final presentation was weak. The host team asked why the visitors had not requested a different format; the visitors had assumed that there wasn't the flexibility to redesign things. The host team had assumed that a stronger critique would happen if the visitors could talk together openly and assumed that the visiting teams wouldn't talk together as openly if the host team were there. Too many assumptions spoiled the stew.

DISCUSSION

The eight frames described above were generated by teams during site visits as they developed theories about their work together as critical friends. These frames suggest that the teams were able to create a rich and subtle environment at site visits within which to keep inquiring into and improving each other's work. In each category, teams visiting and critiquing each other were able not just to diagnose mechanical or structural problems, but to uncover attitudes and beliefs that impeded or aided the teams' effectiveness. They were able to use reflection on their own experiences to predict their colleagues' concerns and design ways of supporting them. They engaged in problem solving and shared strategies for moving their schools forward in the work of restructuring. Their need to focus on the concrete in order to keep restructuring alive in their schools pushed them to experiment with ways of acting in areas that we, as outsiders, could identify as important in only a fairly abstract way. Being peers, having the same experience of the summer workshop and the Trek framework to help structure their work, and having no evaluative power over each other all contributed to the success of the site visits, in their estimation. By modeling facilitation and contributing to keeping the agenda focused on being critical friends, our presence as outsiders helped. But without the interactions of the teams, the site visits could not have been anywhere near as powerful and productive as they were.

Yet one of our hopes is that the critical reflection and peer critique that form the basis for Trek teams' site visits can truly become the cornerstone of cultural self-consciousness and thus of cultural change. Cultural self-consciousness can expose the ideologies that underlie the structures and procedures that have kept schools the places they are, places that sort and de-skill rather than places for learning. To get at those issues, critical reflection must move beyond the micro level that Wilcox identifies as historically the domain of ethnography and take on the "structures and processes at the level of the large-scale social aggregate" that affect "life in schools" (Wilcox, 1982: 478). Little of the teams' reflection on and critique of the Trek site visits or Trek teams' work in their schools demonstrated this shift to the larger domain. As frank and critical as the dialogue at site visits was, clearly more interpersonal comfort, sense of safety, and competence at communication are necessary to move to this next level of work.

12 Through the Eyes of Anthropologists

G. Alfred Hess, Jr.

In this concluding chapter, I attempt to step back from the specific studies included in this volume to gain some perspective on the various efforts now being implemented to restructure America's schools. I also attempt to examine the role of anthropologists in affecting educational policy and the wider networks that will be required if more fruitful connections between anthropologists, other qualitative researchers, and policy actors are to be forged.

ASSESSING SCHOOL RESTRUCTURING EFFORTS

The seven case studies included in this volume have examined different efforts to restructure our nation's schools. True to the ethnographer's bias toward a participant's view of each reform effort, each chapter assesses the developments in the city or state being studied on the basis of the aims of the particular effort. Thus, in one sense, the studies judge the cases on their own criteria. They are ground-level studies using the local criteria as a basis for assessment. But the effort to restructure American education is broader than simply a set of independent experiments. To assess the efforts from a larger, policy-relevant perspective requires adopting a set of criteria that supersedes local goals.

During the latter part of the 1980s, the debate about education reform focused more and more sharply upon the effect of various reform efforts to improve the levels of educational achievement by our country's children. There is a wide debate still raging about how student achievement should be assessed. Some simply focus on results on standardized tests.

Others add a series of other easily quantifiable goals: graduation rates, success in enrolling in college or securing a job, attendance rates, discipline rates, and grade retention rates. Still others prefer measures still under development to assess critical thinking skills and other arenas of competence, emphasizing student essays and portfolios of performance. But however it is measured, there is an emerging consensus that the most important criterion for judging school restructuring efforts is improvement in the levels of student achievement.

Shifting from Inputs to Outcomes

This emphasis on student achievement is in sharp contrast to the traditional approaches of assessing school systems that dominated most of this century. In most states, school accreditation and accountability still focus upon the adequacy of the various components present in a school or a school system. Teachers, or at least most of them, are expected to be properly certified by the state and to be teaching grades and subjects for which their certification applies. Facilities should meet safety codes. Libraries should have the requisite number of books. Schools should provide enough courses for their students to meet state graduation requirements. And if a state wants to toughen its standards, it typically raises the number of required courses or tries to increase the educational credentials necessary to become a teacher. The assumption behind this approach is that if all of the requisite inputs are in place, then differences in student outcomes reflect differences in the students themselves. It is also assumed that all of these resources function in roughly equivalent ways from school to school.

Research over the last several decades, however, has called these assumptions into question (Brookover & Schneider, 1975; Brookover & Lezotte, 1979; Edmonds, 1979; and Purkey & Smith, 1983). Schools with similar inputs are sending forth students with very different outcomes. The well-accepted belief that the primary determinant of these different outcomes was the social and economic class of the families from which the students came (Coleman, et al., 1966) was disputed by the same scholars. Based on comparative studies of schools with similar enrollments of students, these scholars identified some schools as more effective than others, even when the resources at the schools were similar.

If differences in resources and differences in students did not account for the differences in student achievement, then differences in the ways schools operated must be important. Without disputing the importance of family background, these scholars asserted that schools do make a difference! They began to compile a set of characteristics that distinguished effective schools from ineffective ones. Unfortunately, their efforts to turn ineffective schools into more effective ones were less successful.

The new emphasis on outcomes, however, was enthusiastically embraced by politicians and businessmen. It gave politicians a vehicle for holding school people accountable for the billions of dollars states annually provide to local school districts across the country. To the business community, an emphasis on outcomes sounds like something akin to a "bottom-line." But to school people, teachers, principals, district administrators, and the like, this outcome emphasis sounds like schools are being likened to manufacturing plants and students reduced to products. It is probable that most teachers today still would say, "If I come to school every day and teach to the best of my ability, what else can I do? If my students don't learn, it's their problem, not mine!"

Thus one of the struggles behind the effort to restructure America's schools is the struggle to get agreement to the premise that it is proper to evaluate schools on the basis of the achievement levels of their students. This standard, with appropriate allowances for differences in student characteristics, has been widely accepted by politicians, the business community, voters, and most academics. But it is a standard that has not yet been widely accepted at the school and district level, as Muncey and McQuillan point out. Thus there may be a fundamental disagreement about the goals of policy reforms being mandated from above but implemented at the local level. Reformers and policymakers are focused on raising student achievement levels, while school-level educators think they are being as successful as can be expected. This is an important element of school reform implementation that should be more closely examined in future assessments.

Whatever its acceptance at the local level, improvement in student achievement is clearly one of the primary national goals of education reform. To date, there is little evidence that either teacher or parent empowerment efforts can be directly linked to improvements in student achievement. Most of the restructuring efforts are too new to be assessed on the basis of such a criterion. In a recent study, my colleagues and I showed that we could predict, with nearly 90 percent accuracy, which students would eventually drop out of high school on the basis of second-, third-, and fourth-grade attendance and academic data (Hess, Lyons & Corsino, 1989). Thus even if a school district could dramatically improve its primary grades this year, it might be eight years (when the current fourth-graders might be expected to graduate) before dropout rates reflected that success. Other indicators, such as yearly test scores, attendance rates, and grade retention rates, might begin to improve more quickly than that, but the cumulative effect of formal schooling is such that large-scale changes on these quantifiable measures can only be expected to appear after a number of years have passed. Most of the current cases are too new for such assessments.

The longest operating school-based management schemes of recent vintage, excluding the Salt Lake City experiment (cf. Malen & Ogawa, 1988), are the Hammond, Indiana, and Dade County (Miami) teacher professionalization efforts. In Hammond, all schools have been participating in shared decision making since 1987. In Dade County, about half the schools now voluntarily participate in the shared decision making model. In neither district has there yet been a significant improvement in student achievement levels.

More significant claims to improving student achievement have been made for reform initiatives in Pittsburgh; Cambridge, Massachusetts; and New York's East Harlem (District 4). In Pittsburgh, Superintendent Richard Wallace (1986) claims that curriculum readjustment and the retraining of all teaching personnel have resulted in student test scores moving from well below the norm to above the sixtieth percentile. Similarly, in Cambridge and East Harlem, student scores have increased dramatically, though administrators in both cases ascribe the difference to expanded enrollment choice (Peterkin & Jones, 1989; Fliegel, 1989). However, Harrington and Cookson contend program differentiation is a better explanation of the East Harlem success. To date, there are little systematic data showing widespread improvement in student achievement from statewide choice programs, most of which are also only recently implemented. The most radical of the choice programs, Milwaukee's voucher plan, has only been in operation for a matter of months and incorporates too few pupils (less than 500) to demonstrate much more than the legal issues involved in establishing such a plan.

ISSUES EMERGING FROM CASE STUDIES

While it is much too soon to apply student achievement improvement criteria to the restructuring efforts described in this volume, these case studies do raise a series of important issues. Some of these issues relate to conceptual or design flaws in the restructuring efforts that may seriously hamper any significant effect on school instruction and student learning. Other issues represent key contradictions that must be overcome if the reforms are to have a significant impact.

Is Curriculum Change Adequate?

One question is whether altering the curriculum of instruction, either in changing the ways in which math and science are taught or in narrowing the course offerings of secondary schools to focus on the essentials, will radically change the way students learn. The evidence from McGee Brown's studies points to more incremental change than radical alteration, though there are some very interesting developments, such as extending the school day through a bus curriculum, that bear further examination. Such an approach raises some interesting questions of equity. Do all students receive an equal additional opportunity? Is it appropriate that those students who are most inconvenienced, in terms of having the longest rides to school, are the ones who most are exposed to this additional opportunity?

What about Teachers' Vested Interests?

Another, somewhat related, concern is whether schools can overcome the vested interests of teachers and other school personnel in order to produce better school outcomes. Evidence from the efforts of the Coalition of Essential Schools shows how difficult it is for this to happen. Teachers in noncore subjects were reluctant to give up their specialties in order to more narrowly focus on the essential core. In fact, many rejected this differential evaluation of different specialties. In one Chicago high school, not part of the CES network, when the Local School Council president sought to reduce the number of vocational course requirements in order to broaden the precollegiate offerings, the vocational and technical teachers mounted such a fierce counterattack that the LSC president was discredited and stripped of virtually all of his power. If school restructuring means that some teachers or other school personnel either will lose their jobs or will be forced to completely change what they do on a daily basis, it is unlikely that such approaches will be undertaken voluntarily or accepted without significant coercion.

To date there is little evidence that teacher empowerment approaches, whether of the Coalition's variety or the shared decision making variety in Miami and Memphis, ever will have a significant impact upon the wide range of students and their levels of achievement. There is the very real possibility that teachers will be more concerned to use their new roles in decision making to assure better working conditions for themselves, regardless of the impact on students. Inherent in such questions is the internal conflict between reform initiatives designed to enhance the professional status of teachers and the heritage of many teacher unions, which have frequently been more identified with blue-collar worker concerns than those of a professional association.

A frequently noted problem in shared decision making, the lack of planning time for teachers, may be a prime example of such a conflict. As Daniel Brown notes (1990: 173, citing Alexandruk, 1985: 49), "When teachers were asked to nominate *weaknesses* of school-based management . . . leading the drawbacks was the *time demands*, mentioned by 22 percent of teachers" (emphasis in the original). In Chicago, we found principals emphasizing exactly this concern: where do they find the time to do all the things required under school-based management? Yet many parents and some principals have complained loudly about teachers who bolt out the school door only minutes after their students leave but then complain that school-based management is demanding too much time.

One of the conflicts between professionalization and blue-collar unionism is the attitude toward time. For those professionals not billing clients for their time, professionalism frequently means working to the needs of the job, regardless of the time involved. Such professionals regularly work more than forty hours per week without additional compensation. Such professionals are being compensated for their skills and what they accomplish, not for the hours they sell their employers. By contrast, most unionized blue-collar workers sell their time and negotiate over what they should be expected to accomplish during that time. Additional time is sold at an additional price. How teachers and school systems resolve this conflict about the use of time will indicate much about the potential for professionalization approaches to school improvement.

It should be noted that most client empowerment approaches to restructuring start from a position of some antipathy toward teacher unions. Choice notions are frequently associated with explicitly antiunion postures. In the United States, voucher advocates frequently make the comparison that private schools educate students for significantly lower costs than do public schools and imply that an open market system would, therefore, be less costly. Essentially, that posture is a de-unionization position, though frequently unacknowledged as such. To their credit, Chubb and Moe (1990: 48f) are more explicit in their argument that teacher unions are one of the primary problems in public education, driving up costs, forcing incentive-deadening work rules, structuring the teaching role in overly rigid ways, and depriving principals of managerial discretion. Similarly, both the Chicago parent-empowering school-based management scheme and the East Harlem alternative schools program grew out of frustration with union activities. Thus one sharp difference between the teacher professionalization model and the client empowerment models of school-based management and choice is in their posture toward educational professionals. Can they be empowered to surmount the classic limitations of blue-collar union-management confrontation, or should they be challenged to be more creative by holding them more closely accountable to their clients?

Correspondingly, a question that must be answered by the client empowerment model of school-based management is whether the potential client-professional confrontation can be managed in such a way as to win the collaboration of professionals in seeking to improve what happens in classrooms. Ultimately, improvement in education must involve changes in the ways in which teachers and students are interacting. If principals and teachers are not enlisted as active partners in the school improvement process, it is unlikely that much significant change will happen in the classroom (cf. McLaughlin, 1978).

In one sense, the two major restructuring strategies represent two halves of the same apple. Both focus on the relationships among the various major actors in the educational process: principals, teachers, students, parents, and community representatives. The teacher empowerment strategy focuses on teachers and their relationships to their principals and, secondarily, district administrators, while downplaying teachers' relationships to parents and largely ignoring their relationships to members of the community who do not have children in school. In this sense, the teacher empowerment strategy tends to remain a school-bound strategy. The parent or client empowerment strategy focuses on parents and community members and their ability to hold teachers and principals accountable for their performance, either directly through management councils or indirectly through market forces. As Don Moore has powerfully argued, this strategy encompasses the many other "teachers" of students who are not formally employed by school systems. It is a strategy that is not restricted to the formal educational system. This is an important distinction in many inner-city neighborhoods, where the public schools are seen more as colonial outposts of a hostile mainline culture rather than as community institutions (cf. Williams, 1981). Tom Carroll has explained the historical background of the current disconnection between schools and their communities. Still, the two restructuring strategies are not necessarily hostile to each other and are not necessarily mutually exclusive.

Will Local Actors Know How to Improve Schools?

However, behind these concerns about the interactions of actors in the school improvement process lies the question: will professionals know what to do to improve schools? This author's personal experiences with school-level educators prompts more skepticism than optimism on this question, despite the fact that there are some very creative and knowledgeable teachers and principals in the Chicago Public Schools. Outside observers have come to a similar conclusion. Chester Finn and Stephen Clements have been periodically observing the implementation of school reform in Chicago and, on the basis of contacts with a small group of schools, raise the following caution:

> What concerns us is whether this new system, once fully born, will be able to put into place a radically altered educational vision, a profoundly different set of ideas about teaching and learning, school organization and process, curriculum and pedagogy, student assessment and parent participation. (1990: 6)

This concern is equally applicable to the various teacher empowerment and parent empowerment reforms we have been discussing here.

It is to this point that the Pittsburgh plan is so applicable. With leadership from the top of the administration, the school system in Pittsburgh set out to completely retrain its professionals *before* it embarked upon school-based management. It assured itself that its professionals had been exposed to better ways of operating schools before it asked these professionals to take over their management in more autonomous ways. It must be noted that one of the preconditions for the professionalization model to work, whether in Pittsburgh or Hammond or Miami or San Diego or New York, is that there must be top-ranking professionals who are willing to risk greatly in order to improve their schools. Where such leadership is lacking, as it was in Chicago, citizens might be forced to take action themselves. When they do, a client empowerment approach is more likely to be adopted.

Is Authority Shared, Devolved, or Both?

Another notable difference between professionalization models and parent empowerment models is the issue of devolution of authority. There is nothing inherent in the professionalization model that requires altering the current levels at which various decisions are made. There are various mechanisms through which various types of professionals may be included in the decision-making process at all levels of a school system without changing the locus of authority within the hierarchy (i.e., teachers and principals might be involved in districtwide governing committees that still make decisions affecting all schools in the system). In fact, in most professionalization models, as Hanson and her colleagues note for Dade County, there is relatively little new authority invested in school-level decision making and rarely is there any significant reallocation of funding. In the Chicago reforms, a conscious effort was made to reallocate resources to the school level and to attend to the equitability of the resources available at each school. While there is nothing in the professionalization model that would prevent the devolution of authority and resources, neither is it implicit in the approach that such would happen.

Can States Force Change?

Finally, the question still emerges, can a state mandate wholesale change? The conclusions of William Firestone, Susan Fuhrman, and Michael Kirst (1991) in the Center for Policy Research in Education (CPRE) are more doubtful than hopeful. This volume contains two such examples of state-mandated restructuring. In Kentucky, the early evidence indicates a great diversity of response by local districts to state-mandated reform. The financial aspects of the reform effort appear to have been much more easily implemented than either the governance changes (involving school-based management) or the curricular changes (including moving to ungraded primary schools by 1991–92). In Chicago, where governance and finance changes were mandated but curricular change only encouraged, it is not yet clear that large numbers of schools will significantly change the way in which students learn. The school district was forced to alter the way it allocates its resources and the authority of local school personnel has been enhanced, but only a portion of the system's schools have yet taken advantage of the opportunity to change their basic operations.

Major restructuring efforts are under way in cities across the United States. It will be some years before conclusive quantifiable data will be available to assess their success or failure in improving the achievement of our nation's students. In the interim, policymakers will continue to look to implementation studies, such as those included in this volume, to provide some sense of how restructuring is faring and whether midcourse corrections are required. The need for such studies provides an important opportunity for educational anthropologists.

ROLES FOR ANTHROPOLOGISTS

Anthropologists have not been widely involved in the major educational policy debates in the United States during the last half century. Those who have been active have frequently done so through other guises: as sociologists of education, graduate school professors of education, state board of education researchers, or school reform activists. There are few vehicles for anthropologists, within their own discipline, to actively engage in policy formation, assessment, or critique. When anthropologists are so engaged, there are few avenues to report on their doings to others within the discipline. It is much easier to share their efforts through education, political science, and sociology journals than within anthropology. Journals in anthropology seem to be peculiarly abstract, uninterested in the major policy issues being debated in our country, and inappropriately self-congratulatory.

Yet, as Tom Carroll has pointed out, anthropologists bring important values and skills to the policy formation process. Policy debates tend to be heavily dominated by rhetoric about what a projected policy promises to accomplish and by studies of the outcomes that have resulted. Frequently omitted from this debate is much evidence about how these policies actually were being implemented, what problems were being encountered, and what, if any, midcourse corrections might have been appropriate to help particular policies be more successfully implemented. Such implementation studies provide a special opportunity for anthropologists and other qualitative researchers. One of the strengths of ethnographic research is its ability to describe *what* is actually happening as policies are implemented, *why* various actors in the implementation process are acting as they are, either to make the implementation successful or to frustrate it, and *how* these actors are doing what they are doing. The case studies in this volume are examples of the value of such qualitative approaches to the implementation of school restructuring reforms.

Without such implementation studies, politicians and the general public are quick to jump to premature conclusions about the viability of particular reforms. As one of the persons deeply engaged in the school reform movement that culminated in the adoption of the Chicago School Reform Act of 1988 and yet acknowledged locally as one of the knowledgeable but still objective observers of the implementation of the reform effort, I am asked ten or fifteen times a week, "Well, how's reform going? Is it successful?" As the case studies in this volume indicate, the question of success cannot be answered adequately in Chicago or most other cities for another three or four years at a minimum. But policymakers, the media, and the public want more immediate assessments.

While it is too early for quantifiable measures, during the process of policy implementation, those engaged in studying that process can discuss whether the policy is being implemented in the fashion that was envisioned or whether it is already off-track and encountering unforeseen impediments. They can also provide context for the problems encountered in implementing any change in policy: are these the problems envisioned in the policy design, or are they unanticipated obstacles? And as the final results begin to become available, these implementation studies can help to answer the *why* question: why was the policy successful, or why was it unsuccessful? Was the policy the wrong policy? Was it undermined by unanticipated opposition? Was the policy appropriate but the implementation design faulty? Did other, unrelated events intrude to create an impossible situation or to guarantee success for a policy that otherwise might have failed miserably? Is the policy replicable in other settings, or was it successful because of a unique and idiosyncratic set of circumstances that are unlikely to be duplicated elsewhere? These are important questions, frequently overlooked in the political judgments about adopted policies, which are best answered by qualitative research.

Focus on Policy-Relevant Issues

To seize this opportunity, there must be a body of qualitative researchers whose primary focus is on the major policy issues being debated in our nation. Successful qualitative research is cumulative, not a side foray away from an otherwise unrelated academic career. It requires a body of policy-focused researchers who exchange information about the implementation of various policies over many years. But in contrast with meetings of sociologists, political scientists, and educational researchers, a review of the schedule of a typical meeting of anthropologists reveals a dearth of such topics. When such topics do appear on the agenda, they frequently deal with the fringes of major policy debates, focusing on the impact of major policies on small, exotic subgroups, while ignoring the impact of the policy on the major component populations of our society. If anthropologists are to become an important factor in the policy arena, there must be a change in the nature of our discussions when we meet together, which will in turn require a change in the types of research we do and the ways in which we report on that research. Currently, it would appear that health-oriented anthropologists are ahead of educational anthropologists in this regard.

Objectivity and Policy Research

In Chapter 11, John Watkins argues for a more involved research methodology than that which typifies the more traditional positivistic research orientation. He argues for a research strategy that engages those being studied in the research process itself, a kind of mutual studying of each other under the rubric of "critical friends." Others have much more adequately reviewed the literature on research methodology than we can do in this volume (cf. Howe & Eisenhart, 1990, and the scholars Watkins cites), but it seems evident that significant participation in policy formation, assessment, and alteration requires more commitment and less detachment than does academic research focused on expanding basic knowledge. I leave to others the argument that basic knowledge development also requires a more critical methodology than that supported by positivistic assumptions. My own career has been substantially shaped by Jean-Paul Sartre's (1970) observation that "one knows the world by seeking to change it." Such a sentiment is a hallmark of most policy-relevant research and has far-reaching implications for research methodologies, perspectives, and ethics (cf. Deyhle, Hess & LeCompte, 1992).

In my own experience in public-school-oriented research in Chicago, effective policy-relevant research requires a combination of the roles of advocate and reliable researcher/informant. Policymakers and those shaping their opinions and actions need reliable information that is accurate and timely and appropriate to the decisions they are facing. But they also require advice about how that information should be used. They need recommendations as to what should be done about the policy problems that such research seeks to address. Policy-relevant research is not policy-neutral. It leads toward the making of policy decisions that settle upon one possible action or set of actions while eliminating others. Frequently such decisions are not made on the basis of ultimately demonstrable truth, but in response to the best choice among feasible current alternatives, which may later be succeeded by other, (hopefully) better alternatives. This means that policy-relevant research is regularly assessing the relative value of various policy alternatives or seeking to expand the available alternatives by proposing new ones. In policy-relevant research, everyone has a position. Reliable policy research examines all of the possibly relevant data and assesses their impact on the policy decisions to be taken. Less reliable policy-relevant research allows the researcher's advocacy position to shape what information is included and what omitted. Thus for policy-relevant research, the question is the reliability of the researcher to include all relevant materials and the integrity of the researcher to not seriously distort the interpretation of the data included. For policy-relevant research, the question is not the complete disinterest of the researcher, but his or her reliability and integrity. One of the values of the case studies included in this volume is that they demonstrate the possibility of reliable research performed with integrity by interested observers.

Networking with Other Qualitative Researchers and Policy Activists

Anthropologists are unlikely to ever dominate the field of policy-relevant research. Few senior members of the discipline have serious interests in this direction, and the wide scope of the discipline, including every nook and cranny of man's culture, does not lend itself easily to the more focused arenas of public policy formation. Thus it is critical for anthropologists interested in policy research, in addition to forging new opportunities for policy-oriented exchanges within the discipline, to develop and expand the network of interchange with other qualitative researchers and policy activists.

Most anthropologists now engaging in policy-relevant research are already engaged in such networks. Frequently their works appear in the journals of other disciplines, their research is reported in the annual meetings of other disciplines, and their writings draw heavily upon the work of their nonanthropological colleagues. Not infrequently their anthropological identity is unknown or is subservient to their identity in these related fields. Within the discipline, such cross-field networking and identification create barriers to communication and a degree of marginalization. Anthropologists frequently describe themselves as a tribe; many experience it as a tribe that is fairly exclusive and frowns on mongrelization. Thus the irony is that for anthropologists to be more intimately involved in the policy arena, they must expand their networks of relationships beyond their own discipline, which, in turn, may engender the suspicions of their colleagues who remain in the more traditional mainstream of the discipline.

POLICY AND PLACE, THE STRENGTH OF QUALITATIVE RESEARCH

Policies are sometimes designed in the rarefied atmospheres of political think tanks or may be fashioned in the hard give-and-take of political skirmishing. They may be created by the programmatic decisions of bureaucratic administrators or emerge from the negotiations between employees and management. In most cases, policies are created at some distance from the locations where they must be implemented. Rarely can any policy or set of policies take into account all the possible elements that may affect their implementation. But policies, ultimately, must be implemented in particular places, in particular circumstances, and by specific persons.

As the case studies in this volume show, the strength of ethnographic research is in describing what happens in local situations and in explaining how the policy is implemented. In addition, qualitative research, combining observation of events and interviewing of the major actors in the process of implementation, has an advantage in explaining why things happen the way they do. Qualitative research allows Muncey and McQuillan to tell us much more than that Elliston High School withdrew from its participation in the Coalition of Essential Schools. They were able to detail the deterioration of faculty attitudes from tolerance of the actions of the CES advocates, to doubt, to outright opposition, and, thereby, to raise serious concerns about the inattentiveness of the CES strategy to the potential for divisiveness within the faculties of schools in the Coalition. Responding to this research, Coalition replication efforts now focus more directly on these issues, as Watkins shows.

Similarly, Coe and Kannapel, by analyzing carefully the actors in one small rural school district in Kentucky, are able to point out that the Kentucky Education Reform Act, for all its good intent in attacking the politicization of schooling in that state, may have focused on the wrong problem, nepotism, when the real problem was patronage through cronyism. And in East Harlem, Harrington and Cookson, by recounting the history in which one of them personally participated, are able to sort out the appropriate causes of school improvement in that district. By doing so, they assign a more accurate value to the role enrollment choice played in that district, which counters some of the rhetoric of choice advocates.

Studying the implementation of policy at first hand, qualitative researchers are able to give policymakers a better understanding of the problems and progress local actors are having as they struggle with putting the policy into practice. They help policymakers to see needed correctives and to have patience when the public and the media demand unreasonably quick judgments about the effectiveness of recently adopted policies. But to provide such assistance, qualitative researchers have to participate in the policy debates, be aware of the critical issues being discussed and decided, and find appropriate venues to examine the policies being implemented. Then they must be willing to make interim reports long before they are ready to produce a final product—reports that, by their appearance, may alter the implementation the researchers are studying. As Watkins notes, such involved research is messy indeed. But it is the kind of messy research that policymakers need in order to make, or refrain from making, important policy decisions. Would that more researchers were willing and able to participate in this field.

Bibliography

AASA/NAESP/NASSP School-Based Management Task Force. (1988). *School-Based Management: A Strategy for Better Learning*. Washington, DC: Authors.

Adler, Mortimer J. (1982). *The Paideia Proposal*. New York: Macmillan.

Alexandruk, F. (1985). School Budgeting in the Edmonton Public School District. Unpublished master's thesis. University of Alberta, Edmonton.

Alvarado, Anthony. (1991, April 30). Letter to the Editor. *New York Times*.

American Association for the Advancement of Science. (1989). *Project 2061: Science for All Americans*. Washington, DC: Author.

Anderson, Beverly, & Pat Cox. (1988). *Configuring the Educational System for a Shared Future: Collaborative Vision, Action, Reflection*. Andover, MA: Regional Laboratory for Educational Improvement of the Northeast and Islands, and Denver, CO: Education Commission of the States.

Anderson, Gary. (1989). Critical Ethnography in Education: Origins, Current Status, and New Directions. *Review of Educational Research, 59* (3): 249–70.

Ayers, William. (1989). *The Good Preschool Teacher*. New York: Teachers College Press.

Barker, Bruce. (1985). Curricular Offerings in Small and Large High Schools: How Broad Is the Disparity? *Research in Rural Education, 3* (1): 35–38.

Barth, Richard. (1979). Home-Based Reinforcement of School Behavior: A Review and Analysis. *Review of Educational Research, 49* (3): 436–58.

Becker, Rhoda M. (1984). *Parent Involvement: A Review of Research and Principles of Successful Practice*. Washington, DC: National Institute of Education.

Berman, Paul, & Tom Gjelten. (1983). *Improving School Improvement: An Independent Evaluation of the California School Improvement Program*. Berkeley: Berman, Weiler Associates.

Bitner, Betty L. (1990). Year-long In-service Science Workshop: Changing Attitudes of Elementary Teachers toward Science and Science Teaching. *Research in Rural Education, 6* (3): 53–58.

Blank, Rolf K. (1990). Educational Effects of Magnet High Schools. In William H. Clune & John F. Witte (Eds.), *Choice and Control in American Education: Vol. 2. The*

Practice of Choice, Decentralization and School Restructuring (pp. 77–110). London: Falmer Press.

Bradford, David L., & Allan R. Cohen. (1984). *Managing for Excellence*. New York: John Wiley & Sons.

Bredo, Eric, & Walter Feinberg. (Eds.). (1982). *Knowledge and Values in Social and Educational Research*. Philadelphia: Temple University Press.

Bronfenbrenner, Urie. (1974). *A Report on Longitudinal Evaluation of Preschool Programs* (Vol. 2). Washington, DC: Office of Child Development, Department of Health, Education and Welfare.

Brookover, Wilbur B., & Lawrence W. Lezotte. (1979). *Changes in School Characteristics Coincident with Changes in Student Achievement*. East Lansing: Michigan State University.

Brookover, Wilbur B., & Jeffrey M. Schneider. (1975). Academic Environments and Elementary School Achievement. *Journal of Research and Development in Education, 9*: 82–91.

Broudy, Harry S. (1961). *Paradox and Promise*. Englewood Cliffs, NJ: Prentice Hall.

Brown, Daniel J. (1990). *Decentralization and School-Based Management*. New York: Falmer Press.

Bryk, Anthony S., Valerie E. Lee & Julia L. Smith. (1990). High School Organization and Its Effects on Teachers and Students: An Interpretive Summary of the Research. In William H. Clune & John F. Witte (Eds.), *Choice and Control in American Education: Vol. 1. The Theory of Choice and Control in American Education* (pp. 135–226). London: Falmer Press.

Business Roundtable, The. (1991). *Essential Components of a Successful Education System*. Washington, DC: Business Roundtable Education Public Policy Agenda.

Carnegie Forum on Education and the Economy. (1986). *A Nation Prepared: Teachers for the 21st Century*. New York: Author.

Carroll, Thomas G. (1990). Who Owns Culture? In Thomas G. Carroll and Jean J. Schensul, (Eds.), Cultural Diversity and American Education: Visions of the Future. *Education and Urban Society, 22* (4): 346–55.

Center for New Schools. (1977). *Summary: Assistance Strategies of Six Groups That Facilitate Change at the School/Community Level*. Washington, DC: National Institute of Education.

CES Committee on Evaluation. (1988). *Report of the Committee on Evaluation of the Coalition of Essential Schools*. Providence: Coalition of Essential Schools.

Charron, Elisabeth H. (1987). Influences of Classroom and Community on Youths' Understandings of Science. Unpublished doctoral dissertation. University of Georgia, Athens.

Chicago Panel. (1988). Illegal Use of State Chapter I Funds. Unpublished paper distributed by the Chicago Panel on Public School Policy and Finance.

Chicago Public Schools. (1990). *The School Improvement Plans of 1990: What the Schools Will Do*. Chicago: Report of the Department of Research, Evaluation, and Planning, Chicago Public Schools.

Chicago Tribune. (1990, August 15). "Fuzzy" School Plan Rejected. Sec. 2: 1, 8.

Chubb, John E., & Terry M. Moe. (1990). *Politics, Markets, and America's Schools*. Washington, DC: Brookings Institution.

Clark, Reginald M. (1983). *Family Life and School Achievement: Why Poor Black Children Succeed or Fail*. Chicago: University of Chicago Press.

Coalition of Essential Schools, The. (1985). *Prospectus*. Providence: Brown University.

Coe, Pamelia, & Patricia Kannapel. (1991). *Report on Survey of the Initial Impact of the Kentucky Education Reform Act*. Charleston, WV: Appalachia Educational Laboratory.

Coe, Pamelia, Patricia Kannapel & Pamela Lutz. (1991). *Initial Reactions to the Kentucky Education Reform Act in Six Rural School Districts*. Charleston, WV: Appalachia Educational Laboratory.

Cohen, David. (1988). Educational Technology and School Organization. In Raymond Nickerson & Philip Zodhiates (Eds.), *Technology and Education: Looking toward 2020* (pp. 231–64). Hillsdale, NJ: L. Erlbaum Associates.

Coleman, James S., Ernest Q. Campbell, Carol J. Hobson, James McPartland, Alexander M. Mood, Frederic D. Weinfeld & Robert L. York. (1966). *Equality of Educational Opportunity*. Washington, DC: Government Printing Office.

Collins, Robert A. (1988). *Interim Evaluation Report: School-Based Management/Shared Decision-Making Project, 1987–88, Project-wide Findings*. Miami: Dade County Public Schools, Office of Educational Accountability.

Collins, Robert A., & Marjorie K. Hanson. (1991, January). *Summative Evaluation Report: School-Based Management/Shared Decision-Making Project, 1987–88 through 1989–90*. Miami: Dade County Public Schools, Office of Educational Accountability.

Coons, John E., & Stephen D. Sugarman. (1978). *Education by Choice: The Case for Family Control*. Berkeley: University of California Press.

Courier-Journal. (1990, September 13). Law Shuffles Districts' Revenue, Figures Show. Louisville, KY.

———. (1991, February 19). Council Wants Changes in School-Reform Funding. Louisville, KY.

Crandall, David, Jeff Eiseman & Karen Seashore Louis. (1986). Strategic Planning Issues That Bear on the Success of School Improvement Efforts. *Educational Administration Quarterly, 22* (3): 21–53.

Cuban, Larry. (1988). *The Managerial Imperative and the Practice of Leadership in Schools*. Albany: State University of New York Press.

———. (1990). Reforming Again, Again, and Again. *Educational Researcher, 19* (1): 3–13.

David, Jane L. (1989). Synthesis of Research on School-Based Management. *Educational Leadership, 46* (9): 45–53.

Deming, William E. (1982). *Quality, Productivity, and Competitive Position*. Cambridge: MIT Press.

Designs for Change. (1989). *Shattering the Stereotypes: Candidate Participation in the Chicago Local School Council Elections*. Chicago: Author.

Dewey, John. (1914). *Democracy and Education*. New York: Macmillan.

Deyhle, Donna, G. Alfred Hess, Jr. & Margaret LeCompte. (1992). Approaching Ethical Issues for Qualitative Researchers in Education. In Margaret LeCompte & Judith Goetz (Eds.), *Handbook for Qualitative Research in Education*. New York: Academic Press.

DeYoung, Alan J. (1987). The Status of American Rural Education Research: An Integrated Review and Commentary. *Review of Educational Research, 57* (2): 123–48.

District and School Profiles. Miami: Dade County Public Schools, Office of Educational Accountability, 1987 through 1990.

Domanico, Raymond. (1989). *Models for Choice: A Report on Manhattan's District 4—Education Policy Paper 1.* New York: Center for Educational Innovation, Manhattan Institute for Policy Research.

Dornbusch, Sanford. (1986, Summer). Helping Your Kids Make the Grade. *Stanford Journal.*

Dornbusch, Sanford, Philip Ritter, P. Herbert Leiderman, Donald F. Roberts & Michael Fraleigh. (1987). The Relationship of Parenting Style to Adolescent School Performance. *Child Development, 58* (5): 1244–57.

Drucker, Peter F. (1986). *The Frontiers of Management.* New York: E. P. Dutton.

Easton, John Q., Cheryl Johnson, Jesse Qualls & Darryl Ford. (1990). *Securing Participation of Schools for an In-depth Observational Study.* Chicago: Chicago Panel on Public School Policy and Finance.

Easton, John Q., & Sandra L. Storey. (1990). *Local School Council Meetings during the First Year of Chicago School Reform.* Chicago: Chicago Panel on Public School Policy and Finance.

Edmonds, Ronald R. (1979, October). Effective Schools for the Urban Poor. *Educational Leadership, 37*: 15–18.

Elden, Max. (1979). Participatory Research Leads to Employee-Managed Change: Some Experience from a Norwegian Bank. In International Council for the Quality of Working Life, *Developments in Europe* (pp. 239–50). Boston: Martinus Nijhoff.

Elmore, Richard F. (1978). Organizational Models of Social Program Implementation. In Dale Mann (Ed.), *Making Change Happen* (pp. 185–224). New York: Teachers College Press.

———. (1979). Backward Mapping: Implementation Research and Policy Decisions. *Political Science Quarterly, 94*: 601–16.

———. (1990). Introduction: On Changing the Structure of Public Schools. In Richard F. Elmore and Associates, *Restructuring Schools* (pp. 1–28). San Francisco: Jossey-Bass.

Epstein, Joyce L. (1986, January). Parents' Reactions to Teacher Practices of Parent Involvement. *Elementary School Journal*: 277–94.

———. (1987). What Principals Should Know about Parent Involvement. *Principal, 66* (3): 6–9.

———. (1988). *Parent Involvement.* Baltimore: Johns Hopkins University, Center for Research on Elementary and Middle Schools.

Epstein, Joyce L., & Henry J. Becker. (1982a). Parent Involvement: A Survey of Teacher Practices. *Elementary School Journal, 83* (2): 85–102.

———. (1982b). Teacher Practices of Parent Involvement: Problems and Possibilities. *Elementary School Journal, 83* (2): 103–13.

Etheridge, Carol P., Mary L. Hall, Neely Brown & Sam Lucas. (1990). *Establishing School Based Decision Making in Seven Urban Schools in Memphis, Tennessee: The First Year.* Memphis: Center for Research in Educational Policy, Memphis State University.

Etheridge, Carol P., Lennell Terrell & Johnnie B. Watson. (1990). Teachers, Administrators, and Parents Together: The Memphis Model for Managing Schools through Shared Decision Making. *Tennessee Educational Leadership, 17* (2): 43–48.

Evans, Claryce, Margaret Stubbs, Eleanor Duckworth & Christine Davis. (1981). *Teacher Initiated Research: Professional Development for Teachers and a Method for Designing Research Based on Practice.* Cambridge, MA: Technical Education Research Corporation (TERC).

Fernandez, Joseph A. (1990). Dade County Public Schools' Blueprint for Restructured Schools. In William H. Clune & John F. Witte (Eds.), *Choice and Control in American Education: Vol. 2. The Practice of Choice, Decentralization and School Restructuring* (pp. 223–50). London: Falmer Press.

Finn, Chester E., & Stephen K. Clements. (1990). Complacency Could Blow "Grand Opportunity." *Catalyst, 1* (4): 2–6.

Firestone, William A., Susan H. Fuhrman & Michael W. Kirst. (1991). State Educational Reform since 1983: Appraisal and the Future. *Educational Policy, 5* (3): 233–50.

Fliegel, Seymour. (1989). Parental Choice in East Harlem Schools. In Joe Nathan (Ed.), *Public Schools by Choice* (pp. 95–112). Minneapolis: Institute for Learning and Teaching.

———. (1990). Creative Non-Compliance. In William H. Clune & John F. Witte (Eds.), *Choice and Control in American Education: Vol. 2. The Practice of Choice, Decentralization and School Restructuring* (pp. 199–216). London: Falmer Press.

Ford, Darryl J. (1991). *The School Principal and Chicago School Reform: Principals' Early Perceptions of Reform Initiatives.* Chicago: Chicago Panel on Public School Policy and Finance.

Fowler, William J., Jr., & Herbert J. Walberg. (1991). School Size, Characteristics, and Outcomes. *Educational Evaluation and Policy Analysis, 13* (2): 189–202.

Friedman, Milton, & Ruth Friedman. (1981). *Free to Choose: A Personal Statement.* New York: Avon.

Futrell, Mary. (1989). Mission Not Accomplished: Education Reform in Retrospect. *Phi Delta Kappan, 71* (1): 10–14.

Gardner, Howard, & Thomas Hatch. (1989). Multiple Intelligences Go to School: Educational Implications of the Theory of Multiple Intelligences. *Educational Researcher, 18* (8): 4–10.

Gearing, Frederick O. (1970). *The Face of the Fox.* Chicago: Aldine.

Geertz, Clifford. (1973). *The Interpretation of Cultures: Selected Essays.* New York: Basic Books.

Gittell, Marilyn, Bruce Hoffacker, Eleanor Rollins & Samuel Foster. (1979). *Citizen Organizations: Citizen Participation in Education Decisionmaking.* Boston: Institute for Responsive Education.

Gomez, Joseph J. (1989). Restructuring Means Scaling Obstacles. *American School Board Journal, 176* (10): 20–22.

Goodlad, John I. (1984). *A Place Called School: Prospects for the Future.* New York: McGraw-Hill.

Gordon, C. Wayne. (1978). *Social System of the High School: A Study in the Sociology of Adolescence.* Glencoe, IL: Free Press.

Haas, Toni. (1991). Why Reform Doesn't Apply: Creating a New Story about Education in Rural America. In Alan J. DeYoung (Ed.), *Rural Education: Issues and Practice* (pp. 413–46). New York: Garland.

Haberman, Martin. (1987). *Recruiting and Selecting Teachers for Urban Schools*. New York: ERIC Clearinghouse on Urban Education, Institute for Urban and Minority Education, and Resont, VA: Association of Teacher Educators.

Hall, Gene E., Susan F. Loucks, William L. Rutherford & Beulah W. Newlove. (1975). Levels of Use of the Innovation: A Framework for Analyzing Innovation Adoption. *Journal of Teacher Education, 26* (1): 5–9.

Hampel, Robert. (1986). *The Last Little Citadel*. Boston: Houghton Mifflin.

Henderson, Anne T. (1987). *The Evidence Continues to Grow: Parent Involvement Improves Student Achievement*. Columbia, MD: National Committee for Citizens in Education.

Herenton, William W. (1989). *Proposed Comprehensive Reform Plan*. Memphis: Memphis City Schools.

Herman, Joan L., & Jennie P. Yeh. (1980). Some Effects of Parent Involvement in Schools. Paper presented at American Educational Research Association conference, Boston.

Hess, G. Alfred, Jr. (1990a). A Little Reason about the Question of Choice. *Panel Update: A Newsletter of the Chicago Panel on Public School Policy and Finance, 7* (1): 2–3.

———. (1990b). *Chicago School Reform: What It Is and How It Came to Be*. Chicago: Chicago Panel on Public School Policy and Finance.

———. (1991a). Chicago and Britain: Experiments in Empowering Parents. Unpublished paper presented to the American Educational Research Association, Chicago.

———. (1991b). *School Restructuring: Chicago Style*. Newbury Park, CA: Corwin Press.

Hess, G. Alfred, Jr., & Hilary Addington. (1991). Reallocation of Funds in the Chicago Public School System. Unpublished paper presented to the American Educational Research Association, Chicago.

Hess, G. Alfred, Jr., Arthur Lyons & Lou Corsino. (1989). *Against the Odds: The Early Identification of Dropouts*. Chicago: Chicago Panel on Public School Policy and Finance.

Hirsch, Eric Donald. (1987). *Cultural Literacy: What Every American Needs to Know*. Boston: Houghton Mifflin.

Holt, John. (1964). *How Children Fail*. New York: Dell.

Horn, Jerry G., Patricia Davis & Robert Hilt. (1985). Importance of Areas of Preparation for Teaching in Rural/Small Schools. *Research in Rural Education, 3* (1): 23–29.

Hornbeck, David W. (1990). *Recommendations Related to Curriculum, Adopted by the Task Force on Education Reform Feb. 23, 1990*. Frankfort, KY: Legislative Research Commission.

Howe, Kenneth, & Margaret Eisenhart. (1990). Standards for Qualitative (and Quantitative) Research: A Prolegomenon. *Educational Researcher, 19* (4): 2–9.

Hueftle, Stacey J., Steven J. Rakow & Wayne W. Welch. (1983). *Images of Science: A Summary of Results from the 1981–82 National Assessment in Science*. Minneapolis: University of Minnesota.

Illinois Bell. (1990). *Local School Councils Ideas and Success. Chicago School Reform: Year One*. Chicago: Author.

Jinks, Jerry, & Russell Lord. (1990). The Better Elementary Science Teaching Project: Overcoming the Rural Teacher's Professional and Academic Isolation. *School Science and Mathematics, 90* (2): 125–33.

Keesling, J. W. (1980). *Parents and Federal Education Programs: Some Preliminary Findings from the Study of Parental Involvement*. Santa Monica: System Development.

Kentucky General Assembly. (1990). *The Kentucky Education Reform Act of 1990 (House Bill 940)*. Frankfort, KY: Legislative Research Commission.

Kohl, Herbert. (1967). *36 Children*. New York: Signet.

Kozol, Jonathan. (1967). *Death at an Early Age*. Boston: Houghton Mifflin.

Kutner, Mark A., & Laura H. Salganik. (1987). *Educational Choice in New York District 4*. New York: Education Analysis Center for Educational Quality and Equality.

Kyle, William C., Ronald J. Bonnstetter, Maria A. Sedotti & Donna Dvarskas. (1990). ScienceQuest: A Program That Works. *Science and Children, 27* (8): 20–21.

LeCompte, Margaret D., & Gary A. Dworkin. (1988). Educational Programs—Indirect Linkages and Unfulfilled Expectations. In H. D. Rodgers (Ed.), *Beyond Welfare* (pp. 135–68). New York: M. E. Sharpe.

Lieberman, Ann, & Lynne Miller. (1978, September). The Social Realities of Teaching. *Teachers College Record, 80*: 54–68.

Lewin, Kurt. (1964). Group Dynamics and Social Change. In A. Etzioni & E. Etzioni (Eds.), *Social Change* (pp. 354–61). New York: Basic Books.

Lewis, James. (1990). 101 Questions and Answers about School-Based Management. Unpublished manuscript.

Louis, Karen Seashore, & Matt Miles. (1990). *Improving the Urban High School: What Works and Why*. New York: Teachers College Press.

McGregor, Douglas. (1960). *The Human Side of Enterprise*. New York: McGraw-Hill.

McLaughlin, Milbrey W. (1978). Implementation as Mutual Adaptation: Change in Classroom Organization. In Dale Mann (Ed.), *Making Change Happen* (pp. 19–32). New York: Teachers College Press.

———. (1990). The Rand Change Agent Study Revisited: Macro Perspectives and Micro Realities. *Educational Researcher, 19* (9): 11–16.

McPike, Liz. (1987). Shared Decision Making at the School Site: Moving toward a Professional Model—An Interview with Patrick O'Rourke. *American Educator, 11* (1): 10–17, 46.

Malen, Betty, & Rodney T. Ogawa. (1988). Professional-Patron Influence on Site Based Governance Councils: A Confounding Case Study. *Educational Evaluation and Policy Analysis, 10* (4): 251–70.

Malen, Betty, Rodney T. Ogawa & Jennifer Kranz. (1990). What Do We Know about School Based Management? A Case Study of the Literature. In William H. Clune & John F. Witte (Eds.), *Choice and Control in American Education: Vol. 2. The Practice of Choice, Decentralization and School Restructuring* (pp. 289–342). London: Falmer Press.

Manhattan Borough President's Task Force on Education and Decentralization. (1987). *Improving the Odds: Making Decentralization Work for Children, for Schools, for Communities*. New York: Author.

Marburger, Carl L. (1989). *One School at a Time*. Columbia, MD: National Committee for Citizens in Education.

Martin, Brian, Heidi Kass & Wytze Brouwer. (1990). Authentic Science: A Diversity of Meanings. *Science Education, 74* (5): 541–54.

Massey, Sara, & Jeannie Crosby. (1983). Special Problems, Special Opportunities: Preparing Teachers for Rural Schools. *Phi Delta Kappa, 65* (4): 265–69.

Mead, Margaret. (1969). *Culture and Commitment.* New York: Natural History Press/Doubleday.

Meier, Deborah W. (1991, March 4). Choice Can *Save* Public Education. *Nation*: 266–71.

Memphis City Schools SBDM Advisory Council. (1989). *Guidelines for Local School Councils.* Memphis: Memphis City Schools.

Miller, Janet. (1987). Researching Teachers: Problems and Emancipatory Potentials in Collaborative Studies. Paper presented at American Educational Research Association annual meeting, Washington, DC.

Miller, Mary Helen, Keven Noland & John Schaaf. (1990). *A Guide to the Kentucky Education Reform Act of 1990.* Frankfort, KY: Legislative Research Commission.

Moore, Donald R. (1991a). *A Surefire Plan for School Reform Success.* Chicago: Designs for Change.

———. (1991b). Chicago School Reform: The Nature and Origin of Basic Assumptions. Paper presented at the American Educational Research Association conference, Chicago.

Moore, Donald R., & Suzanne Davenport. (1989). *Excerpts from the New Improved Sorting Machine.* Chicago: Designs for Change.

———. (1990). School Choice: The New Improved Sorting Machine. In William L. Boyd & Herbert J. Walberg (Eds.), *Choice in Education: Potential and Problems* (pp. 187–224). Berkeley: McCutchan.

Moore, Donald R., & Arthur A. Hyde. (1979). *Educational Equity and Parent and Citizen Involvement in School District Financial Decisions.* Washington, DC: National Institute of Education.

———. (1981). *Making Sense of Staff Development: An Analysis of Staff Development Programs and Their Costs in Three Urban School Districts.* Washington, DC: National Institute of Education.

Moore, Donald R., Sharon Weitzman Soltman, Lois S. Steinberg, Ularsee Manar & Dan S. Fogel. (1983). *Child Advocacy and the Schools.* Chicago: Designs for Change.

Morris, Donald R. (1991). Initial Patterns and Subsequent Changes in the Staff Characteristics of SBM/SDM Pilot Schools, Relative to Those of Non-Participating Schools. Paper presented at the meeting of the American Educational Research Association, Chicago.

Murphy, Joseph. (1990). *Restructuring America's Schools.* Charleston, WV: Appalachia Educational Laboratory, and Nashville: National Center for Educational Leadership.

Nachtigal, Paul. (1991). Rural Grassroots School Organizations: Their Agendas for Education. In Alan J. DeYoung (Ed.), *Rural Education: Issues and Practice* (pp. 395–412). New York: Garland.

Nathan, Joe. (1989). *Choosing Our Future.* Minnesota: Institute for Learning and Teaching.

National Commission on Excellence in Education. (1983). *A Nation at Risk: The Imperative for Educational Reform.* Washington, DC: Government Printing Office.

National Education Association. (1989). *Site-Based Decisionmaking: A Guidance and Training Manual*. Washington, DC: Author.

National Institute of Education. (1977). *Administration of Compensatory Education*. Washington, DC: Author.

National Science Foundation. (1989). *Directory of Awards by NSF's Directorate for Science and Engineering Education*. Washington, DC: National Science Foundation.

New York Times. (1991, August 23). 62% of Americans Support School Choice, Poll Finds.

Noddings, Nel. (1987). Fidelity in Teaching, Teacher Education, and Research for Teaching. In Margo Okazawa-Rey, James Anderson & Rob Traver (Eds.), *Teachers, Teaching, and Teacher Education* (pp. 384–400). Cambridge, MA: Harvard Educational Review.

Oakes, Jeannie. (1985). *Keeping Track: How Schools Structure Inequality*. New Haven: Yale University Press.

O'Connell, Mary. (1991). *School Reform Chicago Style: How Citizens Organized to Change Public Policy*. Chicago: Center for Neighborhood Technology.

Olmsted, Patricia P., & Roberta I. Rubin. (1982). Linking Parent Behaviors to Child Achievement: Four Evaluation Studies from the Parent Education Follow Through Program. *Studies in Educational Evaluation*: 317–25.

Peterkin, Robert S., & D. S. Jones. (1989). Schools of Choice in Cambridge, Massachusetts. In Joe Nathan (Ed.), *Public Schools by Choice* (pp. 125–48). Minneapolis: Institute for Learning and Teaching.

Peters, Thomas J., & Robert H. Waterman, Jr. (1982). *In Search of Excellence: Lessons from America's Best-Run Companies*. New York: Harper & Row.

Piercy, Marge. (1982). To Be of Use. In *Circles on the Water: Selected Poems of Marge Piercy*. New York: Alfred A. Knopf.

Powell, Arthur, Eleanor Farrar & David K. Cohen. (1985). *The Shopping Mall High School*. Boston: Houghton Mifflin.

Purkey, Stewart C., & Marshall S. Smith. (1983). Effective Schools: A Review. *Elementary School Journal, 83* (4): 426–52.

Ravitch, Diane. (1985). *The Schools We Deserve*. New York: Basic Books.

———. (1990, Summer). Multiculturalism: E Pluribus Plures. *American Scholar*: 337–54.

Raywid, Mary Anne. (1990). Rethinking School Governance. In Richard F. Elmore and Associates, *Restructuring Schools* (pp. 152–205). San Francisco: Jossey-Bass.

Resnick, Lauren B. (1985). *Constructing Knowledge in School*. A report to the National Institute of Education. Pittsburgh: Learning Research and Development Center.

Revicki, Dennis A. (1981). The Relationship among Socioeconomic Status, Home Environment, Parent Involvement, Child Self-Concept, and Child Achievement. Unpublished paper.

Richard Day Associates. (1990). *A Survey of Members of Chicago Local School Councils for Leadership for Quality Education*. Chicago: Leadership for Quality Education.

Rogers, David. (1981). *School Decentralization in New York City*. New York: Educational Priorities Panel (ERIC Document ED 219 466).

Rose v. Council for Better Education. (1989). 790 S.W. 2d 186, 60 *Education Law Reporter* 1289 (KY).

Rosenbaum, James E. (1980). Social Implications of Educational Grouping. In D. C. Berliner (Ed.), *Review of Research in Education, 8*: 361–401. Washington, DC: American Educational Research Association.

Rosenfeld, Stuart. (1983). Something Old, Something New: The Wedding of Rural Education and Rural Development. *Phi Delta Kappan, 65* (4): 270–73.

Sarason, Seymour B. (1971). *The Culture of the School and the Problem of Change.* Boston: Allyn and Bacon.

———. (1990). *The Predictable Failure of Educational Reform.* San Francisco: Jossey-Bass.

Sartre, Jean-Paul. (1970). *Literary and Philosophical Essays.* New York: Collier Books.

Schensul, Jean J., & Thomas G. Carroll. (1990). Visions of America in the 1990s and Beyond: Negotiating Cultural Diversity and Educational Change. *Education and Urban Society, 22* (4): 339–45.

Schlechty, Phillip C. (1989). Remarks made at Leadership Conference. Louisville, KY.

———. (1990). *Schools for the Twenty-First Century: Leadership Imperatives for Educational Reform.* San Francisco: Jossey-Bass.

Schlechty, Phillip C., Donald W. Ingwerson & Terry I. Brooks. (1988). Inventing Professional Development Schools. *Educational Leadership, 46* (3): 28–31.

Shroyer, Gail, & Larry Enochs. (1987). Strategies for Assessing the Unique Strengths, Needs, and Visions of Rural Science Teachers. *Research in Rural Education, 4* (1): 39–43.

Shulman, Lee S. (1986). Those Who Understand: Knowledge Growth in Teaching. *Educational Researcher, 15* (2): 4–14.

Sirotnik, Ken. (1991). Critical Inquiry. Chapter prepared for Edmund Short (Ed.), *Forms of Curriculum Inquiry: Guidelines for the Conduct of Educational Research.* New York: SUNY Press.

Sizer, Theodore R. (1984). *Horace's Compromise: The Dilemma of the American High School.* Boston: Houghton Mifflin.

———. (1989). Letter to all Coalition schools.

———. (1991). Letter to all Coalition schools.

Slavin, Robert E. (1988). Synthesis of Research on Grouping in Elementary Schools. *Educational Leadership, 46* (1): 67–74.

Smylie, Mark A., & Jack W. Denny. (1990). Teacher Leadership: Tensions and Ambiguities in Organizational Perspective. *Educational Administration Quarterly, 26*: 235–59.

Southern Regional Education Board. (1989). *Improving Science Education for Vocational Completers.* Atlanta: Southern Regional Education Board—State Vocational Education Consortium.

Sykes, Gary. (1987). Reckoning with the Specter. *Educational Researcher, 16* (6): 19–21.

Task Force on Education for Economic Growth. (1983). *Action for Excellence: A Comprehensive Plan to Improve Our Nation's Schools.* Denver: Education Commission of the States.

Thornton, Mel. (1991). (Nebraska Mathematics Scholars Program Open-ended Questionnaire Data.) Unpublished raw data.

Tichy, Noel. (1983). *Managing Strategic Change.* New York: John Wiley & Sons.

Timar, Thomas B. (1989). A Theoretical Framework for Local Responses to State Policy: Implementing Utah's Career Ladder Program. *Educational Evaluation and Policy Analysis, 11* (4): 329–41.

Tomlinson, Tommy M. (1981, April–May). Effective Schools: Mirror or Mirage? *Today's Education*: 60 GS-63 GS.

Twentieth Century Fund Task Force on Federal Elementary and Secondary Education Policy. (1983). *Making the Grade*. New York: Twentieth Century Fund.

Tyack, David. (1990). "Restructuring" in Historical Perspective: Tinkering toward Utopia. *Teachers College Record, 92* (2): 170–91.

Walberg, Herbert J. (1991). Improving School Science in Advanced and Developing Countries. *Review of Educational Research, 61* (1): 25–69.

Wallace, Richard C., Jr. (1986). Data-driven Educational Leadership. *Evaluation Practice, 7* (3): 5–15.

Watkins, John, & Sue Lusi. (1989). Facing the Essential Tensions: Restructuring from Where You Are. Paper presented at American Educational Research Association annual meeting, San Francisco.

Weiss, Janet A. (1990). Control in School Organizations: Theoretical Perspectives. In William H. Clune & John F. Witte (Eds.), *Choice and Control in American Education: Vol. 1. The Theory of Choice and Control in American Education* (pp. 91–134). London: Falmer Press.

White, Paula A. (1989). An Overview of School-Based Management: What Does the Research Say? *NAASP Bulletin, 73*: 1–8.

Whyte, William Foote. (1984). *Learning from the Field: A Guide from Experience*. Beverly Hills, CA: Sage Publications.

Wilcox, Kathleen. (1982). Ethnography as a Methodology and Its Application to the Study of Schooling: A Review. In George Spindler (Ed.), *Doing the Ethnography of Schooling: Educational Anthropology in Action* (pp. 456–88). New York: Holt, Rinehart and Winston.

Williams, Melvin D. (1981). *On the Street Where I Lived*. New York: Holt, Rinehart and Winston.

Williams-Norton, Mary, Marycarol Reisdorf & Sallie Spees. (1990). Home Is Where the Science Is. *Science and Children, 27* (6): 13–15.

Worthy, Ward. (1988). College Chemistry to Be Offered via Satellite to Rural High Schools. *Chemical and Engineering News, 66* (36): 15–16.

Yager, Robert E., & John E. Penick. (1986). Perceptions of Four Age Groups toward Science, Classes, Teachers, and the Value of Science. *Science Education, 70*: 355–63.

Index

About the Editor and Contributors

G. ALFRED HESS, JR., is the executive director of the Chicago Panel on Public School Policy and Finance. The Chicago Panel is conducting a five-year project, Monitoring and Researching School Reform in Chicago, with support from the Spencer Foundation, the MacArthur Foundation, the Chicago Community Trust, the Woods Charitable Fund, the Field Foundation of Illinois, and the Fry Foundation. An educational anthropologist, Hess is cochair of the Committee on Ethnographic Educational Evaluation of the Council on Anthropology and Education. He is the author of a participant observation study of the school reform movement in Chicago, *School Restructuring, Chicago Style* (1991).

WILLIAM AYERS is an assistant professor of education at the University of Illinois at Chicago and the author of *The Good Preschool Teacher* (1989).

MARY JO MCGEE BROWN is an assistant professor of educational psychology, teaching qualitative research at the University of Georgia in Athens.

THOMAS G. CARROLL has been deputy director of the Fund for the Improvement of Postsecondary Education since 1986. Prior to this, he was director of policy and planning at the National Institute of Education, to which he had come from Clark University, where he had been an assistant professor of anthropology and education. His research has involved education and work, lifelong learning, experiential learning, and organizational change in schools.

PAMELIA COE is an educational ethnographer with the Appalachia Educational Laboratory in Charleston, West Virginia.

ROBERT A. COLLINS is a supervisor in Dade County Public Schools' Division of Program Evaluation and leader of the team responsible for evaluation of Dade's School-Based Management project.

THOMAS W. COLLINS is a professor of anthropology at Memphis State University. His teaching and research focus on labor segmentation and school preparation for the workplace. During the 1970s he conducted a major study on desegregation in Memphis schools, and he is currently writing a book on the influence of social and economic stratification on school and community cultures in Memphis.

PETER W. COOKSON, JR., is the assistant dean of education at Adelphi University in Garden City, New York.

JOHN Q. EASTON is the director of monitoring and research for the Chicago Panel on Public School Policy and Finance. The Chicago Panel is conducting the major independent effort to assess the effectiveness of that city's school restructuring effort, Monitoring and Researching School Reform in Chicago.

CAROL PLATA ETHERIDGE is an assistant professor in the department of curriculum and instruction and a researcher in the Center for Research in Education Policy at Memphis State University. Her research interests include teacher socialization and empowerment, urban school cultures, and school reform.

MARJORIE K. HANSON is a coordinator in Dade County Public Schools' Division of Program Evaluation and part of the team that evaluated School-Based Management.

DIANE HARRINGTON is director of communications at the National Center for Restructuring Education, Schools, and Teaching (NCREST), a research and technical assistance center at Teachers College, Columbia University. In the 1970s, she was a curriculum developer in District 4 of the New York City Public Schools.

PATRICIA J. KANNAPEL is an ethnographic consultant to the Appalachia Educational Laboratory for the evaluation of the Kentucky Education Reform Act study.

PATRICK J. MCQUILLAN is codirector of the School Ethnography Project and a graduate student in the Department of Anthropology at Brown University.

DONALD R. MOORE is the executive director of Designs for Change, a nonprofit research and advocacy organization in Chicago, Illinois. Moore has directed a series of national studies of urban school reform and has been centrally involved in restructuring the Chicago public school system.

DON R. MORRIS is a coordinator in the Office of Educational Accountability, Dade County Public Schools. His current research interests include dynamic modeling of grade retention.

DONNA E. MUNCEY is codirector of the School Ethnography Project and a postdoctoral research associate in the Education Department at Brown University in Providence.

JOHN M. WATKINS works at The NETWORK, Inc., focusing on ethnographic evaluation, and collaborative action research as a steering mechanism for systemic change, while writing his dissertation at Harvard on the role of teams and peer site visits in restructuring.